Obscenity Rules

LANDMARK LAW CASES

&

AMERICAN SOCIETY

Peter Charles Hoffer
N. E. H. Hull
Series Editors

For a complete list of titles in the series go to www.kansaspress.ku.edu.

WHITNEY STRUB

Obscenity Rules

Roth v. United States and the Long

Struggle over Sexual Expression

UNIVERSITY PRESS OF KANSAS

© 2013 by the University Press of Kansas
All rights reserved

Published by the University Press of Kansas (Lawrence, Kansas 66045), which was
organized by the Kansas Board of Regents and is operated and funded by Emporia
State University, Fort Hays State University, Kansas State University, Pittsburg State
University, the University of Kansas, and Wichita State University

Library of Congress Cataloging-in-Publication Data

Strub, Whitney.
Obscenity rules : Roth v. United States and the long struggle over sexual expression /
Whitney Strub.
p. cm. — (Landmark law cases & American society)
Includes bibliographical references and index.
ISBN 978-0-7006-1936-8 (cloth : alk. paper)
ISBN 978-0-7006-1937-5 (pbk. : alk. paper)
1. Roth, Samuel, 1893–1974 — Trials, litigation, etc. 2. United States — Trials,
litigation, etc. 3. Trials (Obscenity) — United States. 4. United States. Supreme
Court. I. Title.
KF224.R68S77 2013
345.73'0274 — dc23
2013013472

British Library Cataloguing-in-Publication Data is available.

Printed in the United States of America

10 9 8 7 6 5 4 3 2 1

CONTENTS

Whitney Strub's essay on the Roth obscenity case is remarkable in many ways, first and foremost for turning what was, in his own words, a poorly executed Supreme Court attempt to define obscenity into a superb survey of obscenity law. In short, Strub succeeds where Justice William Brennan and his brethren failed. But that is only part of this book's achievement.

Today Samuel Roth lives in the shadows of First Amendment law, his publications no longer read and his case rarely studied. As Strub reminds us, Roth "never became a household name. Without his shady, half-underworld publishing career and the legal case it engendered, however, the erotic media landscape might look very different." In part this is because Roth was not a literary giant like D. H. Lawrence, a First Amendment warrior like Daniel Ellsberg, or a media figure like Larry Flynt. But Roth's case demonstrated how the most good-faith effort to avoid government censorship of prurient materials could end up so inchoate that even its author, years later, would concede his failure.

In *Roth*, the Court tried to strike a balance between material that contained explicit sex but had redeeming literary or social merit and material that was simply pornographic. The problem was that the eye of the beholder was not tutored by the distinction, leaving the Court to face case after case in which the postal service or local authorities prosecuted alleged offenders. As Strub writes, "people could be — and still are — imprisoned for publishing or distributing obscene material."

Using Roth's own private papers along with the records of the various prosecutions and the memos of the justices, Strub brings the case to life. While Roth's ultimate motives may remain a mystery, Strub has gotten closer to them than anyone else has or is likely to do. To this he has added a richly depicted and thoroughly researched essay on obscenity itself: how it came to be a crime, how it came into the High Court, and how subsequent cases and commentaries have handled it. For the story does not stop with Roth's case. Everyone from radical feminists to conservative moral commentators to First Amendment formalists has something to say about the subject, and Strub, who does not hide his own well-formed opinions, gives ample space to theirs.

If, as he writes, "this book, then, tells the history of a failure," the book itself is a great success. It will become the standard citation on the case and will inform every discussion of the subject. Insofar as that subject was a centerpiece of moral tub-thumping during more than one twenty-first-century presidential campaign, this book should have a wide audience.

ACKNOWLEDGMENTS

This book began with a suggestion from Hilary Lowe and Seth Bruggeman over a beer at a bar trivia game, so in turn my thanks begin with them too. From there, Michael Briggs was a receptive, responsive editor, and shepherded this project from proposal to final manuscript with grace and skill. For that matter, everyone at the University Press of Kansas has been a delight to work with, and I truly appreciate all their thoughtful work.

The primary archival bases of *Obscenity Rules* were the Samuel Roth Papers at Columbia University and the various Supreme Court justices' papers at the Library of Congress; on numerous impromptu, often disorganized visits, I was treated warmly and helpfully at both places, and I am grateful for the kindness.

My incredible colleagues and remarkably supportive administration at Rutgers University-Newark are simply unparalleled in the known world, and provided the perfect environment for researching and writing this book. It remains an honor to be a part of this campus community, and my thanks go to effectively everyone here, including my students, on whom I tested a few aspects of my analysis. Jonathan Lurie and Beryl Satter were both willing to read significant portions of the manuscript from the angle of their respective fields of expertise, and I benefited greatly from their wise suggestions.

Series coeditor Peter Charles Hoffer gave the whole manuscript a very useful review. As well, Jay Gertzman, the foremost expert on Samuel Roth, graciously saved me from error and weighed in on a point of confusion. I thank also the anonymous reviewer who gave the manuscript a commendably meticulous scrutiny of the most productive sort.

Since I always enjoy a glimpse at how books were written, here's mine: the largest portion was composed at Grindcore House, South Philadelphia's only vegan coffee shop with a blast beat. Even when I more or less camped out there for days on end with nothing but a bottomless cup of coffee, the friendly staff never gave me the boot, and they seemed to intuitively know how to shift from the morning Elliott Smith and Nico playlist to the harder stuff each day around noon, right as my fading stamina needed it, so my thanks to everyone there.

Other sections were written in Philly's Chinatown, Newark, New York City, and Hemet, California, where my parents, Kris Breza and Ron Strub, remain supportive as always.

Mary Rizzo was the constant backdrop to the writing of this book, not to mention a source of great joy and hilarity in my life. Reading chapters and improving them with her suggestions, spurring me on with her own exemplary scholarship, exploring this fascinating city of ours from the Paul Robeson House to alleys forlorn enough to come out of a Samuel Roth novel, and helping me cope with the crankiest cat that ever did meow, she should—and I note my belief that everyone's entitled to one groan-inducingly awful play on words in their life, and hereby cash mine in—be arrested on charges of being an obscenely great partner, in all the right ways. This book is for her.

Introduction

Before there was Jenna Jameson, before there was Larry Flynt, before there was Hugh Hefner, there was Samuel Roth. Unlike those luminaries of smut, he never became a household name. Without his shady, half-underworld publishing career and the legal case it engendered, however, the erotic media landscape might look very different. The 1957 Supreme Court case bearing his name, *Roth v. United States*, established the relationship between obscene materials and the First Amendment, laying down a doctrine that continues to structure the legal meaning of obscenity over a half century later.

In *Roth*, Justice William Brennan kept obscenity outside the protections of the First Amendment. Because of this, people could be — and still are — imprisoned for publishing or distributing obscene material. Yet Brennan wanted no part of censorship and strove to clarify that not every book, movie, magazine, or image dealing with sex could be considered obscene. Only those completely lacking in socially redeeming value, material whose dominant theme, when taken as a whole, appealed to what Brennan called "prurient interests," could be legally defined as obscene. To remove such items from the public sphere, Brennan thought, detracted nothing from freedom of speech, the exchange of ideas, or the power of the First Amendment.

Brennan was wrong. No less an authority than William Brennan himself would make this case, fifteen years later, once he saw the effects of *Roth*. Scholars agree. The eminent legal historian Lucas Powe pulls no punches, calling *Roth* a "sloppy, unpersuasive effort." Others take a softer tone, but search the scholarly archive far and wide, and you will find opinions generally ranging from lukewarm to dismissive. Celebrations of *Roth* are rare.

This book, then, tells the history of a failure. The failure cannot simply be pinned on Brennan's written opinion. The justice strained in good faith to reconcile competing tendencies in American legal and cultural history, but few have ever been able to effectively bridge the gaps between individual liberties and the enforcement of dominant social values. Obscenity law has satisfied no one, be it the conservatives distressed by the pornographic saturation that the law has seemingly done little to stop, or liberals aghast that in the twenty-first century people can still be incarcerated for selling images of actions that are perfectly legal between consenting adults. *Roth* did not single-handedly create this situation in a vacuum, but it is the case that bears the weight of this history, that somehow *both* opened the cultural gates to a "floodtide of filth" *and* deserves credit or blame each time another citizen stands behind bars for publishing pornography. If *Roth* is a paradox, as it surely is, its flaws go beyond Brennan's efforts to craft a viable obscenity doctrine and speak to a larger ambivalence in the history of American sexuality.

My goal here is not to condemn *Roth*, since its shortcomings are so self-evident they hardly require further haranguing. Neither is my goal to rescue its reputation, an unnecessary act of contrarianism for an opinion that deserves its ill regard. Instead, this book seeks to *understand Roth*, situating it in its historical context to flush out the unspoken tensions, anxieties, and ideologies hiding between its lines, finding tortured expression in Brennan's contradictions and convolutions. It is my central contention that the history of obscenity doctrine can be understood only by taking into account the history of sexuality and gender, as they played out through politics, culture, and law. In this, I am in the good company of the scholars whose work on sexuality and legal history I frequently draw on to tell the story. *Roth* says much more about American sexual values than Brennan's written words necessarily acknowledge.

In the history of obscenity, what we really witness is the history of social boundaries being firmed, tested, and shifted over time. Not just smut, but contraception, homosexuality, and questions over the meaning and significance of pleasure play out through obscenity doctrine. As it moves, so too do the borders of what scholars call sexual citizenship, or the sense of social belonging afforded to various forms of sexuality at any given point. Perhaps the major transition captured by (and in) obscenity doctrine is the advance of sexual liberalism, discussed further in the following chapters but basically amounting to a recognition and validation of sexual pleasure for its own good, as an end in itself, unbound by confinement to its strictly procreative, marital form. These battles frequently recur over time — as any observer of the stunning Republican assault on contraceptive access witnessed, not in the 1960s (when it was more likely to come from Democrats), but in the second decade of the twenty-first century. Well into the twentieth century, as we shall see, contraception itself was legally obscene.

The early chapters here trace the advent of obscenity as a legal concept, following its migration from England into the American common law, and finally into its culminating early moment when the United States adopted a strong federal obscenity law in 1873. Set against this legal story are the evolving sexual mores and notions of free speech that quickly began to chafe against the censorial power invested in national figures such as the late-nineteenth-century anti-smut zealot Anthony Comstock. _Obscenity,_ it is important to note at the outset, is a technical legal term, whose evolving meaning will be fleshed out throughout the book. _Pornography,_ on the other hand, is a cultural term that enters the vocabulary in the mid-nineteenth century and also changes over time; while it always refers to sexually explicit representations, it more specifically describes whichever of them are socially unacceptable at a given moment. It is therefore not a stable label; a book such as D. H. Lawrence's _Lady Chatterley's Lover_ might be deemed pornographic (and obscene) in 1930; four decades later it would be considered a classic, available in most good bookstores.

Beginning in chapter 3, we zoom in from the wide-angle shot of a nation tenuously modernizing to a close-up of a young man whose combination of artistic ambition, classic immigrant quest for upward mobility, and, let it not be disputed, salacious interest in all things sexual generated both a torrent of smutty literature and, ultimately, a Supreme Court case. He never sought to become a First Amendment warrior, but he became one nonetheless through his lifelong defiance of what the government deemed acceptable. It took decades for Samuel Roth to get from crowded New York City courtrooms to the magisterial Supreme Court building. This book is not a biography of Roth, but it is in some sense a biography of his era, for which his life provides a fascinating and useful window. It would be wrong, for reasons that will become all too painfully clear in at least one chapter, to label him the hero of this story. He is, however, the avatar.

In the middle chapters of the book, Roth's three-decade battle with postal inspectors, prosecutors, and smut-chasers serves as a shadow history of obscenity. We cut back to the big picture, of pivotal moments and cases, but we also see how the sexual politics of obscenity played out on a smaller scale for one unscrupulously sleazy smut merchant. Large-scale social changes sometimes rescued him, and they sometimes didn't; Roth spent nearly a decade of his life imprisoned, on several occasions, for the things he sent through the mails. Ironically, the very case that sent him to his longest sentence is the one that ensured that every single thing he had ever sold, no matter how covertly under the table, would be openly available across the nation within years.

If Samuel Roth leads us through the landscape of obscenity, William Brennan steps into its quicksand. His *Roth v. United States* opinion is in some ways the climax of this book, where the contradictions of a society both prurient and repressive, both righteous and sinning, commingle uncomfortably. The late chapters reflect the fallout: a new doctrine that helps usher in the sexual revolution, and also works to contain it. Critics range from conservatives with affronted morals to feminists who locate in obscenity law gender politics William Brennan never recognized, even as he promoted them. From the Nixon years of the late 1960s to the time of George W. Bush's presidency in the early 2000s, we see a society supporting presidents who fight against smut, even as that same society consumes pornography so voraciously that more old-fashioned capitalists who laboriously exploit sex to sell such other products as cars, hamburgers, and perfume can but wish their merchandise so effortlessly sold itself.

Given the tensions of such a society, perhaps obscenity law could never succeed; the inconsistencies run too deep. What's more certain is that, in the actual historical record, it did *not* succeed. In examining the long history leading to *Roth*, and its subsequent impact, we should remember that the failures are not strictly those of a legal doctrine, but rather of the deep-seated, still-operative social values it embodies.

Toward Obscenity

Legal Evolution from Colonies to Comstock

When Justice William Brennan, writing for the majority in *Roth v. United States*, excluded obscenity from the protections afforded by the First Amendment, he strove to ground that outcome in the broader currents of American history. Brennan argued that the Court in 1957 was simply making manifest a status already implicit in the legal record, not carving out a new exception to free expression. Much of Brennan's argument hinged on his assertion that "the unconditional phrasing of the First Amendment was not intended to protect every utterance" and that obscenity had never been understood as a part of the "unfettered interchange of ideas" undergirding freedoms of speech or press.

This historical trajectory played a central role in Brennan's analysis. Yet Brennan's exposition proved remarkably thin. Other justices sometimes delivered major opinions on matters ranging from labor law to interstate commerce regulation in the form of miniature monographs, dense and extensive in their attention to detail. Brennan's survey of history in *Roth* occupied a mere few paragraphs.

Leaping from a 1712 Massachusetts law to the Continental Congress and from there to the 1860s, Brennan's opinion lacked any sense of historical context or social change over time. Its blunt, broad brushstrokes did not, however, err on the core idea: nowhere in the mainstream currents of American legal, political, or cultural thought had free speech ever been absolute, or obscenity ever acceptable. From the preconstitutional social regulation of blasphemy, to the early republic's effortless absorption of obscenity into the common law, and on into the gradual state-level passage of obscenity statutes in the mid-nineteenth century, obscenity had never joined other forms of expression in the imagined marketplace of ideas.

The 1873 Comstock Act began to craft a piecemeal legal regime into something moving toward cohesion. Its passage, though, marked not the beginning but simply the clarification and expansion of obscenity regulation in the United States. Much would change by the time Brennan and the Court upheld its legal structure, but the continuity he saw running from the colonies to the Eisenhower years was not a complete fabrication.

Blasphemous Origins

The evolution of the colonies into states had witnessed very little concern over possible tension between protecting freedom of speech while prohibiting profanity or blasphemy (understood, broadly, as a defamation of religion). Of the fourteen states to ratify the Constitution by 1792, ten guaranteed freedom of speech, with the 1776 Virginia Declaration of Rights leading the way. In strong language, it called freedom of the press "one of the great bulwarks of liberty," which could "never be restrained but by despotick governments." Phrasing among the other states varied, but the theme remained consistent. Yet these broad declarations of liberty coexisted with restrictions. Most participants in these discussions understood the celebrated freedoms to pertain primarily to political speech — and assumed that category as self-evident rather than carefully defining it. Civil actions against slander (purely verbal expression) or libel (written), for instance, were nowhere regarded as infringing on free speech. As Brennan later observed, thirteen of those first fourteen states also made blasphemy or profanity statutory crimes. He linked this to obscenity, showing that a 1712 Massachusetts law had criminalized the publishing of "any filthy, obscene, or profane song, pamphlet, libel, or mock sermon."

But Massachusetts was the only colony to specifically criminalize obscenity. In part, this reflected the simple fact that social concern over obscenity remained minimal among the colonies. Between the virtual nonexistence of the domestic press and the scarcity of foreign texts, the circulation of obscene materials posed little social threat. Even the Massachusetts law mentioned obscenity only in passing, positioning it as merely one corollary form of blaspheming the church through sexualized means. The colonies had imported a hodgepodge assemblage of English common law (law based on the judicial prece-

dents of court decisions, as opposed to the statutory law passed by leg-
islatures), which only in 1727 formally articulated obscenity as a criminal offense, in the case of *Regina v. Curll*.

Technically, obscenity constituted a libel. As a civil offense, libel
consisted of defamatory statements about an individual. When such
defamation targeted monarch or deity, however, it became criminal—
seditious libel or blasphemous libel, respectively. Obscene libel presented a third variant, and *Curll* defined the damage inflicted more
broadly, as against civil society or the public at large (though the book
in question, *Venus in Her Cloister, or, the Nun in Her Smock*, was
directed specifically against Catholicism). Since obscenity was pre-
sumed to undermine the public sphere by short-circuiting its dialogue
with lowest-common-denominator discourse, obscene libel could easily be understood in secular terms.

The ripples of *Curll* crossed the Atlantic rather faintly. As the
colonies developed increasing resistance to their subordinate status,
free expression took on new importance. Escalating resentment of a
corrupt colonial governor led a New York jury to nullify seditious libel
charges against printer John Peter Zenger in 1735, striking a bold
precedent for freedom of the press and weakening the value of seditious libel charges as a means of suppressing dissent. Blasphemy
remained actionable, but secularization and the general decline of
moral policing in the eighteenth century gave it less salience than it
once had. Massachusetts began punishing the technically capital crime
with mere floggings, and the more lax Virginia pursued not one prosecution in the entire century.

In this context, the American common law quietly absorbed
obscene libel without much immediate use for it. When sexual regulation took place, it was more likely against *actions* than texts, in the
form of charges such as lascivious conduct. Sexually themed literature, including sordid anti-Catholic tales and the folk knowledge of
Aristotle's Masterpiece, which provided the closest thing to sex education available to many eighteenth-century Americans, circulated
freely. Most of it was imported from Europe, as the American press
remained in its infancy.

As resistance to British rule ushered in revolution and independence, the new nation celebrated freedom of speech and the press as
core values, enshrined in the First Amendment to the Constitution.

"Congress shall make no law," it declared, "abridging the freedom of speech, or of the press." Yet this rhetorical embrace never amounted to absolute freedom, and in the fraught political situation of the 1790s, even seditious libel was reinstated by an Adams administration eager to quash dissenting voices. Nearly twenty indictments, and almost a dozen convictions, resulted from the 1798 Sedition Act, all against opponents of Adams's Federalist administration, including even a Vermont congressman, who was reelected while imprisoned.

Reconciling the Sedition Act with the First Amendment required careful — some, such as Thomas Jefferson, would have said twisted — parsing of the constitutional language to read abridgment of the press as merely a prior restraint on publication. That is, Congress could not *prevent* publications, but, supporters of the Sedition Act claimed, it could *punish* publishers for what they had printed if the expressions were deemed actionable. The matter never reached the Supreme Court for clarification, with the Sedition Act expiring in 1801. Meanwhile, even Jefferson himself, once elected president in 1800, allowed seditious libel charges (now against Federalists), as long as they happened through *state* laws, which posed no First Amendment issues since they were not enacted by the national Congress. In the years of the new nation, it remained unclear whether the First Amendment granted an affirmative right to expression, or simply freedom from prior restraint.

While the Sedition Act reflected the precarious nature of free speech in the early republic, the federal government showed little interest in moral regulation of the cultural or sexual variety, which it left to states and towns. Even in the face of a vociferous Sabbatarian movement in the 1820s demanding the closing of post offices on Sunday, the federal government refused to act, and without any comparable movement against obscenity, no national legislation regarding it emerged during the first half century of the United States. Indeed, while moral regulation was taken for granted at the state and local levels, no conception of a federal police power that might serve that purpose existed. Blasphemy, while rarely punished, remained on the books and would continue to play a structuring role as obscenity formally entered the legal sphere in the 1810s and '20s.

Two of the more prominent blasphemy cases of the period reflect the influence it would carry. In 1811, when John Ruggles declared,

"Jesus Christ was a bastard, and his mother must be a whore," he inspired a trial that clarified New York's blasphemy law. Chancellor James Kent, as the highest judge of the state was known, did not hesitate to call the United States a Christian nation in his opinion, but carefully grounded his affirmation of Ruggles's conviction in secular logic, calling his statement a form of "licentiousness" that "tends to corrupt the morals of the people, and to destroy good order." Distinguishing such prosecutions from "any religious establishment or the rights of the church," Kent emphasized instead the "essential interests of civil society." In comparing Ruggles's words to other "things which corrupt moral sentiment, as obscene actions, prints and writings, and even gross instances of seduction," Kent concluded that such expressions were legitimately criminalized "because they strike at the root of moral obligation, and weaken the security of the social ties." The Pennsylvania Supreme Court agreed in another 1824 blasphemy case, finding in a public debate over the truth of the Bible "a nursery of vice, a school of preparation to qualify young men for the gallows, and young women for the brothel."

This leap in logic from debate club to brothel collapsed religious transgression into political and sexual transgression. The slippage was perfectly legible in the early republic, where belief in liberty balanced precariously against anxiety over licentiousness. As capitalism, demographic change, and technological development in transportation accelerated urbanization and what historians call the "market revolution," the resulting social transformations highlighted the symbolic meaning assigned to gender and sexuality. The American experiment in democracy and equality had always hinged on a populace possessed of moral rectitude. Only by trusting the judgment of the people could democracy properly function. Ideas of "Republican motherhood," for instance, placed critical importance on women's roles in bearing and raising decent citizens. Cities, with their breakdown of conventional forms of personal regulation and community surveillance, came to symbolize the dangers of licentiousness. "Confidence men" and "painted women" threatened to replace the orderly citizenry with unchecked passions that undermined democratic order.

In this context, sexual propriety played a crucial role in assuring the reproduction of the social order that nurtured democracy. Obscenity slowly entered the legal arena during this historical moment, building off the language of blasphemy while also reflecting the anxieties of the age. Philadelphia, for instance, had hosted what historian Clare Lyons calls a vibrant "pleasure culture" before the revolution, with public expressions of sexuality viewed nonchalantly. Ribald verses and arousing literature, much of it imported from England, had circulated freely in the mid-eighteenth century. Even John Cleland's notorious 1748 novel *Memoirs of a Woman of Pleasure*, better known as *Fanny Hill* — ultimately to inspire centuries of American obscenity cases — was obliquely advertised in newspapers and catalogues by the 1760s.

With independence, however, came a new sexual conservatism that challenged such openness. By the time city officials learned of Jesse Sharpless and a group of friends charging admission to see a graphic painting of a "man in an obscene, impudent and indecent posture with a woman" in 1815, criminal charges ensued. To the local grand inquest, Sharpless and associates were guilty of "being evil-disposed persons, and designing, contriving and intending the morals, as well of youth as of divers other citizens of this commonwealth, to debauch and corrupt, and to raise and create in their minds inordinate and lustful desires," all of which potentially destabilized the social order.

Sharpless's attorney argued that the painting was shown only in private, and no actual statutory crime of obscenity lay on the books. Unconvinced, the Pennsylvania Supreme Court upheld the convictions. Agreeing with the attorney general that "crimes are public offences, not because they are *perpetrated publicly*, but because their effect is to injure the public," the court cited *Curll* to locate obscenity in the common law, thus punishable even in the absence of a specific statute. Employing similar reasoning, the high court of Massachusetts likewise affirmed an obscenity conviction stemming from domestic distribution of John Cleland's *Fanny Hill*. In both cases, the courts agreed that graphic description of the allegedly obscene material need not be entered into the public record, so as to avoid reproducing and disseminating the material. While neither obscenity case contained the religious components of the blasphemy cases, they followed the same logic of justifying the suppression of obscenity in the name of protecting a fragile body-politic easily upset by moral transgression, both rife with such phrases as "debauch," "corrupt," "scandalous," "lustful desires," "lewd," and "wicked."

By the 1820s, states had begun to write obscenity laws, transform-

{ *Chapter 1* }

ing it from a common-law offense to a statutory one, with Connecticut, Vermont, and Massachusetts leading the way. New York, meanwhile, lacked a state law until the late 1860s, despite its urban center of gravity in New York City being responsible for approximately 40 percent of the domestic smut market. A certain permissiveness marked the city, with prostitution tacitly allowed as long as it was kept off the streets and thus only semivisible. Though a female-led moral reform movement against prostitution would develop by the 1830s, sordid literature circulated with relative impunity, with *Fanny Hill* available by the 1820s.

It was only with the emergence of the so-called flash press in the early 1840s that New York City authorities began to move against obscenity, still a common-law offense and a libel. New printing technology had lowered the costs of entrance to publishers, and such spectacles as the 1836 murder of the prostitute Helen Jewett had helped spawn a sensationalized penny press. The flash press consisted of a group of newspapers with names like the *Whip*, the *Rake*, and the *Libertine*, which employed penny-press tactics and directed them toward single young men in the city. Occupying a tenuous class position between the emerging industrial working class and the bourgeois white-collar professionals, many of these readers worked as clerks, secretaries, legal assistants, and other aspirational but not-yet-established positions. The flash press catered to their interests in gambling, boxing, cockfights, and the pursuit of sexual pleasure. Of particular irritation to the authorities were the underhanded activities of several editors in using their bully pulpits to threaten and even blackmail prominent citizens with the publications of exposés (which could be true or false). When ordinary libel charges failed to effectively stop the flash press, the district attorney turned to obscenity.

The advantage of obscenity charges, from a prosecutorial perspective, was the irrelevance of truth as a defense. The elite was hardly seen as sinless by an increasingly class-conscious public, which made it tougher to indict flash-press publishers for character assassination — which juries might find accurate. More effective were indictments based on the moral debasement of the public sphere. Obscenity charges worked: by 1843 the flash press had been largely destroyed, with many of the editors either in jail, in exile from the city, or moving on to other pursuits. Notably, while fighting the charges, the editors had used fiery rhetoric bemoaning everything from prosecutorial hypocrisy to their property rights as publishers, but freedom of speech was not a significant part of their arguments. Such freedom was simply not taken for granted in the 1840s. The First Amendment applied strictly to federal action, certainly not to actions of local authorities, and the New York state constitution's own free-speech clause made clear that "abuse" of that liberty was not to be understood as protected.

Also reflecting the relative insignificance of the First Amendment was its absence from discussion of the first federal obscenity law, passed without debate by Congress in 1842 and directed against the importation of "all indecent and obscene prints, paintings, lithographs, engravings, and transparencies." Included in a larger tariff law, it carried little immediate impact. No meaningful federal mechanisms policed obscene materials once they were inside the country (or were published by the growing domestic smut trade), and since much of the existing obscenity-law enforcement remained strictly local, astute entrepreneurs shifted their distribution from visible newsstands or dealers to mail order.

In this way, as the historian Donna Dennis has shown, the slowly coalescing law of obscenity did not so much stop the smut trade as shape it; the legal gaps of antebellum federalism played a key role in facilitating the rise of mail-order merchants such as William Haines and George Akarman, each responsible for vast proliferations of erotic publications sent through the mail between the 1840s and 1870s. Their wares ranged from racy pamphlets working-class readers could purchase for a quarter to "fancy books" for more upscale readers, costing two dollars and more and bearing cloth binding and even color plates — a differentiated set of product lines for a nation increasingly consuming print media.

Dime novelist George Thompson, for instance, churned out lurid pulp spectacle at a machinelike rate, filling page after page with descriptions of women's "swelling bosoms" and "undulating outlines." Thompson's books wallowed in male sexual privilege that extended sporting-culture attitudes. When protagonist Frank Sydney meets a teenage girl on a nighttime stroll in "the great city of New York" in the 1849 *City Crimes*, he considers rescuing her from the dangers of the city but winds up instead embodying them after succumbing to "those feelings and desires that are inherent in human nature." Overcome with lust, "his heart palpitated violently, his breath grew hurried and irregular, and he could scarcely restrain himself from clasping her to his breast with licentious violence."

What restraint he does show is, of course, short-lived, and Thompson addresses Frank directly as "thy hand plays with those ivory globes" and "thy amorous soul bathes in a sea of rapturous delight!" Like the flash press, Thompson and other dime novelists painted what one scholar calls an "urban porno-gothic" that titillated even as it pretended to warn. Thompson's prose style buzzed with awareness of obscenity law, frequently invoking it to allude to even *more* depraved pleasures whose precise nature could not be elaborated for fear of prosecution. In this way, obscenity law inadvertently contributed to an erotic process of fetishistic concealment.

The federal government revisited obscenity during the Civil War, as concern over the dirty books and pictures bought and shared by soldiers mounted. One of the historical obstacles to federal moral regulation had been southern fear that any governmental powers based on moral foundations would inevitably turn toward slavery, condemned by abolitionists as immoral (for that matter, abolitionist literature often mirrored the graphic language and feverish tenor of dime novels in its condemnations of the South as a giant brothel, based on the sexual exploitation of slaves). With the southern states detached from Congress during the war, no such barrier to federal power stood in the way, and new precedents in federal moral regulation resulted. Among other provisions, the 1862 Morrill Act outlawed polygamy, and an 1865 obscenity bill finally targeted the domestic mails, outlawing the mailing of obscene materials. As in 1842, debate was minimal. Even within the context of a limited federal government, Congress had specific authority over the postal service, making it the natural focus of such legislation. The only substantive objection to the bill involved the postmaster's right to open and inspect first-class mail, which threatened personal privacy in correspondence. With that section struck, the bill passed with little further discussion.

With the Union at war, neither the Morrill Act nor the 1865 obscenity law carried major immediate impact. Both anticipated the reconfiguration of federalism wrought by the war, though, with power shifting from the states to the national government, as reflected most strikingly in the Thirteenth, Fourteenth, and Fifteenth Amendments, which in ending slavery, granting citizenship to freedmen and -women, and ostensibly protecting voting rights also clearly asserted the new centrality of the federal government. These legal and political shifts formed the structural backdrop for the emergence of a strengthened obscenity regime, but the direct catalyst would be an upwardly mobile young man whose forceful personality, lobbying skills, and personal obsessions ultimately left the next four decades of moral policing stamped with his own name as marker of an era.

The Comstock Era

In many ways, the early life of Anthony Comstock mirrored those of the young sporting men who preceded him. Born to humble circumstances in Connecticut, he served in the Union army during the war before joining the ongoing mass urban migration that had seen America's cities exploding in population by 700 percent in the three decades leading up to the Civil War. Working as a dry goods clerk in Brooklyn, he harbored ambitions of establishing himself socially and financially in the middle class.

Whatever demographic affinities he shared with flash-press readers were easily overshadowed by Comstock's radically different disposition. While his army peers enjoyed smutty pictures and texts, as well as the company of prostitutes, young Comstock instead attended religious services with an intense fervor. At a time when the military distributed daily rations of liquor, he poured his out rather than drink or share. Once in New York, he rejected the various pleasures of bachelor life for marriage and family. And while other young men pinned their dreams on the rapidly bureaucratizing corporate world, Comstock saw opportunity in a different economy, with its own emerging bureaucracy: the moral economy.

It was an opportune moment to strike out as a moral entrepreneur. Concerns over urban danger went back decades, but with the social upheavals of the war, increasing immigration, continued urbanization, and the ever-present moral pollutants of prostitution and immoral literature and images finding little opposition from such growing political machines as New York's Tammany Hall, the 1860s *seemed* to those living through them an entirely new crisis, at least in scale and scope. Such moral reform organizations as the Children's Aid Society, established in 1853 by Charles Loring Brace, and the Young Men's Christian Association, imported from England around the same time, had established infrastructures aimed at reforming and protecting, respectively, "street urchin" children and single young men in the city. Opportunity awaited entrepreneurs who might advance these agendas in the midst of postwar confusion.

No reformer in American history would exploit those opportunities as effectively as Comstock. His dedication appeared sincere, even obsessive. After the death of a close friend in the late 1860s, attributed by Comstock to a downhill slide into sexual dissipation that began with the lust generated by reading dirty books, the young clerk began investigating local smut merchants until he had enough evidence to prod authorities into arrests. During this same period, the YMCA was active in New York state politics pushing for an obscenity law, which it finally achieved in 1868, moving obscenity from common to statutory law at last. The clear resonance of Comstock's activities with the YMCA's reform agenda brought him to the attention of its wealthy patrons, and Comstock quickly won YMCA sponsorship, increasing his resources and social prominence.

In late 1872, Comstock made a tactical decision to go after well-known feminist Victoria Woodhull, who with her sister Tennie Claflin published a weekly newspaper that had exposed the adulterous affairs of the Reverend Henry Ward Beecher. While historian Helen Lefkowitz Horowitz has noted several continuities between the flash press and *Woodhull & Claflin's Weekly* in terms of prose and topical focus, the case certainly drew more publicity than activities against the less famous local purveyors Comstock had been targeting—something the enterprising reformer certainly well understood and expected. Woodhull and Claflin faced obscenity charges for their reporting on Beecher, but escaped conviction on a technicality. They had been tried under the federal obscenity law, which did not apply because its provisions did not explicitly include newspapers.

In losing, though, Comstock obtained even greater prominence, catapulting to Washington, D.C., to lobby for a stronger obscenity law, one that expanded postmaster power and included newspapers. His efforts proved successful. With the Credit Mobilier scandal exposing the rampant bribery and corruption of the Reconstruction-era Congress, a convenient assertion of morality found easy favor, and like earlier federal obscenity action, the bill passed with minimal discussion (coming before the House on a Sunday morning at the end of the session). The resulting federal act for "Suppression of Trade in, and Circulation of, Obscene Literature and Articles of Immoral Use," better known as the Comstock Act, finally strengthened the federal obscenity law.

Casting a broad net, the Comstock Act covered every "obscene, lewd, lascivious, or filthy book, pamphlet, picture, paper, letter, writing, print, or other publication of an indecent character," as well as "any article or thing designed or intended for the prevention of conception or procuring of abortion" and "any article or thing intended or adapted for any indecent or immoral use." The term "pornography" had only recently entered the language and was primarily used in the literal sense of its ancient Greek etymology, as descriptions (*graphe*) of prostitutes (*porne*), so remained absent from the law. Penalties were severe. A first offense could result in a $5,000 fine and five years' imprisonment, with each subsequent offense carrying double penalties. Flash-press editors had measured their prison stints in weeks; publishing *Fanny Hill* in 1820s Massachusetts had been a misdemeanor. Suddenly, obscenity law had teeth.

For Comstock, the personal benefits of this legal codification were immense. The YMCA in 1873 gave its moral reform committee institutional autonomy as the Society for the Suppression of Vice and named Comstock its secretary and chief agent, with a salary that doubled his income as a clerk and allowed him to devote himself full-time to smut suppression. Further, appointed by Congress as special agent to the Post Office, he gained the power to make arrests, no longer needing to build cases that convinced other authorities to act. Comstock held both positions until his death in 1915, and the changes were pronounced and immediate. From seven obscenity prosecutions initiated by the Post Office between 1865 and 1872, cases in the next seven years included 100 commenced by Comstock alone.

By the time of his ascent, Comstock had already begun altering the sexual landscape of New York City. When smut merchant William Haines died in 1872, for instance, Comstock arranged for the YMCA to purchase the plates of his publications from his widow, thus foreclosing their reprinting. Neither Comstock nor anyone else could completely eliminate smut, but he did succeed at making it significantly less visible in the public sphere and harder to obtain. Historians have read Comstock's efforts through three primary lenses, all fleshed out below: social control of the "lower" classes; bourgeois self-disciplining; and the policing of gender norms. Because sexual politics are so frequently inconsistent and paradoxical, all three analyses work together collectively to capture the convoluted nature of Gilded Age urban anxieties. Comstock himself had a much simpler explanation: as the "boon companion to all other crimes," lust lay at the heart of all social problems.

"There is no evil so extensive, none doing more to destroy the institutions of free America," he intoned, and he meant it literally. Comstock wrote, lectured, and harangued constantly, but his message remained unwavering for nearly a half century. "Lust has but to whistle, and red-handed murder quickly responds," with smut clearly inspiring the inhalation behind the whistle. Comstock's 1883 manifesto *Traps for the Young* crystallized his worldview. While everything from gambling to quack science wins scorn for its detrimental effect on the young, the central, obsessive focus remains on the "death-traps" of immoral literature. Comstock's prose style utilizes the same sensational tactics as his opponents' and frequently slips into even purpler hues. "This moral vulture steals upon our youth in their homes," he writes, before quickly shifting metaphors. "Like a cancer, it fastens itself upon the imagination," until it succeeds at "poisoning the nature, enervating the system, destroying self-respect, fettering the willpower, defiling the mind, corrupting the thoughts, leading to secret practices of most foul and revolting character, until the victim tires of life, and existence is scarcely endurable."

Shorn of its overheated rhetoric, Comstock's basic argument was that obscenity dealers deliberately targeted children, as easy marks ripe for addiction. The idea of childhood innocence was a recent cultural invention, one that had accompanied the emergence of a large middle class in the mid-nineteenth-century United States. This idea served Comstock well, as it tapped into relatively new social concerns, forging a link between smut and the corruption of children that would reverberate for the next hundred and fifty years. Reading smut, Comstock explained, led to the "secret vice" of masturbation, and from there life might deteriorate immediately, with "pale cheeks, lusterless and sunken eyes" preceding a full collapse into physical turpitude. If that could be avoided, the turpitude would be moral: seeking ever-greater sensual pleasures, boys and young men would pursue sex through manipulation, purchase, or force, leaving young women ruined by sexual defilements running the gamut from seduction to rape to abortion, all of which Comstock considered approximately equal in moral harm. These socially destabilizing outcomes justified whatever drastic action need be taken to quell the immoral merchants of smut and death.

None of Comstock's ideas were radically at odds with mainstream beliefs of the day. Medical science was only on the brink of full-scale professionalization, and notions of a "spermatic economy" through which men could be depleted into sallow frailty remained pervasive. Self-control was a central virtue of the Gilded Age, and obscenity actively undermined it. The middle class, most rapidly adapting to the bureaucratic strictures of corporate capitalism, imagined itself the paragon of self-control. Likewise (and deeply intertwined with class status), white Protestants saw themselves as most fastidiously uphold-ing these tenets. The poor and working class, increasingly composed of Catholic and Jewish eastern European immigrants (such as young Samuel Roth and his parents), represented to the dominant culture the absence of self-control. Social science of the time facilitated this, tending to read lower-class pathology and "immorality" of various sorts as causing poverty, rather than reflecting it.

With classist ideas of working-class/immigrant/non-Protestant immorality circulating so openly at the time, historians have persua-sively read Comstock and the larger antivice movement as "a response to deep-seated fears about the drift of urban life in the post–Civil War years," as Paul Boyer wrote in his influential 1968 book *Purity in Print*. Boyer and other social historians emphasize the ways moral reform functioned as a mechanism of social control, policing and regulating unruly desires and actions to coercively fold the lower classes into social and economic structures that supported existing hierarchies. Controlled, predictable behavior was simply more suited for the new-found emphasis on efficiency that undergirded industrial labor, and eliminating or curtailing smut, prostitution, gambling, drinking, and other forms of profligacy forwarded that end.

{ *Chapter 1* }

Indeed, class bias in its most transparent form was evident in Comstock's activities. While busting sellers of contraception, he was most likely to investigate immigrants, women, and Jews — while leaving untouched the elite men who ran such corporations as Goodyear and Sears, Roebuck, each of which openly sold contraceptive devices in the late nineteenth century. In a startling incongruity that best reflects how "vice" was always viewed through various class and social lenses, millionaire Samuel Colgate was at the same time the president (and a primary funder) of the New York Society for the Suppression of Vice that paid Comstock, *and* heir to Colgate and Company, the New Jersey firm whose products included Vaseline, explicitly marketed for its spermicidal qualities.

If compelling reasons support an analysis of Comstockery highlighting social control of the lower classes, bourgeois self-regulation formed another important component of its logic. In her book *Imperiled Innocents*, Nicola Beisel argues that while class anxieties assuredly formed the backdrop to Comstock's ascent, the real fears of his elite sponsors had less to do with controlling immigrant behavior per se than ensuring that their own children avoided downward mobility into the increasingly dire living conditions of the poor. Obscene materials, as a gateway into more generalized dissipation, threatened to undermine the family reproduction that perpetuated elite standing, by diverting sexuality into vice-ridden pursuits.

Certainly both historical analyses rightly highlight the class anxieties behind Gilded Age moral reform, and the two leading approaches are hardly irreconcilable, differing more in emphasis than substance. What neither disputes is that the ultimate governing logic of Comstockism hinged on sexual politics — if always mixed with other concerns over class, immigration, religion, and other factors, nonetheless still possible to distill into some basic underlying principles. At its core, Comstockism served as a rearguard action to halt the already underway separation of sex from procreation that would flourish in twentieth-century modern sexuality.

The human pursuit of sexual pleasure reaches across epochs, but in the United States, only in the modern era would pleasure for pleasure's sake slowly be afforded social recognition and validation. Arising out of a complex confluence of forces, including urbanization, demographic patterns that resulted in more young, unmarried, unsupervised people sharing close proximity, and the development of a consumer culture that promoted pleasure in order to commodify and capitalize on it, this shift aroused fear over its potential impact on the sanctity of the family, seen as the fundamental unit of the existing social order. That the Comstock Act was written to reassert the procreative nature of sexuality is clear from its otherwise seemingly tangential inclusion of contraceptive and abortion-related devices and information, deemed obscene at the behest of Comstock himself.

Doctors bestowing reproductive insight and pornographers lavishly describing bodies and sex acts might occupy disparate literary terrain, but that map collapsed into a single point for Comstock. Several of his early high-profile cases had nothing to do with pornography, but instead involved practitioners of various forms of birth control. Dr. E. B. Foote, for example, had long promoted contraception, selling informational books and pamphlets, and also devices like the "womb veil," precursor to the modern diaphragm. Attuned to politics and law, Foote testified as the sole dissenter against New York's updated state obscenity law, one of a rash of so-called little Comstock laws that proliferated in the 1870s. He failed to carry the day and, recognizing the turning legal tides, removed the contraceptive information from his publications, including it only in a pamphlet, *Words in Pearl for the Married*, sold only when signed for by two marital partners. Even that restriction failed to satisfy Comstock, who may have held a grudge from the hearings. Arrested in 1875, Foote was convicted for violating the Comstock Act.

Fined $3,500, Foote avoided prison. Not every Comstock target was so lucky. Ann Lohman had spent decades as New York's most prominent abortionist, known as Madame Restell. Always located in a legal gray area, she became an obvious target in the new legal landscape. Using a fake identity to draw her into violating the law through the mail (the same technique he used on Foote and numerous others), the publicity-conscious Comstock brought the press along for a high-profile arrest in 1878. Facing serious prison time, Lohman slit her own throat in the bathtub. Comstock gave no quarter even in death, reportedly declaring, "a bloody end to a bloody life" when told of her suicide.

Punitive prison sentences frequently awaited those who did find themselves convicted. Of particular outrage to Comstock were the freethinkers and free lovers whose scathing attacks on Christianity and marriage fostered a thriving radical culture in the 1870s. Ezra Heywood best personified the free-love movement; along with his wife, Angela, he argued in several newspapers and pamphlets for male and female sexual freedom, understood as the right to both enter into and refrain from sexual relations as an individual saw fit, without legal interference from the government. Heywood's most notorious pamphlet, the 1876 *Cupid's Yokes*, offered itself as a treatise on "sexual self-government," arguing that "vice does not consist in the judicious gratification of sexual desire, but in *repression* and disordered *excess*." While clearly not advocating orgiastic revelry, Heywood's position still hit at the center of Comstock's worldview. Though the Heywoods had married for convenience, to avoid fornication or cohabitation laws, they rejected the coercive power of the institution, described as "legalized prostitution." Not only was marriage unjustly the only avenue to licit sex, they contended, but also it served to conceal the sexual subjugation of wives to their husbands' demands.

For publishing *Cupid's Yokes*, Ezra Heywood received two years of hard labor. Though pardoned by President Rutherford Hayes, Heywood dedicated himself to serving as gadfly, fighting the Comstock Act for his remaining decades. Repeatedly arrested for publishing Walt Whitman's poem "To a Common Prostitute," for selling a contraceptive douche helpfully named the Comstock Syringe, and finally for distributing fellow Comstock-target Moses Harman's radical newspaper *Lucifer, or the Light-Bearer*, Heywood was sentenced in 1890 to two years of hard labor at age sixty-one. Surviving his sentence, he emerged from prison a bitter man, devastated physically and psychologically, and died shortly thereafter.

Comstock's arrest ledgers in these years included ample sex radicals, educators, and pornographers, but no case exemplified the state of American obscenity law as well as that of D. M. Bennett, arrested repeatedly in the late 1870s and ultimately convicted for selling Heywood's *Cupid's Yokes*. A prominent freethinker, whose paper the *Truth Seeker* offered strong polemics against Christianity and organized religion more broadly, Bennett roused Comstock's ire with a particularly inflammatory 1875 "Open Letter to Jesus Christ," which posed a long list of questions to the Christian savior. With obvious mockery, Bennett positioned Christ's wine-making ways against temperance reformers of the day. Strongly insinuating that as the "youngest mythology," Christianity was a "plagiarism," Bennett's letter had little in the way of sexual content beyond a bold questioning of Jesus's conception, asking whether love had been involved in the "transaction," and most controversially, whether it had been "an example of 'free-love.'" Reflecting obscenity's link to blasphemy, Comstock had Bennett arrested for the open letter and a tract on marsupial reproduction.

These charges failed, but when Bennett sold a copy of *Cupid's Yokes*, fully aware the sale served as provocation, new charges came and stuck. A month before his trial, Bennett published an open letter to Samuel Colgate, calling his obscenity charges a "pretext" and calling himself "no more a violator of the law than yourself," quoting Vaseline ads to the antivice funder. Defending *Cupid's Yokes* as a "dry, argumentative production" that avoided titillation in making its case, Bennett compared Comstock to "a vicious dog." Powerfully written, the letter little mattered; in 1879, the sixty-year-old intellectual was convicted, sentenced to thirteen months of hard labor. He appealed, and the resulting federal circuit court opinion set the course of obscenity law for decades to come.

Reviewing the case for the federal circuit court, Judge Samuel Blatchford (soon to go on the Supreme Court) saw few problems with how the trial had run. The district attorney read portions of *Cupid's Yokes* to the jury, and when the defense wanted to read the pamphlet in its entirety, the judge refused. The obscenity charge stood or fell on the particulars, and based on the statute, "the necessity of reading the whole book is not apparent," the trial judge explained. Bennett's defense had also requested several jury instructions, mostly pertaining to the context and intent of the pamphlet. The key instruction asserted that "where words which might otherwise be obscene or indecent, are used in good faith, in social polemics, philosophical writings, serious arguments, or for any scientific purpose, and are not thrust forward wantonly, or for the purpose of exciting lust or disgust, they are justified by the object of their use." The judge refused to so instruct the jury.

In place of Bennett's suggested framing of obscenity, the court adopted standards imported from the 1868 British case *Regina v. Hicklin*. The proper test of obscenity established in this case was "whether the tendency of the matter is to deprave and corrupt the morals of those whose minds are open to such influences, and into whose hands a publication of this sort may fall." As the court made explicitly clear, texts were to be assessed on the basis of their obscene *parts*, rather than how those parts fit into works as organic wholes; susceptible minds, meanwhile, included "the young and the inexperienced," thus setting the bar for depraving and corrupting distinctly low. In affirming these so-called *Hicklin* standards, circuit judge Blatchford formalized a precedent that would define American obscenity law for nearly eight decades. While President Hayes had pardoned Ezra Heywood for selling the same pamphlet, not even a 200,000-name petition for Bennett's freedom, the largest such campaign of the century, helped him win the same release. Comstock himself personally met with the president to argue for imprisonment, though historian Roderick Bradford contends that the first lady, a devout Methodist known as "Lemonade Lucy" for her teetotaling mandate for White House events, played the most influential role. In any case, to hard labor Bennett went.

As Bennett, Heywood, and others contested Comstock's legitimacy, the Supreme Court signaled its approval of the national obscenity law without yet taking on any obscenity cases directly. Two late-1870s cases reflected its stance, with *Ex parte Jackson* (1877) upholding Congress's right to ban lotteries from the mail. In passing, the Court also alluded to a "matter deemed injurious to the public morals" as falling within the congressional purview. Hearing D. M. Bennett's appeal soon after, Judge Blatchford suggested that *Jackson* had "definitively settled" the Comstock Act's constitutionality. Meanwhile, in *Reynolds v. U.S.* (1878), the Court upheld Congress's ban on polygamy, suggesting expansive federal power over morality. Both cases hinted at previously undeclared federal police powers, reflecting the readjusted Reconstruction-era federalism of rising national power.

When the Court finally turned directly to Comstock in the 1890s, it was a series of nearly unqualified victories for the vice crusader. One of Comstock's most controversial tactics involved his use of pseudonyms to order material in building cases against his opponents. Defendants complained bitterly, likening it to entrapment in the ways it commissioned the committing of crimes. In the 1895 case *Grimm v. U.S.*, emanating out of a western vice agent's use of a fake name to inquire about "fancy photographs" from a St. Louis merchant, the Court unambiguously upheld the tactic as constitutionally sound. The next year, the Court heard its first obscenity case, involving a paper, *Broadway*, with "pictures of females" in "different attitudes of indecency," including pictures coated in black lamp that could be wiped off to expose more revealing sights. Affirming publisher Lew Rosen's conviction, the Court cited the *Bennett* case and quoted its obscenity criteria in full, promoting the *Hicklin* standard to law of the land. The Court also cited several state-level cases from earlier in the century to agree that allegedly obscene material was "not proper to be spread upon the records of this court" and so need not be reprinted in indictments or court documents as long as it was clearly identified, for fear of courts themselves becoming unwitting smut publishers. Juries would still bear the burden (or, perhaps, thrill) of examining the material.

A few months after *Rosen*, the Court reversed an obscenity conviction, this one involving the Kansas publisher of the *Burlington Courier*, a paper guilty of using "coarse and vulgar" language, the Court averred, but not obscene (editor Dan Swearingen had written a fierce invective against an anti-Populist enemy as a "redheaded mental and physical bastard" who would "pimp and fatten on a sister's shame," among other vivid denunciations). Attempting to clarify the law, the Court explained that *obscene* and its synonyms *lewd* and *lascivious* "signify that form of immorality which has relation to sexual impurity." The Court distanced obscenity from its roots in blasphemy, but left intact the shared moralistic origins. With that, the Court determined it had clarified the parameters of obscenity; not until *Roth* in 1957 would it again directly and substantively confront them.

"Sexual impurity," of course, remained a broad category, and Anthony Comstock pushed hard to even further expand its boundaries. Women who violated gender norms inspired his particular wrath. Not only did Victoria Woodhull undermine marriage through her endorsement of free love, for instance, but her very visibility in the public sphere (as Spiritualist, first female presidential candidate, and first female stockbroker on Wall Street, among other signature achievements) constituted a challenge to the reigning Victorian beliefs in women's proper domestic place. As historian Jesse Battan suggests, one of the reasons Anthony Comstock found the free-love press so noxious was that its print culture placed a literal, physical manifestation of women's expressions of desire into the public sphere.

Anti-obscenity activism was never a strictly male affair, with the Women's Christian Temperance Union most prominently mobilizing around women's supposed moral purity to rally against smut in the 1870s and beyond. But the institutional enforcement of obscenity law remained male territory, from Comstock himself through the various judges, juries, and prosecutors who comprised the legal system of the era. Most importantly, the *logic* of obscenity stemmed from patriarchal sexual values that hinged on male control over women, which is why women who resisted their designated places aroused such antagonism in Comstock.

One final example shows the dangers to women who resisted these strictures. Ida Craddock, a Chicago-based mystic and sex reformer, repeatedly fell afoul of obscenity laws in the 1890s for her pamphlets *Right Marital Living* (1897) and *The Wedding Night* (1899), which took bold feminist stances calling for men to attend to women's pleasure. Even though Craddock always situated sexuality within the confines of marriage, her clinical description of semen and vaginas, as well as the suggestion that "a woman's orgasm is as important for her health as a man's is for his," butted against the prevailing Victorian ideology of women's "passionlessness." Politicized by her legal troubles, Craddock moved to New York to more directly contest Comstockism at its heart. Having avoided prison to that point, she found herself quickly sentenced to three months for *The Wedding Night*. The trial judge called the pamphlet "blasphemous," once more invoking the history of obscenity as an outgrowth of blasphemous libel—despite the Supreme Court's apparent severing of that link. It was not the last time a lower court would either disregard or misunderstand the Supreme Court's doctrine.

Devastated by her prison experience, Craddock returned to freedom only to face immediate rearrest on new charges by Comstock. Again convicted, she this time faced an unthinkable five-year sentence. In 1902, she committed suicide rather than serve her term. Her public suicide note acted as final condemnation of Comstock. Blaming him directly for her death, Craddock called him a "sex pervert" and a sadist, "unctuous with hypocrisy," and accused him of deriving pleasure from his own lurid prose about the dangers of smut.

The twentieth century thus began with the Comstock Act adding one more casualty to its body count. In death, though, Craddock called for a future more imminent than she may have realized. "I earnestly hope," she wrote in her final missive, "that the American public will awaken to a sense of the danger which threatens it from Comstockism." Massive social and cultural shifts, already under way but rapidly accelerating in the self-consciously new century, helped facilitate a mass sentiment of modernism eager to dissociate itself from a Victorian past. Comstock entered the century with tremendous, barely accountable legal power, but increasingly found his cultural position relegated to one of relic from a repressed, and repressive, past.

Modernizing Free Speech
Politics, Sex, and the First Amendment
in the Early Twentieth Century

In retrospect, one defense against obscenity charges remained con-spicuously absent from the courtroom as the new century began. The conspicuousness was *only* retrospective, however; in the legal atmos-phere of 1900, few in the mainstream would have assigned the First Amendment any position of centrality in the debates over obscenity. Free-speech activism began in the last quarter of the nineteenth cen-tury, but several decades passed before it attained social or political prominence.

When the egregious civil liberties violations of the Wilson admin-istration during World War I helped awaken broader awareness of the need to protect freedom of speech and the press, a more robust First Amendment than ever before emerged out of the contentious court battles. Yet even as freedom of speech slowly moved into the pantheon of fundamental democratic values, obscenity remained excluded from its provinces. Most theorists of free speech still thought primarily in terms of *political* speech and relied on traditional notions of what that meant; rarely was sexuality conceptualized as inherently political. No powerful or influential participant in the debates over free expression ever suggested allowing pornography into the public sphere.

While obscenity's suppressed status remained constant, however, its parameters shifted. As the American people embraced ideas of modernism in technology, culture, and identity, they also tenuously endorsed modern sexuality. Though perpetually ambivalent about lust, prurience, and various forms of "deviant" sexuality, a broad national consensus coalesced around increasing frankness in education and entertainment, as well as an expanding zone of personal privacy that butted against invasive Comstockian regulations. No definitive legal doctrine would develop until the Supreme Court finally returned to the fray in the 1950s, but well before that it was evident that the broad trajectory in obscenity law was one of liberalization — which followed the currents of what historians have labeled "sexual liberalism," the modern form of sexuality that began to contest Comstock's values.

Forming the Free-Speech Lobby

The Comstock Act had never gone unchallenged. Victoria Woodhull, D. M. Bennett, Ezra Heywood, Ida Craddock, and many others had both sharp critiques of the law's censorial impact and pointed words to describe Comstock's own behavior in enforcing it. But with the strongest critiques coming from freethinkers and free lovers, the arguments were easily marginalized on the basis of their speakers' positions on the fringes of society.

Mainstream political organization against Comstock began with the National Liberal League, mobilized around Dr. E. B. Foote after his run-in with Comstock in 1875. By 1878, the League had obtained a remarkable 70,000 signatures on a petition sent to the House Committee on the Revision of Laws. Though Foote and his son E. B. Foote Jr. led the petition effort, it quickly became associated with its most famous signatory, prominent freethinker Robert Ingersoll. Horrified by Comstock's public comments about using obscenity law to eradicate publications with "infidel" messages, the famously agnostic Ingersoll knew that standard implicated his own speeches and writings. Ingersoll hardly proved a free-speech extremist, though. The petition called for the "repeal or modification" of the Comstock Act, and he went to some lengths to clarify his preference as the latter. "No one wishes the repeal of any law for the suppression of obscene literature," he wrote, adding, "for my part, I wish all such laws rigidly enforced."

The debate over repeal or modification of the Comstock Act ruptured the barely formed organization. Ingersoll and his affiliates wanted the Comstock Act clarified to expressly prohibit Comstock's use of it to enforce his religious beliefs, but they took little interest in further reform. Pitted against them, the other major faction, unwilling to leave sex radicals vulnerable, demanded more categorical resistance. With tension devolving into impasse, the more expansively minded faction regrouped as the National Defense Association

(NDA) in 1878, dedicated specifically to providing legal aid to Comstock defendants.

With the Footes continuing in key roles, the NDA built off the National Liberal League's infrastructure, spearheading the massive petition effort that led President Hayes to pardon Ezra Heywood. It failed to secure similar exoneration for D. M. Bennett, however, or to achieve its goal of overturning the Comstock Act. The NDA consistently assisted sex radicals and freethinkers, famous and otherwise, from Ida Craddock to the Kansas freethinker John B. Wise. Debating a minister in 1894, Wise had sent postcards with graphic sexual quotes from the Bible, resulting in obscenity charges. While the NDA's legal assistance failed to prevent a conviction and $50 fine, the fact that even the Bible could be held legally obscene under the Comstock Act served as potentially effective propaganda for free-speech advocates — though perhaps too inflammatory, since it went largely unused at the time.

While the NDA limited its focus specifically to victims of the Comstock Act, its next notable compatriot, the Free Speech League (FSL), went further, espousing a radical libertarianism that advocated absolute freedom of expression for all citizens, under all conditions. In practice, this meant the sex radicals, health and medicine writers, and pornographers prosecuted by Comstock, as well as such political radicals as communists and anarchists. Formed in response to governmental crackdowns on anarchists after the 1901 assassination of President William McKinley, the FSL directed much of its attention toward the defense of revolutionary political sentiment, especially after Congress passed the Alien Immigration Act of 1903, allowing for the exclusion of foreign advocates of anarchism.

Despite the urgency of defending besieged radicals, FSL founder and leader Theodore Schroeder found time to write the most direct and powerful attack on obscenity law yet undertaken. As a young man, informed by the free thought of Robert Ingersoll, Schroeder had written anti-Mormonism tracts, resulting in a turn-of-the-century obscenity charge for a pamphlet accusing Joseph Smith, founder of the church, of being an abortionist. In 1911, after amassing an unsurpassed knowledge of obscenity law, Schroeder published what amounted to his manifesto, *"Obscene" Literature and Constitutional Law*. Declaring obscenity laws "not within any express or implied power of

Congress to enact," Schroeder flatly conceded that their absence would allow "real smut" to circulate. Without applauding this fact, he simply chalked it up to the conditions of freedom.

Schroeder's positions were outside the mainstream. While *"Obscene" Literature* won positive reviews, it hardly marked the beachhead of a major movement. Indeed, as Schroeder increasingly turned his attention to psychoanalysis in the 1910s, the FSL was left to wither. Combined with the death of the NDA's E. B. Foote Jr. in 1915, the result was an atrophied free-speech movement. What would emerge from its crumbling was a distinctly less radical and libertarian activism on the issue of obscenity. In the American Civil Liberties Union (ACLU), the free-speech lobby would finally find a sustained and influential organizational base. To do so required trading the categorical opposition to Comstockism that demanded free expression for all, no matter how distasteful or offensive, for a more limited, if also less aggressively unpopular, version of free speech.

The ACLU's roots took soil during the buildup to World War I, in the pacifist American Union Against Militarism. When the Union's early faith in President Woodrow Wilson to avoid entering the European conflict proved misplaced, a collaborative relationship turned combative. As the Wilson administration grew increasingly aggressive in its efforts to suppress dissent, the Union found itself caught in the middle, with the government moving to the right on civil liberties issues as the Union's Civil Liberties Bureau radicalized. In 1917 the bureau took independent form as the National Civil Liberties Bureau (NCLB). Under the leadership of pacifist Roger Baldwin, the NCLB became the most outspoken critic of Wilson's staggering wartime repression.

Domestic wartime measures were drastic. The 1917 Espionage Act criminalized the deliberate causing of "insubordination, disloyalty, mutiny, or refusal of duty," as well as obstructing military recruitment, and the 1918 amendment known as the Sedition Act went even further, targeting "unpatriotic or disloyal" language. The Wilson administration interpreted all of this language broadly, commencing a national crackdown on antiwar rhetoric, as well as anarchism, labor activism, and other radical doctrines. More than 2,000 criminal cases resulted, most won by the government. Meanwhile, Postmaster General Albert Burleson, empowered by the new legislation to ban advo-

{ *Chapter 2* }

cacy of treason in the mails, engaged in particularly punitive measures, largely destroying the socialist and left-wing press. Encouraged by these coercive actions, nongovernmental vigilantism also ran rampant.

In this chilling political climate where dissent was literally criminalized, the majority of activists, intellectuals, and organizations kowtowed to power, with even pacifists often endorsing the war or simply keeping quiet. As a rare voice of resistance, the NCLB found itself a target. The Justice Department raided its New York offices, and the Post Office denied it mailing privileges, even, ironically, for its pamphlet *Freedom of Speech and the Press*. With the raising of the draft age to thirty-five now including the thirty-four-year-old Baldwin, the pacifist NCLB head refused to sign up for the selective service and consequently received a maximum yearlong prison sentence. Far from breaking his spirit, the experience further radicalized Baldwin. As a young man involved in the Progressive movement he had not taken an inherently adversarial stance toward government, but in prison he came to a new understanding of the modern state as a tool of the business class, designed not to promote democracy but rather to perpetuate inequality.

Baldwin emerged from prison vigorously committed to the fight for civil liberties, but society was not yet with him. The public had accepted Wilson's crackdowns in the name of wartime exigencies. When Attorney General A. Mitchell Palmer attempted to extend these measures into peacetime, however, expressions of resistance grew more audible. Capitalizing on panic over the 1917 Russian revolution, in which communists had toppled the czardom, as well as multiple anarchist attempts to bomb him, Palmer launched a massive roundup of foreign- and native-born communists, anarchists, and labor radicals, all in the name of national security. With thousands arrested and hundreds deported, the excesses of Palmer's 1919–1920 Red Scare finally drew protest from liberal media outlets, Department of Labor officials, and even some members of the Justice Department. Greater awareness of the need for civil liberties to curtail such heavy-handed tactics ensued, though not before Palmer managed to devastate the national labor-union movement, setting its progress back a full decade.

Reorganized in 1920 as the American Civil Liberties Union (ACLU), the NCLB capitalized on this dawning sentiment. Its 1920 report on the unconstitutional actions of the Justice Department excoriated Palmer. Baldwin's radical affiliations and uncompromising rhetoric kept the early ACLU firmly outside the political mainstream, but its 1920 report did win the signatures of several influential law professors, including Harvard's Zechariah Chafee, whose 1920 monograph *Freedom of Speech* quickly achieved prominence, even if his writing put him under fire at his Harvard post. The ACLU still had its work cut out for it in forging a mass consensus around free speech and civil liberties, but a half century after the Comstock Act, its opponents finally had the beginnings of a sustained organizational infrastructure.

Incorporating the First Amendment

As shown in chapter 1, the First Amendment occupied a marginal role in nineteenth-century debates over obscenity. With the Bill of Rights understood primarily as a restraint on the *federal* government, the First Amendment had never guaranteed absolute individual freedom of expression; state and local restrictions were uncontroversial. Meanwhile, although the First Amendment did expressly prohibit Congress from "abridging the freedom of speech, or of the press," when Congress did just that with the Comstock Act, general consensus situated this more in the realm of protecting morality. While the extent of federal police powers remained rather unclear, the consolidation of federal power during and after the Civil War made the Comstock Act and other morally based feats of state-building more feasible than they would have been in antebellum years. The greatest achievement of the ACLU and its allies would be to counteract this legacy by positing a robust First Amendment as the crucial underpinning of a democratic society. The process would take years, decades even, but persistent civil liberties activism gradually found growing support from the American public.

Going into the twentieth century, First Amendment claims hardly found a receptive audience in the court system. Historian David Rabban identifies "a pervasive judicial hostility to virtually all free speech claims" in the years before World War I, extending up to and including the Supreme Court. Labor injunctions against striking workers were a common tool of industrialists to break union efforts, and the courts consistently upheld them, even to the point of directly silencing unions. One particularly fraught injunction case involved Chicago railroad workers who were barred from urging other workers to walk off their jobs. When it reached the Supreme Court in 1895, such was the marginal position of the First Amendment that labor lawyer Clarence Darrow did not even cite it in making his case. Nearly a decade later he did try to cite it, defending English labor radical John Turner from deportation after the 1903 Alien Immigration Act impinged on the free expression of immigrants who supported anarchism. The argument won no traction with the Supreme Court, which upheld the law in 1904.

American Federation of Labor leader Samuel Gompers raised the First Amendment when an injunction barred the AFL from including an antiunion St. Louis company on its "unfair" and "We Don't Patronize" lists. When Gompers and other union leaders were imprisoned for violating the injunction, the case reached the Supreme Court in 1911. Unmoved by Gompers's claims, the Court — no more supportive of labor rights than free speech — dismissed his argument with a curt assertion that the AFL's boycotting tactics should be understood not as protected speech, but rather as conspiratorial restraint of trade. The Court showed reluctance to fully articulate its understanding of *speech* in the case, but seemed to suggest that speech that inspired action could simply be considered part of the action and regulated as such.

Other Supreme Court opinions showed similar disregard for the amendment's ostensible protections. When Thomas Patterson, a longtime U.S. congressman from Colorado, was held in contempt of court for publishing scathingly satirical political cartoons in his newspaper mocking the corruption of the Colorado Supreme Court, he attempted to adjust First Amendment law to political reality. Noting that the Fourteenth Amendment guaranteed individual due process rights of life, liberty, and property at the *state* level, an explicit shift from the Constitution's historic application at the federal level, Patterson asserted that the Fourteenth Amendment thus incorporated his First Amendment rights against the state of Colorado's intrusion. The Court pointedly disagreed.

While Justice Oliver Wendell Holmes's majority opinion left

"undecided" the question of the Fourteenth Amendment's impact on the First, he held the issue moot, declaring that even if Patterson were right, it would not "prevent the subsequent punishment of such as may be deemed contrary to the public welfare," leaving state officials massive latitude to suppress even political cartoons. A few years later, in 1915, the Court upheld film censorship, excluding motion pictures from inclusion among the First Amendment–protected press and instead classifying them as "a business, pure and simple, originated and conducted for profit, like other spectacles."

These recurring defeats reflected a growing assertion of First Amendment rights, even as the Supreme Court's unwillingness to support free expression generated cynicism among some observers. The revolutionary Industrial Workers of the World offered its own satirical version of the First Amendment in 1913: "Freedom of speech shall be guaranteed to all capitalists, politicians, preachers, and other representatives of law and order in good and regular standing. It shall be abridged to socialists and utterly denied to anarchists, to the I.W.W. and to all inciters of strikes and other riots." Even the radical Wobblies, as IWW members were known, would be taken aback by the Court's rejection of free speech during the Red Scare, as cases from World War I measures percolated up through the judicial system to reach its highest court. Upholding governmental prerogatives over individual rights at every step, the Court delivered a crushing blow to civil liberties, albeit one laced with biter irony as it sowed the seeds of a new First Amendment regime.

As the first Espionage Act cases reached the Court in 1919, it affirmed several convictions. Charles Schenck, general secretary of the Socialist Party, had been convicted for sending a pamphlet calling military conscription a form of despotism, urging young men called to service to "assert your rights." The Court affirmed the conviction. Eugene V. Debs, a major leftist activist who had won nearly a million votes as Socialist candidate in the 1912 presidential election, was arrested in Ohio after a 1918 antiwar speech and sentenced to a draconian ten-year prison term. This, too, the Court affirmed. As in the past, speech connected to actions could be folded into the actions — even if they had not actually occurred.

In his *Schenck* opinion Holmes had presented the key legal question as "whether the words are used in such circumstances and are of such a nature as to create a clear and present danger that they will bring about the substantive evils that Congress has a right to prevent." He did not belabor the question. In a time of war, he simply believed, the socialist pamphlets clearly met the standard. Holmes did not seem to assign much immediate significance to his phrasing, since he did not repeat the "clear and present danger" language in subsequent related cases of the October 1918 term that stretched into 1919, such as *Debs*.

A 1919 article by legal scholar Zechariah Chafee, however, highlighted the "clear and present danger" standard as a bold intervention in free-speech doctrine. Though the progressively inclined Harvard scholar knew full well the Court's hostility to First Amendment claims, Chafee devised a deliberately revisionist history of American free speech that situated Holmes — despite his clear record of resistance to First Amendment claims — as a modern pioneer in civil liberties. The historian David Rabban has persuasively argued that Chafee disregarded historical accuracy in order to promote a free-speech agenda and that it proved remarkably successful when Holmes, ironically enough, embraced the image of himself that Chafee had invented.

Whether or not Holmes found himself under the sway of Chafee's against-the-grain reading of his own opinion, his position did in fact shift. When the Court resumed for the October 1919 term, Holmes suddenly found himself dissenting against a majority still committed to affirming Espionage and Sedition Act convictions. In the first major case, *Abrams v. U.S.*, a group of Russian-born radicals had handed out circulars in New York City, even throwing some from a window. Presenting the war as a capitalist conspiracy, the pamphlets called President Wilson a hypocrite and a coward, and went on to urge workers and immigrants to "spit in the face of the false, hypocritic, military propaganda" and instead begin a general strike. Sentenced to twenty-year terms, the five defendants insisted that their real grievance had been not with the war itself, but rather with Wilson's illegal military intrusion into Russia in the hopes of squashing the revolution. An unimpressed Supreme Court affirmed their convictions.

The affirmation was not unanimous, however. Holmes, author of the key repressive speech cases last term, now dissented. Working hard to distinguish the facts of the case from *Debs*, *Schenck*, and other earlier cases, Holmes downgraded the allegedly seditious material to "a silly leaflet by an unknown man," unlikely to foment much threat to national security. Returning to his own phrase that Chafee had imbued with meaning, Holmes for the first time explicitly valorized the First Amendment, asserting that only "speech that produces or is intended to produce a clear and imminent danger" of "certain substantive evils" could be constitutionally suppressed. Denying that this constituted an about-face, Holmes simply cited *Schenck* as consistent with his *Abrams* dissent.

Only Justice Louis Brandeis, the progressive reformer appointed by Wilson in 1916, joined Holmes in dissent. Writing as a minority, they could not spare the five radicals from prison. Yet the dissent was understood immediately as a clarion call against the wartime and postwar excesses. Slowly, the First Amendment was rising in significance, moving toward the centerpiece of the American political tableau. "Whatever political or economic opinion falls within the scope of the First Amendment," Chafee wrote at the start of *Freedom of Speech*, "ought to be safeguarded from governmental interference." An unrepentant Eugene Debs ran for president again in 1920, again receiving nearly a million votes as Socialist Party candidate, this time from his prison cell. By 1921, with the threat of sedition (and further socialist votes) past, President Warren Harding commuted the sentences of Debs and twenty-four others on Christmas Day. In 1923, President Calvin Coolidge followed suit with more commutations. Perhaps most importantly, the ACLU won its first major free-speech victory in a Paterson, New Jersey, labor conflict where Roger Baldwin and others had violated an injunction by marching with American flags and reading out loud the First Amendment.

Almost as an afterthought, the Supreme Court incorporated the First Amendment through the Fourteenth in 1925, granting its fundamental significance in one of the more perversely understated monumental moments in American legal history. A few recent cases involving education had suggested a shift in this direction, when the Court invalidated a Nebraska ban on teaching foreign languages in primary schools and an anti-Catholic Oregon law mandating public-school attendance, both on Fourteenth Amendment grounds of individual rights against state actions, but the doctrine remained undeveloped. Meanwhile, Benjamin Gitlow, a revolutionary socialist, had been convicted of criminal anarchy in a New York state court for such writings as *The Left Wing Manifesto* and *The Revolutionary Age*. "For present purposes," wrote Justice Edward Sanford, "we may and do assume that freedom of speech and of the press which are protected by the First Amendment from abridgment by Congress are among the fundamental rights and 'liberties' protected by the due process clause of the Fourteenth Amendment from impairment by the States." Sanford offered no further analysis, and the declaration was rendered even more underwhelming when it failed to prevent the Court from affirming Gitlow's conviction. Invoking the clear and present danger test, Sanford described Gitlow's fairly boilerplate radicalism as "not the language of philosophical abstraction" but rather "direct incitement."

A terse Holmes again dissented, with Brandeis signing on. Wasting no words, he simply charged Sanford and the majority with misunderstanding both the clear and present danger test and also Gitlow's tracts, whose socially marginal position ensured that they posed no real danger. Two years later, Brandeis delivered his own definitive free-speech statement, in the case of Anita Whitney, convicted under California's Criminal Syndicalism Act for her membership in the Communist Labor Party. Justice Sanford's opinion again distinguished between free expression and conspiring to overthrow the state, a distinction Brandeis savaged in a critical opinion. Denying that communist organizing posed a tangible threat, he put it in perspective with a biting quip: "Men feared witches and burnt women." Outlining his own First Amendment stance, Brandeis explained, "No danger flowing from speech can be deemed clear and present unless the incidence of evil apprehended is so imminent that it may befall before there is opportunity for full discussion." Invoking the nation's founders, he noted that "those who won our independence by revolution were not cowards."

Even more so than Holmes's *Abrams* dissent, Brandeis's *Whitney* opinion laid out a broad civil libertarian platform, enshrining a virtual ACLU stance in the official word of the Supreme Court. Yet, for all the fierce critique of Sanford's majority opinion, Brandeis's was in fact a concurrence, supporting affirmation of Whitney's conviction. Though Brandeis made clear where he stood on the matter, ultimately he believed the Court must defer to the state of California in defining what constituted a threat; it was a question not just of free speech, but also of federalism. In a rushed pair of closing paragraphs, Brandeis conceded that while neither Whitney nor her communist group had actually conspired to commit crimes, the California courts had decided that the industrial-sabotage tactics of the IWW "would be furthered by the activity of the society of which Miss Whitney was a member," and it was not the place of the Supreme Court to question that assessment — however much Brandeis might want to.

As a dissent and a concurrence, neither major Supreme Court declaration of First Amendment rights had yet spared the plaintiff from prison. Yet Brandeis in particular pioneered a new analytical model of free speech; in contrast to earlier libertarian radicals such as Theodore Schroder, whose valorization of speech rights emphasized the individual, Brandeis came out of a Progressive tradition more concerned with social interests. He strongly supported free expression, but less as an individual right than as a *social* one — namely, as the cornerstone of a democratic society. As such, free speech was not absolute, but always a matter of balancing individual rights against broader social interests. The idea was as old as James Madison, but Brandeis's gloss on it was as modern as the automobile.

When Charles Evans Hughes took the chief justiceship in 1930, he recognized the tension in free-speech jurisprudence. Brandeis had compellingly described free expression as "essential to effective democracy," and yet even as such theories imbued the First Amendment with ever-greater protective functions, the Court continued to allow both federal and state governments wide latitude in defining "threats" that exempted various forms of political participation from the realm of speech.

Determined to rectify the incongruities, Hughes wrote opinions for two 1931 cases that decisively put the increasingly robust First Amendment into meaningful practice at last. Striking a 1919 California law against red flags as unconstitutional suppression of (communist) political speech, Hughes signaled that radicals would begin to have the same access to free expression as those within the political mainstream. And in rejecting a Minnesota gag order against the scurrilous newspaper the *Saturday Press*, Hughes called the order "the essence of censorship." While publisher Jay Near was later described by his chronicler as "Anti-Catholic, anti-Semitic, antiblack, and anti-labor," his repugnant opinions did not exclude him from the "immunity from previous restraints or censorship" that Hughes found in the First Amendment.

Under Hughes, the amendment moved from rhetorical device to tangible tool. What that meant for obscenity remained unclear. While Hughes noted in *Near v. Minnesota* that "the primary requirements of decency may be enforced against obscene publications," it was a mere aside, issued without citation or explanation. This embodied the Court's behavior for the first half of the twentieth century. As the First Amendment's slow ascent into fundamental underpinning of American democracy took shape, the Court never weighed in with more than asides to how this impacted obscenity doctrine. Instead, that debate was left to the lower courts — and even more importantly, to the evolving social and cultural mores of the times.

———

Sexuality, Culture, and Obscenity

If twentieth-century politics began with a bang as a gunshot felled President William McKinley in 1901, modern sexuality followed suit a few years later with its own symbolically resonant assassination, as Harry Thaw shot wealthy architect Stanford White for having "ruined" Thaw's wife, Evelyn Nesbit, in an earlier relationship. The first great sex scandal of the century, the 1906 incident quickly came to represent the many cultural shifts already under way. As a sometimes-nude painting and photograph model, Nesbit reflected the increasingly public nature of female sexuality, parleying her prominence into further fame as an actress on stage and screen. Quickly adapted into multiple films, the case proved perfect fodder for the emerging mass entertainment culture driven by the new medium. And while endless press coverage of sensationalized scandal was nothing new, the frank discussion of pre- and extramarital sex showed a society publically acknowledging and negotiating the tenuous boundaries of acceptable sexual behavior, adjusting to the rising awareness that Victorian norms failed to dictate urban modes of living.

The graphic nature of some recountings of the Thaw-White-Nesbit story even inspired obscenity charges, as newspapers in Louisville, Kentucky, faced them for reprinting graphic testimony from Thaw's trial. Such episodes reflected the growing tension between restrictive laws and changing cultural norms that butted up against them. In that case, the public's prurient interests won, as a judge exonerated the newspapers in the name of the trial's public interest and significance. Other similar incidents fared less well for sexual modernism. The Massachusetts Supreme Judicial Court in 1909 upheld the obscenity of Elinor Glyn's novel *Three Weeks* for its adulterous content, though the book's best-seller status revealed widespread interest in its tale.

Perhaps no medium better reflected these tensions than the cinema. First appearing as a "low" form of entertainment in nickelodeons intended for immigrants and poor workers in the 1890s, film exploded in popularity as the new century began. New York City alone expanded from fewer than 50 theaters in 1900 to more than 500 by 1908, with other cities following suit. The new medium found few defenders when progressive reformers pushed for official censorship boards on the condescending grounds that its audience was insufficiently sophisticated to critically engage with the sensational imagery. To these reformers, smut or even sensationalistic cinema was, as Paul Boyer writes, "as much a part of the urban environment as were sweatshops and unadulterated food" — and in just as much need of regulation.

Partly inspired by scandalous films such as the Thaw-White adaptation *The Unwritten Law* (1906), Chicago launched the first, police-operated, censor board in 1907, and on Christmas Day the next year New York City mayor George McClellan Jr. revoked all licenses for theaters to operate. Exhibitors won an injunction against McClellan's sweeping gesture, but the battle was on. Censor boards proliferated at the state and local levels, with the Supreme Court upholding them in 1915 — but at the same time, public hunger for cinematic thrills drove filmmakers and studios to perpetually push against their constraints, with "white slave" films about prostitution in the 1910s, alluring "flappers" such as Theda Bara and Clara Bow appearing shortly thereafter, and Cecil B. DeMille's opulent, sexualized biblical spectacles tremendously popular by the 1920s.

What film showed was that law could not always contain broad cultural swings. When it came to obscenity, few other than libertarian radicals of Theodore Schroeder's ilk questioned the *existence* of obscenity law, but the rise of what historians John D'Emilio and Estelle Freedman call "sexual liberalism" began to constrict its *extent*. Sexual liberalism encompassed a great variety of ideas and behaviors, but at its heart it involved the modernizing of Victorian norms, generally within such existing structures as marriage and heterosexuality. Thus, marital sexual pleasure, and even some premarital sexual experimentation, became increasingly acceptable, aided by the sexualized consumer culture and its accompanying advertising industry sprouting at the time, as well as the new discourse of psychoanalysis, whose pioneer Sigmund Freud insisted on sexual undercurrents even in regard to seemingly nonsexual thoughts and dreams. In keeping with nineteenth-century understandings of "liberalism," this modernization privileged individual freedom over state regulation.

Sexual liberalism revealed itself taking shape in regard to birth control and the Comstock Act as early as the late nineteenth century. Under the Comstock Act, even basic information about contraception and abortion was deemed legally obscene. From the start, women and men resisted this restriction on their reproductive options, often successfully. Comstock had one woman, Sarah Chase, arrested five times between 1878 and 1900; only once, in the case of a botched abortion, did she serve any prison time. Otherwise, she sold contraceptive devices with relative impunity, and juries repeatedly refused to indict her. The historian Andrea Tone uses Chase and others to argue for an unspoken "zone of privacy" that developed informally. While a strong majority of approximately 75 percent of Comstock's arrests resulted in convictions, 38 percent of persons charged for selling contraceptives or contraceptive information avoided conviction. Those convicted nearly always received lenient sentences.

If the contraceptive zone of privacy remained unspoken outside sex radical circles, by the early twentieth century the social changes of sexual liberalism opened space for more public discussion. Coming out of the labor movement, activist Margaret Sanger saw the human toll inflicted by the Comstock Act on poor women trapped in cycles of unwanted pregnancies and unsafe, illegal abortions. As she wrote of Comstock in her book *My Fight for Birth Control*, "his stunted, neurotic nature and savage methods of attack had ruined thousands of women's lives." Dedicating herself to combating his denial of reproductive self-determination, she launched a newsletter, *The Woman Rebel*, which was declared unmailable by the Post Office almost immediately in 1914. Indicted on obscenity charges, Sanger hopped bail and went into European exile.

Returning to the United States in 1915, Sanger beat the charge when the district attorney abandoned the case, citing, in part, her "nervous condition." The sexist condescension of the comment masked the fact that Comstock Act action against contraception was on the wane. While Sanger's ex-husband William did receive a monthlong jail term for distributing her pamphlet *Family Limitation* while she remained out of the country, reformer Mary Ware Dennett continued publishing her educational pamphlet *The Sex Side of Life*, written for her own sons in 1915, without incident for several years even after postal authorities declared it obscene and unmailable in 1922.

Concurrent with this social pushback against the Comstock Act came judicial manifestation of sexually liberal attitudes. The most important obscenity case of the early century emanated out of the federal court for the southern district of New York, where a complaint from Anthony Comstock had led to an obscenity indictment involving Daniel Carson Goodman's novel *Hagar Revelly*. The novel detailed, as a court reporter put it, the "several amorous misadventures" following the seduction of the title character, ending with "a loveless marriage and the prospect of a bleak future." Its moralistic message did not preclude Goodman from reveling in description of the seduction, where, "intoxicated by the cataclysmic enormity of her first real entrance into the secrets of sexual passion," Hagar Revelly "clung to" her seducer, "returning throb for throb, pulsation for pulsation," until "through the light fabric of her thin silk skirts she could feel the warmth of his body penetrate into her own."

While the state prosecutor honed in on this passage, publisher Mitchell Kennerley (facing the 1913 criminal charge) demanded consideration of the full book rather than sensational passages, asking the federal court to intervene. In a pretrial hearing on that motion, Judge Learned Hand, who would display free-speech sympathies during World War I as he supported the radical magazine *The Masses* against postal suppression, felt bound by precedent stretching back to *Bennett* and denied Kennerley's request. Yet unwilling to pass judgment without comment, he added a plea for further consideration at a higher judicial level. "The rule as laid down," he wrote, "however consonant it may be with mid-Victorian morals, does not seem to me to answer to the understanding and morality of the present time." Not only did Hand advocate a modernized obscenity doctrine that did not "reduce our treatment of sex to the standard of a child's library in the supposed interest of a salacious few," but he also called into question the *Hicklin* standard that set the bar for obscenity at the most susceptible reader. Calling that a "fatal policy," Hand invoked "the average conscience of the time" as a better yardstick.

Hand's sexual liberalism failed to spare Kennerley a state trial, though the growing prevalence of similar attitudes could be seen when three jury members had to be excused for what the *New York Times* called "prejudice on their part against Anthony Comstock." Back in the criminal court, the judge delivered slanted instructions to the jury, emphasizing the *Hicklin* standards and heavily suggesting conviction. They refused, deliberating just over five hours before acquitting Kennerley. An apoplectic federal attorney exclaimed, "I am at an utter loss to understand the verdict," but the logic was clear: while Judge Hand could not overrule *Bennett* or the *Hicklin* standard given credence by the Supreme Court, the jury could, and did, silently nullify them.

Comstock's death shortly thereafter in 1915 invites historical interpretation as marking the passing of an era, and not without cause. While the *New York Times* still commended Comstock's work in its obituary, sexual liberalism continued amassing influence, achieving social consensus at least in the urban world. Certainly it stunted the relentless quest of Comstock's New York Society for the Suppression of Vice (NYSSV) successor John Saxton Sumner to continue the battle against indecency. Sumner aimed high, ambitiously targeting books from respected authors and publishers during and after World War I, but historian Paul Boyer terms the result "humiliating failure," with most cases failing to win convictions, and frequently even indictments. By 1924 vice society arrests dropped to twenty-five, the lowest in years.

Yet while the iconic speakeasies and flappers of the 1920s certainly suggested an urbane decade striving to normalize expressions of sexuality and desire, the Jazz Age never went uncontested. Those same years also witnessed the social conservatism of Prohibition and a resurgent Ku Klux Klan, whose headline-grabbing racism, anti-Semitism, and anti-Catholicism overshadowed its conservative sexual politics, which it exerted in numerous ways. Obscenity law continued to operate as an instrument to police the boundaries of the socially permissible, with censorial power claiming some significant victories.

Sumner managed a conviction against the Greenwich Village publishers of the avant-garde magazine *Little Review* in 1921 for including a section of James Joyce's modernist landmark *Ulysses*, notorious for its stream-of-consciousness style and blunt descriptions of sexual thoughts and acts. Five years later the Watch and Ward Society, Boston's answer to the NYSSV, banned sixty-five books in what became known as the "Boston Massacre," with such respected authors as Sinclair Lewis, Ernest Hemingway, and William Faulkner caught up alongside less prestigious works.

To that point, the ACLU had shown little interest in obscenity or censorship. Coming out of the bruising battle for wartime political expression, the group never assigned these issues primary importance in its agenda. Nor did it question the basic validity of the Comstock Act. Despite Theodore Schroeder's voluminous writings on obscenity, Zechariah Chafee excluded him from his ostensibly comprehensive history of free speech, paying only the most fleeting attention to obscenity in *Freedom of Speech*, which quickly became the bible of civil libertarians as Schroeder's work receded from memory and view. Like profanity, Chafee explained, in obscenity law "the words are criminal, not because of the ideas they communicate, but like acts because of their immediate consequences to the five senses." This separation of obscenity from the realm of "ideas" would prove influential.

A few years later in 1924, ACLU founder and head Roger Baldwin simply said, "censorship on the ground of morality . . . has been accepted for several centuries." Though historian Leigh Ann Wheeler notes that Baldwin and several other founding ACLU members led sexually unconventional lives and used the organization to support birth control activists, nudists, and those accused of obscenity in various ways from negotiating with public officials to providing legal aid, in a formal capacity the ACLU made little dent litigating against obscenity laws in the 1920s.

The national politics of the 1920s were discernibly more conservative than the urban culture, with a rightward swing that saw a steady stream of pro-business Republicans elected president across the decade. This left the ACLU grasping to achieve social legitimacy, and culture proved one way to do so. The infamous 1925 Scopes Monkey Trial in Tennessee brought the ACLU some of its first positive national attention beyond radical circles when it defended teacher

John Scopes's right to teach evolution. Fighting censorship, the group realized, was another effective means to secure a reputation, and after the 1926 Boston Massacre, it increasingly turned to freedom of speech, a cause far more popular than the rights of radicals and labor organizers. Member Morris Ernst defended Radclyffe Hall's British lesbian novel *The Well of Loneliness* against obscenity charges in 1928 and 1929, and won.

Mary Ware Dennett helped push the group along when she was indicted on obscenity charges in 1928, having sent *The Sex Side of Life* through the mail undisturbed since the 1922 postal declaration of its obscene nature. Dennett, a longtime ACLU member, encouraged the organization to expand its vision of free speech. Calling the pamphlet "pure and simple smut," the prosecutor read passages from the dry, educational pamphlet in a lurid voice, infusing them with a salaciousness otherwise absent from the page. When a jury convicted Dennett, she refused to pay the $300 fine, preferring jail to accepting her work's obscenity. Both an appeal and the formation of the ACLU's National Committee on Freedom from Censorship were promptly launched. Newspaper editorials across the nation expressed outrage that a civic-minded grandmother could face jail time for something so unpornographic as the pamphlet.

Dennett won on appeal in 1930, and sitting judge Augustus Hand (cousin to Learned) went on in 1936 to allow a New York gynecologist to import Japanese contraceptives to be used between married partners when pregnancy was medically inadvisable. Though the language of the Comstock Act was categorical in suppressing such devices, Hand read it through the lens of modern life, claiming, "the articles here in question ought not to be forfeited when not intended for an immoral purpose." Untroubled by the literal language of the law, Hand simply imagined that Congress surely intended to ban contraceptives only for those immoral purposes — leaving unsaid but implied that nonprocreative marital sex might too claim such protection. Or, as Dennett more acidly noted in her 1930 book *Who's Obscene?*, even members of Congress, while unwilling to defend contraception, "obviously represented family limitation," as few had large families, but "the majority of them were neither sterile nor ascetic." American practices clearly departed from official American doctrine.

In advancing the cause of sexual liberalism by fighting the Comstock Act on multiple fronts of free speech and contraceptive access, neither Dennett nor the ACLU ever argued against the *existence* of obscenity law, only its forms of *enforcement*. That sheer pornography could be constitutionally suppressed as obscene went largely unquestioned, with no prominent voices carrying the torch of Theodore Schroeder's radical libertarianism that would grant absolute freedom of expression, even to smut. Instead, the specific points of contention lay largely in the *Hicklin* standards, which allowed suppression based on *parts* of a work rather than its organic whole, and based the criteria for obscenity on the most susceptible minds, including children or the mentally unbalanced. Free-speech enthusiasts called for the average adult citizen as a better test; otherwise, as Learned Hand had warned in *Kennerley*, this reduced American bookshelves to that literature fit for children.

Finally, dissatisfaction with the procedural elements of obscenity law that placed inordinate power in the hands of Comstocks, Sumners, postmasters, and customs officials butted against the values of many Americans, especially given the backdrop of nascent European fascism, which saw power consolidated in antidemocratic ways. Power should inhere, many believed, in juries, not dictatorial figures. Historian Andrea Friedman calls this bundle of values "democratic moral authority," and it represented the dominant ideology of sexual liberalism, calling not for radical, unregulated freedom, but for the modernization and democratization of law to better mirror the evolving sexual mores of the twentieth century.

No case better crystallized democratic moral authority and sexual liberalism than the victory of James Joyce's *Ulysses* against customs officials who sought to have it excluded in 1933. Clearing the book for entry through customs, federal judge John Woolsey, clearly inspired by Joyce's challenging but brilliant style, composed an artful opinion that carefully distinguished the book from the pornographic "leer of the sensualist." Dismissing the "words which are criticized as dirty" (describing sexual and other bodily functions) as "old Saxon words known to almost all men," Woolsey introduced the notion of intent into his assessment; as a "sincere and honest book" rather than "dirt for dirt's sake," *Ulysses* "did not tend to excite sexual impulses or lustful thoughts." Elsewhere Woolsey added, "nowhere does it tend to be an aphrodisiac."

A judge comfortable with the social shifts of modernism, Woolsey had two years earlier declared nonobscene and thus importable books by British sex reformer Marie Stopes, including *Married Love* and even *Contraception*. "A considered attempt to explain to married people how their mutual sex life may be made happier," he called the former. Between the Stopes opinions and his defense of *Ulysses*, Woolsey made a compelling case for the legitimization of public sexual discussion — always within reputable frameworks of marriage, education, medicine, and high art, though, never as mere lustful aphrodisiac. Woolsey showed an almost casual dismissiveness toward the *Hicklin* standards, approaching *Ulysses* as a whole and not just in its specific "dirty" parts, and explicitly positioning its "effect on a person with average sex instincts" as the proper barometer of obscenity.

Woolsey's case stood as precedent only in the federal district for southern New York, though it was given a boost when Augustus Hand affirmed at the appellate level (with Learned Hand sharing the bench and concurring). Endorsing all of Woolsey's main points and extending them even further, Hand questioned whether the *Hicklin* standards had ever been given the explicit imprimatur of the Supreme Court. "That numerous long passages in *Ulysses* contain matter that is obscene under any fair definition of the word cannot be gainsaid," Hand admitted, but the critical determinant was "the net effect," which he found "pitiful and tragic, rather than lustful."

With the Supreme Court remaining on the sidelines, it fell to the lower courts to modernize obscenity doctrine. While the *Hicklin* standards remained alive and well in numerous state and federal courts, the pioneering efforts of such judges as the Hands and Woolsey reflected the broad influence of sexual liberalism on the legal system by the 1930s. Left unanswered in these judges' proud declarations of modernism was the question of disreputable sexuality. Certain forms of public explicitness were sanctioned by the courts, but what of that material that fell short of James Joyce's artistry or Marie Stopes's pedagogical integrity? With *Ulysses* "rated as a book of considerable power by persons whose opinions are entitled to weight," Hand clearly felt impelled to defend it in part because of its status as a "sort of contemporary classic" — to do otherwise would reveal retrograde cultural sympathies, and by the 1930s few wanted association with the obsolete Comstocks of the world.

The early career of Samuel Roth speaks to this legal and cultural gray zone, showing what happened to freedom of speech when the material in question lacked such valorization. Long before his pivotal 1957 Supreme Court case, Roth's decades of scuffles with obscenity law showed the vulnerability of that "dirt for dirt's sake" that none in the legal, cultural, or political mainstream saw fit to defend. Roth's legal biography provides as well a history of obscenity law's convoluted borders at the ground level as it evolved for over half a century without guidance from the Supreme Court.

CHAPTER 3

Samuel Roth, From Art to Smut

Of the few things Samuel Roth is remembered for, none are flattering. Yet his life embodied many American narratives, some myth, some historical reality: that of the lowly immigrant achieving middle-class comforts through hardscrabble labor and ingeniousness; that of the white ethnic outsider seeking elusive inclusion in the American body politic; and that of a developing mass culture with eyes toward aesthetic loftiness and mind frequently in the gutter. Most of all, in both his personal obsessions and his long conflict with the law, Roth represented a parallel American history to the iconic moments of the Jazz Age, the Great Depression, World War II, and suburbanization, marked instead by evolving but persistent fixations and anxieties about religion, identity, and, most of all, sex.

Roth was not a free-speech activist, until he needed to be; while it is impossible to fully untangle his motivations for pursuing a life of publishing smut, they undeniably ranged from the monetary to his unwavering personal interest in the matters at hand in his various publications. Even in these overlapping layers, he remained quintessentially American, in a society where sex was simultaneously policed, fetishized, and turned into a commodity.

While Roth's 1957 Supreme Court obscenity case is generally the index through which he enters the historical record, the three decades up to that moment are just as important in charting the legal and cultural struggles over obscenity and the boundaries of the socially permissible. Because Roth's many court battles transpired locally, primarily in New York City, and held little significance as precedents to be cited in other cases, they have drawn little attention from historians devising genealogies of modern obscenity doctrine. If marginal to the organic congealing of doctrine, though, they reveal much about the employment and intentions of obscenity law, amounting to a shadow history of obscenity as it played out well below the Supreme Court's purview. It is to Roth's early legal and cultural tumult that this chapter turns.

Toward the Obscene Underbelly of
Culture: Roth in the 1920s

Born to a family of Austrian-Polish Jews in 1893, Samuel Roth entered a social world marked by the poverty, instability, and violent anti-Semitism that spawned a wave of Jewish outmigration from eastern Europe during the period, part of a much longer diasporic history that would haunt Roth throughout his life. Immigrating into the United States at age seven and taking refuge, like hundreds of thousands more eastern European Jews, in New York City, the young Roth arrived just in time to experience the dawning of a new century, matching his new homeland's bristling energy with his own boundless aspirations.

Young Roth grew up against a backdrop of President Theodore Roosevelt's spirited celebrations of fitness and vigor as masculine traits to be adopted by both individual men and the nation itself, and he seemed to absorb some of that rhetoric, proudly writing to a cousin in 1915 that "I run, wrestle, swim, and do pole-vaulting." But even as an adolescent his attention turned primarily to literature, through which he explored politics, religion, and sex, in varying proportions. Roth later claimed that his literary interests grew out of childhood punishment in which his father made him write as penance for various wrongdoings, until he had devised a complete history of the world in verse. As a teenage Zionist, he edited a Jewish-American journal, and despite his humble origins (and the noted anti-Semitism of the school) his poetic efforts landed him a scholarship to Columbia University, where he edited a literary magazine. By 1917 he published his first book, *First Offering: A Book of Sonnets and Lyrics*. If composed primarily of lovelorn-young-man clichés involving "moonless nights and sunless days" alongside tributes to Columbia and a few aimless free-verse experiments in the vein of Walt Whitman, it certainly announced ambition, an excited reach if not yet a matching grasp.

Classified as 4F and thus unfit for combat on account of his poor eyesight, Roth spent World War I working for the Jewish Welfare

Board, teaching literacy to immigrants. After war's end and his departure from Columbia, he founded the Poetry Bookshop, but not even the budding Greenwich Village bohemian scene of the time could keep such a heady establishment financially afloat, and he soon took off for London, hoping to get by as an interviewer for the *New York Herald*. When this also failed to work out as planned, Roth returned to the United States and ran the English Institute, utilizing the teaching skills he had developed during the war.

In the midst of all this, Roth married. Pauline Roth would be not only his lifelong companion, but also his colleague and even legal decoy when circumstances demanded. Their marriage reflected the patriarchal gender norms of the era, as Pauline dealt quietly with Sam's blatant infidelities (his own daughter would later describe him as a "womanizer," and his pursuits ranged from actresses to prostitutes). The Roths did, however, share genuine affection; in another reflection of their times, her voice has been preserved only in dispersed archival traces, while his is scattered across numerous published texts, but her actions over the years showed care for her partner.

As they raised two small children, Sam spent four years running the English Institute but never lost his hunger for literary pursuits. Indeed, any failures of this period were offset by remarkable successes as well. His second book of poetry, *Europe: A Book for America* (1919), was less stiff than his debut, and in its sharp consciousness of colonialism and anti-Semitism it produced periodically striking imagery, as in Roth's excoriation of "England who has a noose for every neck in Europe." By 1920 Roth was placing poems in such magazines as the *Nation*, which also offered a positive review of *Europe* that commended its "bitterish, Old Testament concreteness that will hold some ears a good while."

Roth maintained an impressive social network of literary masters. "I should be glad to call on you" at the Poetry Bookshop, T. S. Eliot wrote in 1921, and other correspondents included the poet known as H.D. and Ezra Pound. During the years that he ran the English Institute he never stopped writing, from poetry to nonfiction, such as his 1925 book *Now and Forever: A Conversation with Mr. Israel Zangwill on the Jew and the Future*, one of his many efforts to grapple with the complexities of his Jewish identity and heritage in an anti-Semitic society. From automobile producer Henry Ford, to the resurgent Ku

Klux Klan, to the World War I–era red scare, hostility to Jews ran rampant. The historian Eric Goldstein suggests that the American public saw Jews as a "mirror of American modernity," linked to the pleasures and the dangers of urbanism, intellectualism, capitalism, mass culture, and social change. To a large extent, Roth agreed—though what to make of this, neither he nor the Gentiles could ever quite decide.

Best known as the author of *The Melting Pot* (1908), the play that crystallized belief in American immigrant assimilation and coined a lasting phrase, Israel Zangwill had engaged in robust debate over Zionism with Roth, who had renounced his youthful endorsement and now believed "Jews who are first of all European have no business returning to Palestine. They are Europeans." In his book, Roth presented a somewhat unfair dialogue between himself and an imaginary Zangwill. Unsurprisingly, Roth got the best lines, including a prediction of rising American anti-Semitism in which "it will be the old melting pot, Mr. Zangwill, but we will be the only ones boiled in it." Roth concluded the philosophical dialogue with an apocalyptic vision, declaring, "I expect to be living when they will be roasting Jews alive on Fifth Avenue." Despite some disquieting comments from Roth about the unattractiveness of Jewish women, the book won praise as "enlightening" from the *New York Times*. In a preview of ethical dubiousness to come, though, Zangwill wrote the author an irritated letter complaining that his preface to the book had been written several years earlier for another project entirely and the concluding acknowledgment that his dialogue in the book was imaginary "comes too late" to be anything but misleading.

In 1926, a reenergized Roth returned to fulltime literary pursuits, this time as publisher of several periodicals. *Two Worlds Quarterly* and *Two Worlds Monthly* aimed highest, as literary journals devoted to cutting-edge fiction and poetry; *Casanova Jr.'s Tales* combined contemporary and "classical" stories, linked by an overriding emphasis on sex; and *Beau* initiated the modern "men's magazine," with journalistic pieces intended to help men cultivate female admirers through effective consumer habits, personal grooming and style, and various other "social arts." From that start, each flirted with the boundaries of obscenity; *Time* noted them in October, calling Roth and his cohort "an exceptionally bold and literate group of Manhattan pornographers," a somewhat unjustified label that nonetheless did capture the undeniably prurient tone of Roth's efforts. Labeling Roth an "able, not unphilosophical editor," *Time* called oblique attention to his Jewishness in describing him as "a foreign looking man . . . with a round, soft, plump face, irregular mouth and a liking for pink-checked neckties, striped flannel shirts."

Casanova Jr.'s Tales debuted first, in April. A mailed circular advertisement for a typical issue promised contents "containing a study of Virginity and Its Traditions, A Defense of Incest, and the suppressed Sixth Satire of Juvenal concerning married life in ancient Rome." The very nature of these taboo-flouting topics seemed to solicit obscenity charges, but as the *Time* report noted, the magazine was "shipped to customers by sly express," making it less visible to John Sumner's agents at the New York Society for the Suppression of Vice.

Beau, with its mainstream aspirations bringing greater visibility, did meet more direct threat of suppression. The magazine's contents included alluring photographs of women that tried to package maximum erotic charge in minimal actual explicitness; reflecting the cultural tenor of the decade, actress Helen Gahagan Douglas gazed directly at the viewer, no demure Victorian, while a shot of Myrna Darby embodied the growing sexual assertiveness of women, with her bared shoulders suggesting a decided confidence. If these images fell well within the confines of the cultural mainstream, not even approaching some of the more outlandish brazenness coming out of the Hollywood film industry's sexualized products, *Beau*'s articles mounted a more aggressive challenge to social norms.

The sexual liberalism of the 1920s increasingly validated heterosexual pleasures as legitimate, but in *Beau* Roth regularly tested the limits. A December 1926 article on the "Confessions of a Homo-Sexualist" courted controversy with its defense of "this alleged perversion." Abortion made repeat appearances in articles, even drawing clumsy and offensive joking in a Roth-penned story about the amorous misadventures of a young bookseller. While these rather daring pieces managed to elude targeting, the dedicated smut-fighter Sumner did informally threaten *Beau*'s distributors over a leering essay on finding women in Paris and, strangely, a reprinted Ben Franklin letter to the Academy of Brussels on the topic of flatulence. From the start, reprinting Franklin's infamous "suppressed" work had been a motif in

Beau, and Sumner's choice may have been arbitrary, since the letter had much less sexual content than Franklin's "Choosing Your Woman," which had graced the first issue, suggesting that, "as in the Dark all Cats are grey, the pleasure of corporal enjoyment with an old woman is at least equal and frequently superior" to that with a younger woman. Though much of this approach to sex, and even his brief experiences as a postwar expatriate in Europe, located Roth within the orbit of the famous 1920s "Lost Generation," none of these efforts attained anything near the critical respect bestowed on Ernest Hemingway or John Dos Passos.

Roth's negotiations with would-be censors revealed the unsure footing of both prosecutor and prosecuted in the shifting obscenity landscape of the 1920s. While Sumner had won against the *Little Review* for their *Ulysses* selections, he lost a 1920 case involving the novel *Madeleine*. After scoring an obscenity conviction against Clinton Brainard for publishing and distributing the book, Sumner saw his victory reversed on appeal. Though the book chronicled the life of a prostitute, it did not, the appellate Supreme Court of New York averred, contain "a single word or picture which tends to excite lustful or lecherous desire." Sordid subject matter could pass legal muster, it seemed, as long as it managed to convince the authorities it had higher purposes than wallowing in prurience.

Further chipping at Sumner's authority was a more dramatic setback in 1922, when book dealer Raymond Halsey not only beat an obscenity charge for a translation of Theodore Gaultier's nineteenth-century French novel *Mademoiselle de Maupin*, but even won a $2,500 malicious-prosecution charge against Sumner, leaving the New York Society for the Suppression of Vice to pay damages. When Sumner contested the decision, the New York Court of Appeals, the highest court in the state, delivered a thorough defense of the book, noting that although the *Nation* had called the book "pornographic and dull" on original publication in 1893, Gaultier's status among the premier French authors, and the book's widespread sale in reputable venues, merited account. Further, joining the growing chorus rejecting the *Hicklin* standards, the court insisted that the book "must be considered as a whole," thereby allowing for a certain quotient of questionable content if absorbed into a broader whole that justified it.

If the trajectory appeared to swing toward liberalization, though, it did so inconsistently. Even at decade's end a case involving the play *Hands Around* (which Roth also sold) resulted in a conviction for Philip Pesky, upheld on appeal in 1930. This time, the Supreme Court of New York took note that "the efforts of the author were not a lesson in morality, nor an attempt to uplift the mind of the reader, but . . . an attempt to depict, in a manner that might possibly be called clever, adulterous relationships, vulgar and disgusting." The book presented itself as a morality play mapped out along a sexual chain of overlapping lovers, and Pesky's defense pointed out that it ultimately served as a critique of infidelity. The court brushed off this argument with scorn, noting, "This is the usual cry of the libertine who is attempting to justify his own life or writings." Morality could legitimize some textual excursions into immorality, but only so long as its alibi was not undermined by leers or smirks. Obscenity law made judges into literary critics, and they remained as inconstant as the ones in magazines.

Within this unpredictable context, it made sense that when Sumner took issue with *Beau*, Roth and his lawyer visited the NYSSV. At least claiming in print to find Sumner "amiable and apparently amenable to reason," Roth described discussing legal precedents with him, with Sumner agreeing to consider Roth's arguments overnight. The next day, though, Sumner made clear his intent to prosecute if the magazine went to press; Roth apparently disregarded the threat, because he told the story in the next issue with an offer to readers to purchase the "suppressed" issue, with his autograph, for an inflated two dollars.

Roth may have exaggerated or misrepresented the episode to profit off the newly "forbidden" collector's edition, but his recounting gels with the course of other concurrent episodes. A leader of the Boston Watch and Ward Society wrote in March 1927 to "disapprove entirely" of several "distinctly offensive" segments in *Beau*, singling out the article on homosexuality. "I am anxious to meet you halfway and to avoid even the appearance of being hypercritical," the would-be censor quickly added, noting that "if only in your editing you could yourself make some concessions to a judgment and taste which may not conform to your own, I feel sure there will exist no difficulties between us." The conciliatory tone itself spoke volumes about the waning sense of power felt by the disciples of Comstock.

Some responses to the episode also displayed a growing sense of frustration with the limits censors placed on sexual expression. One young man, in a mid-1927 personal letter to Roth, applauded his work and condemned the "abnormally sexually obsessed America, whose constant repression" drove "the saintliest of minds to slovenly imaginings that place orgies in sheep's wool." As an eager subscriber to Roth's various publications, the fan compared Sumner's intrusion to "the psychology of a local Inquisition."

If the *Two Worlds* journals were the most conventionally literary of the bunch, publishing an esteemed roster that included D. H. Lawrence, poet Paul Verlaine, Ernest Hemingway, and Carl Sandburg, among others, they also most closely skirted the lines of legal danger for Roth. Anticipating this, Roth opened the second issue of the monthly by noting that it had appeared "on the one hundred and fiftieth anniversary of the founding of the American republic, with its concomitant guarantee of the right to speak and print freely," invoking a heritage of free speech that, as the prior chapters have shown, did not yet exist but whose rhetoric carried social currency. The first issue of *Two Worlds Monthly* in 1926 began a serialized publication of James Joyce's *Ulysses* — a risky endeavor given the successful prosecution of the *Little Review* for having done the same a half decade earlier. And indeed, the law came quickly calling. A citizen complaint involved both *Beau* and *Two Worlds Monthly*, with the "strongest objections" being to *Ulysses*, resulting in a hearing before a local magistrate in March 1927.

Roth beat the rap, with charges dismissed in court. Clearly, the publication of his various magazines exposed softening standards of obscenity, as new cultural directions found legal accommodation. Any sense of victory Roth might feel was quickly stolen away, though, by the international protest that erupted over his publishing of *Ulysses* without permission. The vagaries of copyright law ordained that because the book had been found obscene, it did not qualify for copyright. Joyce sued Roth in 1927 over the use of his name in advertising, and Roth accepted an injunction, but the real penalty came culturally, not legally. Perceiving Roth as an unscrupulous pirate, 167 writers and intellectuals, ranging from Ernest Hemingway to Albert Einstein, issued a formal protest and a scathing denunciation of his work. Other published attacks on Roth proliferated, often employing loaded anti-Semitic code words of "vermin," "lice," or "parasite."

To his death, Roth would insist he had been unjustly vilified in the protest, and that he did indeed have Joyce's initial permission to publish. Joyce scholars have long viewed Roth's claims with skepticism, but literary historian Jay Gertzman, the foremost expert on Roth, has offered a nuanced assessment that evaluates Roth's permission as unclear (a key piece of correspondence from intermediary Ezra Pound that might have resolved things having disappeared from all known archives) but in any case un*timely*, in that Joyce's alleged consent came in 1922 and Roth made no use of it until 1926, making any actual agreement long obsolete regardless. Certainly this fits the pattern of loose regard for other writers' concerns already seen in his casual reappropriation of Israel Zangwill's preface, intended for another book entirely. Whatever the possibly unknowable truth of the Joyce controversy, the result was clear and unambiguous: the expulsion of Roth from reputable literary circles.

His bridge to respectability thoroughly burnt, Roth found himself cut off from his claims to cultural legitimacy. Abandoned by the world of the literary salon but now committed to publishing as a profession, Roth turned of necessity to more brazenly sexual material without the legitimizing aspects of his earlier high-culture ambitions. As always, his motives were mixed; smut promised profits, but financial success could also provide the personal validation he sought. In his various autobiographical writings, Roth often portrayed himself in grandiose terms as a bold crusader for sexual freedom, though these writings served as fairly transparent attempts to justify his various publications. Though not particularly invested in free speech as a cause, Roth never tried to hide his personal fascination with all things sexual — which made him a political figure whether or not he saw himself that way. Meanwhile, emboldened by some success, Sumner continued an obvious vendetta against Roth. The result was a cascading spiral of arrests and trials.

The law fell swiftly upon him; arrested in 1928 for selling an illustrated version of Richard Burton's 1866 translation of the "exotic" fifteenth-century Arabic sex manual *The Perfumed Garden*, Roth took his lawyer's advice and pleaded guilty, receiving a two-year suspended sentence. Probation left Roth vulnerable, and Sumner made use of his precarious position; aggressive raids in June 1928 swept Roth up along with several other alleged obscenity merchants, as Sumner confiscated nearly 2,000 volumes altogether. Roth's holdings ranged from classical erotica to D. H. Lawrence's controversial *Lady Chatterley's Lover*, unpublishable in the United States because of its graphic sex scenes. Roth received a three-month sentence for possessing and selling obscene books this time; from that moment forth, the law of obscenity would never be less than a tangible, palpable presence in his life. Since he had no support from free-speech organizations, lawyers would also become a constant, expensive necessity, to his endless dismay.

Sumner's arrests came fast and furious, and not every book that landed Roth in court approached *Lady Chatterley* in explicitness. Two stories from Giovanni Boccaccio's centuries-old *Decameron*, "Pasquerella" and "Madonna Babetta," bound together in 1927, told tales neither more nor less tawdry than those in Chaucer's canonical *Canterbury Tales*, with the former involving accidental mother-son incest that leads to tragedy and the latter following a similar arc of lust resulting in a fall. None of this went beyond the salaciousness of *Beau* or *Casanova Jr.*, but scattered amidst the stories were drawings by the late-Victorian sketch-artist Aubrey Beardsley, featuring fully naked, albeit undetailed, male and female bodies; Sumner declared the volume obscene. An October 1929 raid again returned Roth (and his brother Max, among other colleagues) to court, on the basis of 3,000 copies of dozens of titles, including *Lady Chatterley* and Frank Harris's notoriously graphic autobiography *My Life and Loves*. Seeing no way to further damage his reputation, Roth had also become the pirate Joyce accused him of being, publishing an unauthorized, unexpurgated *Ulysses* as well.

A somewhat ungracious Roth, counting on the legal system to treat women with a more paternal gentleness, attempted to deny his connection to the confiscated material by claiming his wife, Pauline, actually ran the Golden Hind Press, the latest of his ever-shifting company names; under oath in court, she denied it. Fortunately for Roth, the machinations of his opponents were frequently of equally dubious integrity. One arresting officer claimed to find books containing "photographs and drawings depicting male and female figures in the nude in acts of sexual intercourse and degeneracy," but could not produce them in court and backtracked on cross-examination. Sumner's own testimony could be jumbled too, contradicting itself on details and failing to convince of its accuracy.

Beneath the squabbling in which quite possibly every party was lying resided an actual legal debate. A memorandum of law filed by Roth's attorney after his contested October 1929 arrest insisted that the "meaning of a whole book, not of any particular sentences contained therein determines its character," and the judge seemed responsive to the notion. Sixteen years after the *Kennerley* decision, the old *Hicklin* standards had eroded substantially, reflecting an increasing viability of the taken-as-a-whole defense. Judge John Knox, hearing the case, signaled his sympathies, noting that he had refused to issue a warrant against Roth a few months earlier for an unspecified book that "approached, if it did not pass, the boundary of indecency." *Lady Chatterley's Lover*, though, discovered on the premises of Roth's Golden Hind Press, he found "disgustingly filthy and obscene." Though he called Roth "a man of some literary ability," Judge Knox still sent him to prison for violation of parole, writing, "Whatever the merits of censorship, or lack of it, a man cannot defiantly violate a law which he does not like." Four months, Roth would actually serve this time. Immediately upon his release in mid-1930, he was rearrested and extradited to Philadelphia, where *Ulysses* had been found obscene and he was held accountable as publisher: a sixty-day sentence for that.

Fortune finally favored Roth, if briefly, in 1931 when he fought off another Sumner attack. The books in question were *Celestine* and *Eastern Shame Girl*. The former, written in 1902 by French author Octave Mirabeau, purported to contain the diary of a chambermaid, while the latter was a collection of Chinese folk tales translated from a French version. Roth's attorneys launched an impassioned defense; Mirabeau was a writer "of considerable standing and literary reputation," and their brief noted that the book had sold even at the respectable department store Macy's, reconnecting Roth to mainstream cultural ground. Both books contained sexual innuendos but must be considered as wholes, by "the mores of the day," the brief argued. When *Celestine* did detail its narrator's semicoerced first sexual experience at age twelve ("Violated? No, not exactly. Consenting? Yes, almost"), it lavished more description on the "old, hairy, ill-smelling man, whose face was nothing but a dirty mass of beard and hair" than the act itself. Puffing their chests a bit, Roth's legal team went on, "the standards of yesterday, the abhorrence of any mention of sex, the excessive prudery, the silly squeamishness . . . are definitely as dead today as are the puffed sleeves and the bustle, the horse-drawn carriage and the donkey-engines on the Elevated. We have developed sturdier tastes. And we have grown wiser in the process. We have found that it is better to encourage freedom of expression than to risk the evils of suppression."

Roth's defense also made careful note that these books held "none of the emphasis upon sexual perversion found in *The Well of Loneliness*," which served to distance them from unacceptable forms of sexuality by linking them to the heterosexual pleasures of sexual liberalism. Such tactics proved effective, and Roth beat the charge in May 1931. The freedom he maintained was, he knew, tenuous. Now marked as a smut dealer, banished from reputable literary circles, Roth knew his cultural place. He would spend the 1930s carefully limning his legal position, trying to promise readers sensational, sexualized material while staying just inside the law. For much of the decade it worked, until suddenly it didn't.

Law and Culture in the 1930s

If John Sumner held the power to define Samuel Roth legally, Roth could define Sumner culturally. Under the pseudonym Hugh Wakem, Roth put out the short book *Diary of a Smut-Hound* from Philadelphia in 1930, purporting to be the revealed personal writings of a thinly disguised Sumner. Some of the sections seemed designed simply to infuriate the uptight censor, wallowing in personal attacks: "If I had married a beautiful woman instead of a church-going one," Roth's Sumner ponders, "my attitudes towards nudes would most certainly have been different." Beyond the puerility, though, lay a genuine clash of cultural values. Scrutinizing one potentially dirty book, the narrator muses, "The effect on the mind of the person reading it is that it is possible to manage one's sex life for pleasure rather than procreation. If that isn't filthy, I'd like to know what is?" In one short passage, Roth struck at the core struggle behind sexual liberalism's challenge to Victorian norms.

This theme resonated throughout Roth's prodigious published output. Some of it he wrote, some he merely published, much of it he simply stole and pirated. The quality of the works varied wildly, with some impressive high points and mountains of dreck and drivel. His personal motivations shifted with the texts, from art to profit to sheer vindictiveness. But etched across Roth's uneven bibliography was an unwavering commitment to sexual liberalism, evident in nearly everything he wrote, published, or sold. After his three prison stints, Roth in the early 1930s modulated his stance, accommodating his position as bold cultural warrior to the legal tenor of the times. The result was a spate of books whose overbearing self-awareness of obscenity law's parameters saturated their texts.

Writing to Pauline from his Philadelphia prison cell in August 1930, Sam reflected his tangible awareness of obscenity law. Discussing a manuscript he had planned on publishing, he conceded, "it will have to be toned down." The decision was clearly legal, not aesthetic. Indeed, upon his release, Roth published a voluminous amount of sluggish tripe under his William Faro, Inc., imprint (named after a prison friend, but with a modification to prevent Roth's enemies from seeking out Bill Paro), with sexual themes still occupying the foreground but the content tamed.

A small cavalcade of *Lady Chatterley*–themed books reflected this new Roth demeanor. After the D. H. Lawrence estate rejected Roth's own safely expurgated version of the original novel, Faro released two anonymously written sequels (in addition to publishing the expurgated book anyway). *Lady Chatterley's Husbands* (1931) followed Constance Chatterley past the first novel into a new marriage with her former groundskeeper Mellors. Then in the next book, *Lady Chatterley's Friends* (1932), Constance tires of Mellors and goes on a globetrotting tour with three male friends, keeping rotating intimate engagements with all of them.

The book's sexual trajectories continually broach the boundaries of the potentially obscene but always pull away; when a scene features Constance "tasting the sweet wine of sexual anticipation," whatever comparable anticipations were aroused in the reader were perpetually dashed off into coy hints rather than graphic delivery. If one lover's "fingers stroked the undulating rose marble of her flesh, in the room's dim glimmer," the book never quite clarifies which segment of her flesh; scenes promising insights on "Oriental methods of rousing the tempests of love" as the crew travels to Egypt again insinuate rather than describe exoticized sexual practices. Aspiring to sexual allure, the book allowed obscenity law to constantly rein it in. A climactic scene proved tame enough to have passed Comstock's own muster: "She melted into his arms, like day into the arms of night, like life into the arms of death."

Roth could hardly feign interest in these books. In a telling introduction to his 1931 dramatization of *Lady Chatterley*, published under his own name, he admitted that he never saw in the original "more than a mildly interesting novel," but once it drew publicity for its shock value, he viewed it "purely with an eye to business" as a means to "recoup my finances" after his other legal battles. The dramatized version, he candidly confessed, "is probably very dull" — an understatement, for as a three-act play full of interminable discussions, with the sex elided between the acts, *Lady Chatterley* achieved its arguably all-time worst incarnation. Equally underwhelming was *The Intimate Journal of Rudolph Valentino*, a spurious diary capitalizing on the silent film's star's early death. Promising sensationalism, the book delivered nothing but stagnant, tepid prose devoid even of lurid appeal. "Always there were women and women and women," the faux-Valentino wrote, but he offered none of the salacious detail readers were solicited by the title to expect.

Even as Roth shied away from testing the legal waters in the early 1930s, his publications evinced a commitment to confronting sexual boundaries that seemingly went beyond sheer pecuniary motives. Wary as he was during this period, Roth still published such works as Donna McKay's *A Gentleman in Black Skin* (1932) and pseudonymous Robert Scully's *A Scarlet Pansy* (1933). The former book examined white American fascination with African American sexuality, while the latter told a queer love story. While neither traipsed too far into the sort of graphic descriptions that could land Roth in court, their themes alone took oppositional (and potentially risky) cultural stances, clearly challenging the sexual ideologies of Comstock and Sumner. Roth obviously sought to make money off the fascination of American readers with topics deemed perverse, but he just as clearly showed his steadfast political resistance to social norms simply by continually returning to such controversial terrain.

A roughly contemporaneous book, bearing Roth's own name as author, embodied the tensions of his work at William Faro. *The Private Life of Frank Harris* (1931) told the biography of the notorious writer and publisher, from his British education through his varied experiences in the urbanizing United States of the late nineteenth century, ranging from Kansas cattle ranching to urbane literary circles. Sex stands as the book's central preoccupation. From young Harris's observation of homosexual encounters between British teachers and schoolboys, to a teenage seduction of a girl in which "he kissed and caressed her until she lay tingling and gasping, every inch of her," and on through a fellow rancher's contracting of gonorrhea from a prostitute, the book frames Harris's personal development as a shifting set of engagements with sex and sexuality. In this capacity, the book displayed the distance traversed since the death of Comstock; a few decades earlier, these themes alone would have sufficed as criteria for obscenity.

And yet, the teenage gasping was as explicit as it got. Roth put in Harris's mouth repeated denunciations of obscenity law: "There is no smut, except in the minds of the Comstocks and the Sumners. Old Theodore Schroeder proved that. You let two smutty minds befoul the whole current of creative art of a land," he rants at one point. Holding the American public accountable for their complicity in the enforcement of these laws, he later adds, "If it thrills his Puritan-ridden hypocritical American soul, he'll squirm with rapture over it, and tell every man or woman what a dreadful immoral book it is: and they will, as he expects, at once go out and get a copy." Indeed, even the backstory to the book — Roth having lifted large portions of it whole from Harris's actual autobiography *My Life and Loves*, whose several volumes remained unpublishable because of their intensely graphic sexual depictions that went far beyond Roth's toned-down version — made obscenity the invisible structuring force of the book.

The cultural climate into which Roth launched these books was, to be sure, a changed one from the past decade. If, as chapter 2 suggested, the "Roaring Twenties" image of the Jazz Age with its wild speakeasies was a somewhat simplified vision that masked a greater national ambivalence (much of the "roar" being sparked by Prohibition, after all), historians of gender and sexuality do agree that a resurgent sexual conservatism marked the 1930s. With the economic downturn of 1929 that commenced the Great Depression and left millions of men out of work, the economic basis of the patriarchal nuclear family fell apart, undermining both masculine breadwinner and feminine homemaker roles. Conservative gender politics developed as a way of reasserting traditional gender identities.

In this context, cultural representations assumed greater importance in shoring up and securing those identities. Thus the Hays Production Code of 1930 (effectively enforced beginning in 1934) swerved Hollywood away from the fairly wild excesses of 1920s films into a newly regulated schema with strict limits on the display of such topics as sex and drug use. Characters like the one played by Barbara Stanwyck in *Baby Face* (1933), who used her sexual wiles to climb the social ladder, rapidly disappeared from American film. After a decade on the defensive against relaxing social mores, antismut rhetoric rose in volume as well.

One early Depression-era skirmish began with an effort by Utah senator Reed Smoot to reverse a 1929 tariff-bill revision that had prevented customs officials from destroying imported obscenity based solely on their own judgment. Preferring that the officials hold that authority, Reed declared, "I'd rather have a child of mine use opium than read these books," while his South Carolina colleague Coleman Livingston Blease further upped the ante: "I'd rather see the democratic and republican form of government forever destroyed if necessary to protect the virtue of the womanhood of America." Much of this eruption centered on *Lady Chatterley's Lover*, which *Time* noted circulated in bootleg form for $15–30.

Roth remained one of those "bookleggers." While his "official" efforts recognized obscenity law, he maintained a concurrent, illicit trade in precisely such works as the two senators decried. When the law did come calling in 1931, Pauline Roth took the rap, winning an acquittal for selling the unexpurgated *Chatterley* by asserting under oath that it was Sam conducting the business. Fortune favored her husband, who dodged the charge that time. It was a gendered game the Roths would play repeatedly in their family business: hope Pauline could draw more sympathy as a woman than Sam, and put her legally on the line to test the theory. Postal inspectors understood the ruse, writing to Sam's probation officer already in late 1929 that "his wife is being used as a 'blind.'"

The stakes grew higher for Roth as Depression gender politics clashed with urbane New York social politics. The latter initially held sway, as Mayor Jimmy Walker resisted efforts to block the renewal of

Times Square burlesque theater licenses and famously declared that no woman was ever ruined by a book. By 1934, however, the tides were shifting. Patrick Joseph Cardinal Hayes, archbishop of New York, proclaimed a "crusade for Christian decency" early in the year, and the incoming Fiorello LaGuardia mayoral administration rushed to establish its antismut bona fides by sending out a circular to magazine dealers forthrightly demanding they remove lurid magazines from the stands. Internal administration memoranda carefully listed "Magazines Taken Off the Stands in 1934," including such titles as *The Nudist*, *Studio Art*, *French Art Classics*, *Spicy Stories*, *Modern Art*, *Sexology*, *Sex Life*, and the concisely but unimaginatively named *Sex*.

Defenders of the magazines failed to find an effective public voice; one such publisher, Harry Donenfeld, called the magazines educational. "Take a girl of 18 or 20. They get educated in the sex life and are better able to defend themselves," he insisted, but the argument found little traction anywhere. More influential were the Catholic groups that formed during the 1930s. The Legion of Decency and National Organization for Decent Literature policed films and publications, respectively. Avoiding legal censorship, the groups instead relied on lists of unacceptable titles, hanging them over theaters and merchants with boycott threats. With the gender politics of the Depression favoring male leadership, such groups began to replace earlier women's groups like the Women's Christian Temperance Union.

As these tensions flared, Roth understood that his pariah status, as Jay Gertzman aptly labels it, made him a desirable target for headline-hungry prosecutors. While he kept his William Faro line profitably sensationalized, he often focused on attention-grabbing topics beyond sex. John Hamill's *The Strange Career of Mr. Hoover—Under Two Flags* (1931), for instance, generated great controversy (and sales) through scurrilous attacks on the president. Even when he shifted focus, Roth could not shake his reputation; in covering the Hoover spectacle, *Time* observed, "the notorious Samuel Roth . . . specialized in smutty publications."

As a publishing firm, William Faro won occasional praise; the Roth-penned poetry volume *Songs Out of Season* (1932), for instance, was widely and positively reviewed, a rare return to legitimacy that must have pleased him immensely. More often, though, Roth and Faro remained perceived, not without reason, as mere tawdry amusements. The *New York Times* offered a condescending review of Clement Wood's 1931 *Pope Joan: The Woman Who Was Pope*, calling the book "naïve and appealing as a child's belief in Santa Claus" for its apparently sincere belief in the mythical medieval pope. Meanwhile, the *New Yorker*, reviewing a few Faro titles in early 1932, called them "unbelievably dull, but quite, quite harmless."

If Roth could coast lucratively on this perception of benign banality, bad decisions such as an expensive ten-volume version of French philosopher Voltaire's *Philosophical Dictionary* at the height of the Depression helped deplete Faro's reserves. Roth blamed not himself, but defrauding at the hands of his creditors and false friends, for Faro's sudden decline. Roth had always had a fraught relationship with his attorneys, whom he perpetually distrusted and blamed for any of his misfortunes (writing from prison to Pauline in 1928, Sam had called his attorney a "dirty dog"), and believed himself especially betrayed this time. His response, which became his major work of the 1930s, could not be brushed aside so lightly as Faro's more frivolous titles. Lashing out at Jewish "shyster lawyers," Roth delivered *Jews Must Live*, published under his own name, a horrifying litany of anti-Semitic stereotypes presented as historical truths.

Beginning with the assertion that "it dawned on me suddenly, blindingly that all the evils of my life had been perpetrated by Jews," Roth went on to list both autobiographical and world-historical examples of Jewish mendacity and corruption. Acknowledging the rising Nazi persecution of Jews, Roth nonetheless adopted and mirrored much of their language. "Our major vice of old, as of today, is parasitism," he wrote, also calling Judaism "subversive" and a "moral gonorrhea." Using anecdotes of lecherous, greedy bankers, lawyers (including his own), and others, Roth concluded that global anti-Semitism was natural and deserved, and admitted to thinking "in terms of their destruction."

The book was unconscionable by any standard. Roth himself would spend the rest of his life atoning, explaining, rationalizing, and regretting it. Biographer Jay Gertzman sees Roth's writing of the book as a "neurotic identification" with "the Christian moral authorities who spoke for decency" and had been prosecuting him. Roth had "internalized their contempt, and to exorcise it wrote an anti-Semitic tract."

While mainstream responses ranged from fury to silence, *Jews Must Live* did win praise in provincial and anti-Semitic corners, with the *Charlotte News* in North Carolina calling it the "most frank, unadorned, and authentic volume concerning the Jews already published." While it lacked the sexual content to draw obscenity charges, Roth maintained that it brought law enforcement back after him. Despite his lifelong paranoia and persecution complexes, he may have been right.

Economic trials pressed Roth more than legal ones at mid-decade. His primary battle on the latter front involved *Anecdota Americana*, a collection of ribald stories, jokes, and aphorisms. When John Sumner went after Roth for it, Sumner won, but Roth avoided jail time with a $500 fine. Sumner sensed his powers waning; at a 1933 meeting called by the Greater New York Federation of Churches, the only suggestion the veteran vice crusader could offer was to bring cases before particular magistrates known to be sympathetic. Opponents to the end, Roth and Sumner still shared a keen awareness of the countervailing forces playing out through obscenity law, the longer arc toward sexual liberalism balanced against a more localized 1930s conservatism.

Roth had smartly hedged his bets with his official products under William Faro, but with the firm's decline, he leaned increasingly on more clearly unlawful merchandise. By 1936, the FBI had opened a file on Roth, with J. Edgar Hoover instructing local agents to keep the Roths under observation. Though an effort to "purchase some alleged privately printed world suppressed books, including such titles as *The Secret Places of the Human Body*," failed, the FBI was not wrong in its suspicions that the Roths were engaged in illicit enterprise.

For Sam, hiding behind Pauline continued to offer some cover. She had been charged, yet again, for selling a long list including such titles as *Altar of Venus* and even *Fanny Hill* (just over a century since it had been found obscene in Massachusetts) through the mails in 1935. Once more, Sam played the foil, as Pauline denied accountability and won an acquittal. This was a delicate tightrope for the couple to walk, and when they finally fell, the thud came hard. Pauline beat the charge in December 1935. By September 1936, though, both Roths were back under indictment, and this time the outcome would be more dire.

This time, the material that landed the Roths in trouble was unquestionably obscene by the standards of the day. *Lady Chatterley's Lover*, still too graphic by far, remained also too lucrative to leave behind despite the dangers it had already repeatedly posed for the Roths; likewise for *Fanny Hill*. Books like *Kate's Secret Tryst* and *The Amatory Experiences of a Surgeon* carried little veneer of artistic merit. *Memories of an Hotel Man* was a plainly pornographic pamphlet whose textual recountings of sordid sexual shenanigans were matched by explicitly drawn cartoon sketches. Two French imports, the anonymous *Wide Open* and *Nirvana* (by "Dr. Desernet"), were equally explicit in both prose and drawings.

That the Roths would be found guilty for selling these items was a foregone conclusion. They were the filthiest books he'd ever seen, insisted the prosecuting U.S. attorney, who also pointed out that the Roths' teenage son and daughter had been employed in the family business. The jury took a mere fifteen minutes to convict, on twenty-two counts of conspiracy and using the mail to distribute obscenity. Potential sentences sprawled out to a 107-year maximum. Judge Grover Moscowitz, born only a few years before Roth and sharing a Jewish identity, had pursued a different course in life, one of assimilation into respectability. He was a frequent presence in the Jewish press for his charitable work, though he had come close to impeachment in 1929 after Congress investigated him for seeming improprieties in his handling of bankruptcy receivership cases. Barely weathering the storm, Moscowitz had held on to his position — and a lingering cloud of suspicion. In the Roths, he surely saw a reverse image of himself. Under Moscowitz's rule, Pauline received a three-year suspended sentence with five years of probation. Less fortunate, and perceived as more guilty, Sam drew three years. It was his sixth conviction.

Even as Roth headed for Lewisburg Federal Penitentiary in eastern Pennsylvania, obscenity law evolved around him. His graphic, salacious wares too openly solicited sexual arousal, but other texts and products with interests in sexuality managed to win legal validation. Esar Levine, a fellow distributor of dubiously exploitative books, had been convicted on obscenity charges but saw his conviction reversed in federal court early in 1936. Judge Learned Hand, now a veteran of such cases, assessed Levine's merchandise with a wary eye; while *Black Lust*, a fictional tale of "an English girl captured by the Dervishes at the fall of Khartoum and kept in a harem," possessed "considerable literary merit," it would also "arouse libidinous feelings in almost any reader." Meanwhile, *Crossways of Sex* purported to be a scientific study of sexuality but "its good faith is more than questionable," while *Secret Museum of Anthropology* contained photographs of "nude female savages" and staked an "extremely tenuous" claim to legitimacy as serious anthropology.

Nonetheless, Hand reversed Levine's conviction. The technical grounds were procedural, based on the trial judge's jury instructions to weigh the possible effects of the books on "the young and immature, the ignorant and those who are sensually inclined," who could all be triggered to action by a single lustful passage. Hand rejected these standards, insisting that the books be taken as a whole and the effects be weighed against the entire community, not its most susceptible components. Using his opinion to launch a broader statement of purpose, Hand also declared: "This earlier doctrine necessarily presupposed that the evil against which the statute is directed so much outweighs all interests of art, letters or science that they must yield to the mere possibility that some prurient person may get a sensual gratification from reading or seeing what to most people is innocent and may be delightful or enlightening. No civilized community not fanatically puritanical would tolerate such an imposition."

If Hand's implied critique of Anthony Comstock and Victorian sexual mores remained just barely indirect, similar sentiments were also on display more openly in another case before the Second Circuit Court of Appeals later that same year. Margaret Sanger, in her continuing quest for women's reproductive rights, had helped engineer the sending of 120 contraceptive rubber pessaries from Japan to Manhattan doctor Hannah Stone. When customs officials confiscated the devices, Brooklyn federal judge Grover Moscowitz — seeing in these items more legitimacy than in Roth's — ordered the pessaries released and delivered, on the grounds of their medical utility in saving women's lives (they were being used only for married couples with health issues).

When the case reached the appellate court, Augustus Hand delivered a decisive victory for Stone. Reading the Comstock Act rather against its clear legislative intent, Hand privileged sexual liberalism over strict historical accuracy, insisting that the law "embraced only such articles as Congress would have denounced as immoral if it had understood all the conditions under which they were being used" and had not been intended to "prevent the importation, sale, or carriage by mail of things which might intelligently be employed by conscientious or competent physicians for the purpose of saving life or promoting the well being of their patients." What Hand could not quite bring himself to articulate, but which remained clear and unambiguous even if unspoken, was that "well being" had come to include nonprocreative sexual activity.

The limits were clear: the sex sanctioned by the court system remained between a husband and a wife. Yet within those confines, sex for pleasure — the centerpiece of sexual liberalism — had risen to legal legitimacy. It was culturally and socially acceptable, and it was not obscene. The American public hurried to distance itself from the Comstock era — "the late gorilla-like prude," *Time* now discourteously called the once-dominant figure in covering the contested pessaries. Hand's deference to the medical authority and expertise of the "competent physicians" provided powerfully *modern* cover for the sexual changes contained within that expertise; in the background echoed American concerns over avoiding the course of the repressive fascist and Nazi policies across the Atlantic, too.

These advances, momentous as they were, proved cold comfort to Samuel Roth as he prepared for his three-year sentence. As sexual liberalism solidified its mainstream position, questions lingered about the role of obscenity law in policing and distinguishing legitimate from illicit versions of sexuality. "Well being," "literary merit," and the other phrases invoked in the defense and exoneration of challenged works carried value judgments about the nature of the sexualities solicited by the works; so too did "lustful" and "prurient," words that transformed moral positions into legal doctrines. These words all too often went unquestioned, taken as axiomatic or simply understood, towering over public discussions of obscenity but entering the discourse primarily in shadow form — shadows large enough to blot out the freedom of Samuel Roth.

The Absent Supreme Court
Obscenity Doctrine in the 1940s

The three years, ending in 1939, that Samuel Roth spent in federal prison took their toll. Though he gradually eased into his sentence, he was forced to experience his children's growth from adolescence to early adulthood primarily through the letters he sent and received (as always, Pauline soldiered on in running the family business affairs). He emerged back into society, as his daughter Adelaide wrote in her unpublished memoir, "more tentative, more subdued." In some ways Roth's experiences of the 1940s repeated those of the '30s. After spending the first half of the decade only flirting with the overtly sexual themes that had landed him in repeated legal troubles, he gravitated back to them, only to find the law still waiting to pounce. This time Roth's legal troubles came primarily from the Post Office, in the form of battles over the mailability of his books. While the publisher avoided a return to prison during the 1940s, his protracted legal struggles took him to the Supreme Court, to which he appealed after finding the system unresponsive at the lower levels.

Little result came of Roth's appeal. In fact, the Supreme Court showed great reluctance to deal directly with obscenity law in the 1940s. Its very limited engagement with the topic left the lower courts to hash out doctrine in piecemeal fashion, without great consistency or clarity. Consequently, pressure mounted on the high court to provide resolution. Roth's appeal in 1949, challenging an anomalous circuit court opinion that called the very tenets of obscenity law into question, seemed to demand an answer, but the Supreme Court refused to hear it. The case nonetheless served as a precise dry run in many ways for Roth's later, better known, 1957 obscenity case — except the stakes for Roth were higher in the later case, sending him back to prison once more. This chapter examines the developments of the 1940s through Roth's first failed run at the Supreme Court, and the next moves into the case that would ultimately set the precedent in 1957.

———

Wartime Diversions of a Smutmonger

Roth returned to a New York City in turmoil. Ethnic tensions flared as Europe went to war, and the social conservatism of Mayor Fiorello LaGuardia sought to capitalize on Depression-era gender politics and anxieties. In 1940 the mayor launched another crusade against news-stand smut, with a threatening letter sent out to newsdealers asking them to make lists of their sexually themed merchandise and then vol-untarily promise not to sell it. The voluntary nature of the endeavor was called into question by the mayor's curt dismissal of free-speech concerns. "There is no question of freedom of the press here. It is not censorship that I am seeking to invoke," LaGuardia insisted. Rather, "the Mayor has [the] power of sewage disposal, and if necessary, I will get rid of these dirty magazines as filth."

The mayor's efforts to stretch a metaphor into official action drew mixed results. Calling his efforts "prudish," one angry citizen wrote a letter invoking the looming Nazi menace in Europe, telling him to "call off your Gestapo hounds." The more staid *New York Times* cau-tiously warned, "We do not want to set up a precedent in suppressing smut that will afterward be used to suppress any ideas that some other Mayor does not like." The New York Society for the Suppression of Vice, on the other hand, sent warm word that it was "glad to note the energy and persistence" of the mayor.

The most important response, however, came from the newsdeal-ers, who at least tried to signal their compliance. In his correspon-dence, a pleased LaGuardia noted that most "have been very cooper-ative." A more accurate assessment would probably label them as fearful of prosecution, since the coercive aspects of LaGuardia's "vol-untary" program were hardly implicit (the trial transcripts of one dealer, Murray Winters, discussed below, featured John Saxton Sum-ner invoking the mayor's "banned publications" list in setting up an arrest). Though he continued to insist that there was "not even the remotest suggestion of censorship here" and couch his "request" in polite language, holding a meeting with publishers and distributors

{ *Chapter 4* }

where he asked them to "kindly conform to the requirements of decency," the mayor seemed almost eager to deploy the police in a show of moral governance.

A chastened Samuel Roth had no desire to serve as symbolic bogeyman. Still on probation, he was allowed to continue publishing, so long as he avoided direct mail orders. But the allure of the illicit yet beckoned, and under such imprints as Coventry House he continued churning out *Studies in the Sexual Life of African Savages*, *A Study of 1400 Cases of Rape*, *Cities of Sin*, and *The Body's Rapture*, the titles generally more sensational than the content. Irritated authorities demanded revocation of his parole, though they fell short of calling the books obscene. Only Rhys Davies's *A Bed of Feathers and Tale*, a turgid *Lady Chatterley* knockoff Roth had first published in 1935, was declared unmailable, somewhat surprisingly given the novella's tame prose.

Judge Moscowitz, who sent Roth to prison in 1936, signed an arrest warrant for both Samuel and Pauline (also on probation) in April 1941. Improbable circumstances favored the publisher: while in Lewisburg Penitentiary, Roth had learned of saboteurs planning to attack American industries if war broke out, and he had informed the Brooklyn Naval Intelligence agency of the scheme. Farfetched as the tale sounded, it might have carried some truth. Roth certainly seemed bound for reimprisonment, but Judge Moscowitz's handwritten note after the May hearing simply read, "proceedings adjourned without date," apparently after contacting the authorities to verify the story (at least, so Roth later claimed; given that he would also allege Moscowitz was susceptible to bribery, other possible explanations do exist). When Moscowitz resumed the case in 1942, he found the Roths guilty, but simply extended their probation through 1944.

A smut merchant could capitalize only so much on an act of prison patriotism, and with his favors thus called in, Roth tread carefully. Negotiations with down-on-his-luck Harlem Renaissance author Claude McKay failed to yield a publishable novel, but as the nation moved closer to war, Roth found fertile new ground for exploitation. *Inside Hitler*, he promised in late 1941, would "become important in the propaganda to consolidate national sentiment against the Nazi regime," with its purported psychoanalysis of the Fuehrer. Roth even secured a brief introduction from novelist and leftist activist Upton

Sinclair. While he gave hardly a ringing endorsement of the book ("You will not read it for its graces of style, but for the information it gives you on an important subject"), Sinclair's name nonetheless bestowed respectability – though an aggrieved Sinclair wrote to the author expressing irritation over the failure of the publisher to pay his $100 fee.

If enlisting in the national cause proved both safe and profitable, Roth made his ultimate bid for respectability at mid-decade when he turned his attention to metaphysics and philosophy. *Peep-hole of the Present* arrived in 1945, offering "an inquiry into the substance of appearance," as its subtitle declared. In a somewhat rambling but not inarticulate manner Roth attempted to pull together modern physics, art, religion, and whatever else crossed his mind in a given chapter. He dedicated the book to Albert Einstein (despite Einstein's having signed the 1927 protest that destroyed Roth's legitimate career), and he managed to extract a preface from Cambridge astronomer Sir Arthur Eddington – who spent his two pages mostly politely dismissing the book, but whose very presence in its pages again acted to legitimize it.

Roth's interest in philosophy was clearly sincere, and indeed, his commitment to the themes on which he published had always coexisted with his profit motives. Nothing in Roth's behavior suggested he would separate the two. Even as he strove to reinvent himself as a legitimate publisher, sexual themes recurred throughout his work. Revamping *Inside Hitler* as the more sensationalized *I Was Hitler's Doctor*, Roth advertised it as "the record of the most daring excursion ever made into the sexual aspects of the paranoid human ego."

Most telling, perhaps, were his differing circulars for *Parisian Nights* in 1945. One emphasized the book's heritage, as the work of renowned nineteenth-century French writer Guy de Maupassant, calling it the "complete-unabridged-as you've always dreamed Maupassant would be in the right kind of edition." The other circular replaced an Arabesque drawing with a showgirl picture and downplayed the author, instead emphasizing the "hotels, clubs, and bordellos" that "have made Paris the Mecca of the pleasure-bound world." Literature, erotic enticement, and profit: for Roth they bundled together effortlessly.

These circulars were comparatively mild. Like much of what Roth had now sold for decades, they carried little serious political content in a conventional sense. But their commodified sexuality nonetheless took on political hues, by sheer force of their endorsement of pleasure for pleasure's sake, which resisted the dominant moral conventions of the era. Nothing in them was cause for great legal concern, and indeed, Roth coasted through the war years unmolested by the government. His strategic swerve away from borderline material provided security, and so too did the general upheaval of wartime. With domestic social mores relaxed as women took traditionally male jobs to replace men mobilized for military service, and with national security taking policy priority, the gender anxieties of the Depression receded, and with them any national sense of urgency about obscenity.

The Search for Doctrinal Clarity

By the mid-1940s the Supreme Court had elevated the First Amendment into a "preferred position" among constitutional rights. As Justice Hugo Black declared in a 1941 opinion, "The First Amendment does not speak equivocally. It prohibits any law 'abridging the freedom of speech and the press.' It must be taken as a command of the broadest scope that explicit language, read in the context of a liberty-loving society, will allow." The Court's understanding of the First Amendment undeniably expanded, as it upheld labor unions' rights to picket and distribute literature without permits, and the right of Jehovah's Witness children to refuse participation in mandatory flag salutes at school. Yet the Court had virtually nothing to say about obscenity, evading the topic across the decade.

With the Supreme Court absent from the debate, obscenity doctrine was left to the lower courts. The clear if inconsistent trajectory of the twentieth century had been liberalization from the Comstock era. Yet "liberalization" meant different things to different courts. Broad agreement had been forged over the necessity of examining works as wholes rather than in arbitrary parts, and certainly sexual liberalism had forced a broader acceptance of sexual themes, so long as they remained within prevailing standards of decency — which is to say, heterosexuality in its broad contours had escaped the strict confines of marriage and procreation, but queer and "perverse" sexuality remained on very precarious legal ground. The parameters of the permissible, however, shifted over not only time but geography as well, with standards varying in ways that left obscenity a very murky concept despite its power to incarcerate those found guilty of it.

Cases involving nudist magazines best reflected the tensions contained within obscenity and the lack of agreement among the lower courts. A May 1940 federal appellate opinion, *Parmalee v. U.S.*, set a striking precedent for the rights of nudist publications. After the British import *Nudism in Modern Life* had been confiscated by customs officials, who prevailed in the district court, the Washington, D.C., Court of Appeals reversed, clearing the book for entry. Obscenity, the court noted, "is not a technical term of the law and is not susceptible of exact definition," since "such intangible moral concepts as it purports to connote, vary in meaning from one period to another." Building off such earlier cases as *Kennerley*, the court went on to assert that "nudity in art has long been recognized as the reverse of obscene." Then, following Judge Woolsey's distinction from the *Ulysses* case, it called the book "an honest, sincere, scientific and educational study."

This was the crucial component; because the book could be positioned as other than merely prurient or voyeuristic, it took on legitimacy in the eyes of the law. The court went out of its way to maintain this distinction, insisting, "it cannot fairly be said" that the book's full-frontal nude images of men and women "were intended to promote lust or to produce libidinous thoughts." Were they so intended, the book would indeed be guilty. What mattered the most was not the actual content, but the alibi it supplied: naked bodies depicted for sexual excitement remained obscene, but those inspected as part of a "sociological phenomenon" passed legal muster.

The ideological bent of the case was rather transparent. Obscenity doctrine served less as a clear legal principle than as an agent of moral policing in distinguishing acceptable sexuality from unacceptable – or more specifically in *Parmalee*, which sorts of interest in naked bodies were acceptable (namely, the nonprurient). Yet in clearing the path for the circulation of naked images, it nonetheless advanced the cause of sexual liberalism, with its claims of scientific rationalism.

The Supreme Court of Arkansas, however, cared little for the D.C. court's analytical efforts. When a photographer for nudist magazine *Sunshine & Health* was fined $50 for an obscenity conviction, the state's highest court affirmed in 1943. Its opinion showed little awareness or interest in the modernizing impulses of recent decades. Referencing the "much more comprehensive" case law archive of New York, the Arkansas court cited nothing more recent than 1884. The legal definition of obscenity it arrived at was simply "something offensive to modesty or decency." Since nudist magazines "exposed portions of the body which modesty would conceal," simple syllogistic logic drove the court's conclusion.

In 1945, Massachusetts' highest court affirmed the obscenity of Lillian Smith's novel *Strange Fruit* despite admitting its "literary merit," and endorsed the *Hicklin* standards in its opinion. Meanwhile, that same year the New York Court of Appeals affirmed the conviction of Murray Winters for violating a statute against selling "printed paper devoted to accounts of deeds of bloodshed, lust, or crime, in violation of statute." The court reasoned that such lurid pulp could "be so massed as to become vehicles for inciting violent and depraved crimes against the person." Despite the Supreme Court's specific restriction of obscenity to matters sexual all the way back in its 1896 cases, the New York court allowed for a definition of "indecent or obscene" that included publications with intents other than "excit[ing] sexual passion."

By mid-decade, the federal judiciary remained a generally stronger defender of free-speech rights than state courts. Overzealous government officials often saw their actions overturned, as when a federal appellate court reversed a postal ban on the American Institute of Family Relations' pamphlet *Preparing for Marriage*, which mentioned contraception. Likewise, when the postmaster revoked *Esquire* magazine's second-class mailing privileges for falling into what he called "that obscure and treacherous borderland zone where the average person hesitates to find them technically obscene, but still may see ample proof that they are morally improper," appellate court judge Thurman Arnold dismissively overturned, scorning the "utter confusion and lack of intelligible standards" on display.

Surveying the "confused state of the law regarding obscenity" in 1946, the *Virginia Law Review* could point to such broad trends as "the general breaking down of the *Hicklin* standards," the use of texts as wholes rather than isolated parts, and the use of the "reasonable man" test instead of youth or the overly susceptible as a metric for the

effects of salacious materials. Beyond that, no firm or unified definition existed. This state of affairs proved both problem and opportunity: problem in that obscenity remained a patchwork legal term varying widely from court to court; opportunity in that a growing
free-speech movement mobilized around the First Amendment might
impact obscenity doctrine in its contingent condition. As it turned
out, free-speech activists shied away from direct attacks on obscenity
law. They played a role in shaping it, but in doing so also validated its
core principle that sexually nonconforming material deserved suppression at the hands of the state.

The Free-Speech Lobby in the 1940s

By the 1940s, freedom of speech held a so-called preferred position
not only within the law, but within the social and political values of
the nation as well. With the excesses of the Red Scare long in the
rearview, Americans prided themselves on their open marketplace of
ideas. European fascism provided a stark contrast, as freedom of
speech undergirded a domestic sense of the United States as a democratic, progressive nation. "Censorship," in this context, increasingly
became a disreputable activity — Hitler burned books, Americans read
and debated them, or so the narrative went (recall the reference to
Mayor LaGuardia's censorial "Gestapo hounds" from the disgruntled
New Yorker).

This ideological disposition seemed clear and consistent, at least
on the surface. But it broke down under closer inspection, as in the
case of film censorship, still widely accepted by the public. Obscenity
best reflected the tensions contained within the growing free-speech
consensus. The developing free-speech lobby held some strong beliefs
about obscenity: it wanted widespread adoption of the sexual liberalism already endorsed by the key federal courts, with books and magazines read as wholes, mature adults used as the proper barometers of
their content, and wide latitude given to works that approached sex
frankly but did not wallow in lewdness or salaciousness. Even as pro-
ponents of free speech demanded procedural safeguards for obscenity trials, though, they almost never questioned the basic underpin-
nings of the very criminalization of the obscene. "Prurience," always

{ *Chapter 4* }

defined through a hall of synonym-mirrors, remained unacceptable, its suppression somehow separate from "censorship," though the logic of this distinction was rarely articulated. The liberals who most loudly demanded free-speech rights, then, ultimately proved complicit in upholding a system of sexual regulation and policing that would land Samuel Roth back in prison several years later.

What historian Andrea Friedman calls "democratic moral authority" prevailed by the end of World War II. Emanating not just out of courtrooms and elite venues, it also coalesced as a broad popular sentiment, as the public asserted its right to read what it chose, free from censorial interference. In 1944, Fiorello LaGuardia's commissioner of licenses wrote the mayor to suggest another letter campaign to purge the city's newsstands. This time, the mayor balked. When he did invoke his licensing powers to close the lesbian-themed play *Trio* the next year, expecting to be celebrated as the protector of civic virtue, the city instead "greeted his action with outrage," Friedman writes. Caught off guard, a retreating LaGuardia promised not to close any further plays without first securing obscenity convictions in trials — to do otherwise reeked of authoritarianism at odds with democratic moral authority, which demanded a jury at the very least.

Popular images of the censor fell short of flattering. Writing for the *Nation* in 1941, Jonathan Daniels repeatedly referenced Hitler and the Nazis. "It is time," he wrote, "to stop talking about the honest motives, not to speak of the prayerful piety, of people out to destroy freedom of books." A few years later in the same magazine, social critic Philip Wylie presented censors as themselves perverted: "the censoring of 'obscenity' is the work of the impure, to whom all things are impure." Censorship, Wylie demanded, "should be stopped, both in the name of democracy and in the name of truth." Meanwhile, sexual liberalism reached previously uncharted grounds. Surgeon General Thomas Parran had successfully shone light on the problem of syphilis in the late 1930s, and by 1944 journalist Hannah Lees claimed the once-shunned masturbation "has an important function" in an article titled "The Word You Can't Say."

One measure of democratic moral authority's popular resonance could be seen in the monthly reports of John Saxton Sumner, still vigorously chasing smut at the New York Society for the Suppression of Vice. His declining legal fortunes were paralleled by withering public support. Though he launched about two dozen investigations of smut in candy stores, novelty stores, and Times Square newsstands in March 1944, they came in response to a mere two recorded citizen complaints, one of which pertained to prostitution rather than porn. For November 1945, the header to the "complaints" section of his report was rather plaintively struck out — there were none. This did not stop Sumner from pursuing another two dozen investigations, but the absence of public enthusiasm was evident. By the next year the NYSSV would evolve with a whimper into the Society to Maintain Public Decency, to no discernible public acclaim. Responding to criticism that it was "opposed to freedom of the press, and engaged in a program of censorship," the group's annual report for 1946 called such charges "of course ridiculous." Even the group Anthony Comstock had built wanted no ties to censorship.

If democratic moral authority took shape as both a burgeoning legal consensus and a popular grassroots belief, it certainly found its most vocal institutional proponent in the American Civil Liberties Union. The ACLU's radical early years were discussed in chapter 2. By the late 1930s it had begun a dramatic shift toward the political mainstream. Historian Judy Kutulas argues that fighting for the right to teach evolution in Tennessee brought the organization its first real positive publicity in the mid-1920s, but only with the New Deal of the 1930s did the ACLU truly move beyond the political margins. As President Franklin Roosevelt presided over the first administration ever to support labor rights, long a central ACLU platform, activists stopped seeing government as the enemy and began working *with* it. The 1935 Wagner Act, in particular, protected union rights, and as labor's political fortunes ascended, so too did the reputation of the ACLU for its long hard work in the streets and courtrooms to secure those rights.

The ACLU had never bestowed great attention on censorship. Its traditional vision of First Amendment rights had more to do with freedom of assembly for labor unions on strike than freedom to publish sex-themed material. But the rising tide of democratic moral authority coincided precisely with the heyday of the ACLU, and as the First Amendment took center stage among American conceptions of civil liberties, the group with that phrase in its very name followed suit.

The ACLU-affiliated National Council on Freedom from Censorship operated as the main watchdog body, and by 1940 its approach was established. When Mayor LaGuardia sent his threatening newsstand letter that year, the Council responded that it "view[ed] with concern" his threatening campaign. It rushed to qualify, though, that the Council "of course, holds no brief for pornographic literature." For the ACLU, the price of newfound respectability involved remaining within certain social conventions. Its hotly debated internal purge of communist board members that same year reflected one such concession. With regard to obscenity, though, the ACLU's stance represented less strategic public-relations maintenance than simple default positioning. The group had never endorsed a categorical right to free speech for pornography, and it continued not to.

While ACLU member Morris Ernst had broken new free-speech terrain in his defenses of *The Well of Loneliness* and *Ulysses*, even he in his 1940 book *The Censor Marches On* saw nothing incongruent about condemning censorship while allowing for the prosecution and suppression of smut. Pornography was simply not a First Amendment issue — even though both of the landmark books Ernst defended had been labeled precisely that. Another prominent ACLU member, scholar Alexander Meiklejohn, wrote arguably the most influential treatise of the decade, *Free Speech and Its Relation to Self-Government*, in 1948. The book found obscenity unworthy of discussion, though its argument for the defense of art on the basis of its "social importance" would resonate in the next decade. In both cases, obscenity fit into an aesthetic hierarchy — when lofty, if frank and graphic, works like *Ulysses* could claim status as *art*, they deserved defending against obscenity charges; since such lowbrow efforts as Samuel Roth's mailings contributed nothing to culture, their suppression mattered little.

ACLU founder and head Roger Baldwin's interactions with the Post Office in the mid-1940s best exemplified the group's stance. Postal authorities had continued to harass distributors of nudist lifestyle magazines, and while the ACLU argued for the rights of the magazines, it did so without challenging the fundamental legitimacy of obscenity law. Baldwin went so far as to draft a letter in 1947 suggesting possible standards for obscenity; "of a character intrinsically to arouse" was one. Some members were outraged by the idea that the ACLU would actually *assist* in facilitating prosecutions. Connecticut playwright Elmer Rice sent Baldwin a heated objection to his proposal. "Such words and concepts as lurid, suggestive, immoral, prurient," Rice argued, "should have no place in the vocabulary of the ACLU."

Not even Rice was ready to exempt the obscene from the law, though. The National Council on Freedom from Censorship, where he played a lead role, continued to call for replacing "administrative censors" like postal authorities with jury trials rather than the complete abolishment of obscenity law. Describing its work as the defense of "serious books, plays, and pictures banned for alleged 'obscenity,'" the Council had little to say about material that fell short of seriousness. Instead of confronting obscenity per se, the ACLU evaluated allegedly obscene material, choosing its battles on the grounds of this "seriousness," be it scientific, artistic, or other.

Civil libertarians understood the tension contained in their position. In a 1948 letter, Morris Ernst conceded that the ACLU "has always been squeamish with respect to matters sexual." Reluctant to endorse the rights of smut, but troubled by the inconsistencies of a limited free-speech agenda, Ernst called for the application of the clear and present danger test to sexual publications. Elmer Rice agreed. Yet instead of taking a categorical stand against obscenity prosecutions, the ACLU continued to evaluate them on a case-by-case basis, enlisting its support only for those cases involving the aforementioned "serious" material.

As 1948 drew to a close, Roger Baldwin sent a revealing personal letter to John Sumner. "We have never campaigned for the repeal of obscenity laws," he wrote. He was right. Ostensibly mortal enemies, what the ACLU and the NYSSV really disagreed on was semantics. Butting heads over what should be defined as obscene, neither of them disputed that whatever it was, it should be suppressed.

None of this boded well for Samuel Roth.

———

Postal Woes

Despite his years on the front lines of the obscenity battle, Roth kept little company with the free-speech lobby. From his vantage point, the ACLU surely appeared too meek in its efforts. For the union's part, Roth's debased reputation kept him firmly removed from the realm of the serious literature they defended. By war's end in 1945, Roth seemed comfortable churning out middling works with just enough lurid allure to grab the eye of potential readers, but not so much as to warrant legal intervention from moral watchdogs.

Bumarap, Roth's first proper novel (or at least first published under his own name), captured the tenor of his mid-1940s work. Telling the story of a working-class Italian immigrant as he drifts first into radicalism (calling for "rablooshum"), then into the mansion of a millionaire, its artless prose and lack of narrative momentum hardly made for a riveting book. While the literary world paid little attention, Roth won warm reviews in some small-town newspapers.

Bumarap's faltering story only briefly detoured into sex, as the oblivious title character falls into the arms and bed of a wealthy uptown New York woman — or, as Roth's description had it, "She was not a woman — but a world." The book's sole sex scene offered little graphic detail, and indeed, no less than John Sumner himself, longtime dogged pursuer of what he called "Sam Roth, old offender," in his May 1947 report reluctantly concluded on the basis of a postal inspector's report that *Bumarap* was "not actionable."

"His advertising may be excluded from mails," Sumner's report briefly noted. In this quick aside lay years of struggle for Roth. For while the late 1940s would pass without criminal charges, the Post Office would turn his book's *non*obscenity on him. In a perverse irony, the very fact that *Bumarap failed* to possess a prurient aspect led to its effective suppression. As the Post Office explained, *Bumarap* was not obscene, but its advertising suggested that it was. Thus, Roth's publication could be suppressed on the grounds of "falsity and fraudulence," since his advertising circulars for the book offered "pretenses, representations, and promises . . . to the effect that the said publication as a whole is obscene, lewd, and lascivious."

Specifically, according to the postal authorities, the book's circular featured an illustrated image emphasizing "the cut-line of a female scantily covered by a web-like gown" with a caption in red ink, "He began by kissing her toes." It also quoted such snippets as "The woman was in a state of undress and yet not quite nude" and a description of "the whiteness of her thighs," promising "a really hot offering" to readers. "Any reasonable reader or viewer thereof," the post office contended, "would reasonably derive the impression" that the book was obscene.

This put Roth in a bind: if the circular was misleading, he was guilty of fraud; on the other hand, by the postal definition, if it was not misleading, he would be guilty of obscenity, a potentially criminal charge. Roth filed an official legal answer to the charges in October 1947, delicately attempting to reframe the issue. First, he claimed that the Post Office was not using "the words 'obscene, lewd, and lascivious' within their meaning as defined in recent decisions" of the federal courts, especially *Walker v. Popenoe*, the 1945 case that had criticized both Comstockism and postal authoritarianism in allowing the *Preparing for Marriage* pamphlet into the mails. In trying, somewhat forcedly, to link *Bumarap* to that pamphlet's educational imperative, Roth described the book as being "written in an introspective, philosophical style, without any hint of obscenity."

That the circular played up a sex angle could not, however, be avoided, and Roth confronted it headfirst. "We do not deny that *Bumarap* is a desirable book for people who like sexually stimulating reading," his answer continued, but denied that it went any further than the social mores of the day; any hint of perversity "would have to be supplied by the mind of an abnormally curious reader." The title character's virginity, for instance (terminated by the only sex scene in the novel), was carefully psychologized, as seen by his "inordinate affection for animals" — it being "an established fact" that such affection was a typical displacement. Finally, to show that the circular did not misrepresent the book, Roth noted that hundreds of copies had sold through the mail, all with a money-back guarantee for dissatisfied readers, and not a single refund had been demanded. Clearly, readers got what they expected from the book.

Roth's response had refuted the charges thoughtfully, if perhaps slightly unconvincingly in regard to *Bumarap*'s turgid content. The effort to locate "sexually stimulating reading" within the legal mainstream of the day was a more assertive approach than the ACLU took in 1947. It was also less effective. After hearings in late 1947, the fraudulence of Roth's circular was affirmed in April 1948. Due process having been officially served, the postmaster general thus issued a fraud order that barred Arrowhead Books, Roth's latest incarnation, from sending or receiving mail. *Bumarap* would not send Roth to prison, but it would also not send money into his bank account.

Ever nimble with his publishing houses, Roth simply repackaged the book under a new imprint, Hogarth House. Having simply crossed off the name Arrowhead and inserted Hogarth, Pauline Roth made the tactic mistake of contacting the Post Office to confirm that money orders would be payable to the new firm. Alerted to what it considered the "utter and willful defiance" of the Roths, the office quickly issued a new fraud order, forbidding any payment of postal money orders and returning all mail with a "fraudulent" stamp.

This pattern of chasing and evasion marked Roth's interactions with the postal authorities for the final years of the decade. Less interested in proving First Amendment points than running a smooth operation, Roth attempted to negotiate with the postal authorities, offering to allow their prescreening of his mailings. Postal solicitor Frank Delany gave no quarter, refusing to advise Roth. "You have been advised of the postal fraud statutes," he curtly wrote, "and you will have to assume full responsibility for any advertising."

Neither side gave much ground in this standstill. When Roth published a book called *Self-Defense for Women*, he advertised it with his customary leer, warning of "wanton physical attacks on women" and declaring the book's intent "to combat these brutal sensualists." Never one to let subtlety obscure his point, Roth's circular added, "The wonderful part of it is that the book is not a book of words but a book of photographs posed by a handsome young man and a beautiful young woman." In a precise repeat of the *Bumarap* contest, the Post Office promptly declared Roth's latest house, Psychic Research Press, fraudulent for again promising obscene content not actually delivered by the book.

The legal centerpiece of Roth's postal battles of the 1940s was *Waggish Tales of the Czechs*, published under his pseudonym Norman Lockridge. Roth employed the Lockridge alter ego for some of his folkloric forays, and the invented author had even been offered an honorary membership by the president of the International Mark Twain Society in 1936 for his *Golden Treasury of World's Wit and Wisdom*. Roth seemed to invest a fair amount of care in his Lockridge efforts, and *Waggish Tales* proved no exception. Purporting to consist of a recently discovered and translated fifteenth-century Czech manuscript, the book opened with Lockridge's editorial introduction, comparing the tales to Balzac's *Droll Stories*—a savvy move by Roth, in terms of invoking the nineteenth-century French text for legitimization. In a playful gesture, Lockridge acknowledged that the tales might be forgeries by literary critic Alexander Woollcott, then followed this with a further introduction by Woollcott.

Woollcott's essay showed recurring concern for ensuring the legality of the book. Beginning with an observation that "intimate subjects" were common medieval and Renaissance topics of discussion, it then offered the analysis that their "sought-for end" is "simply gargantuan laughter rather than the sexual excitation of the reader." For that matter, three of the ninety-eight original tales were omitted for unspecified "peculiarly gross obscenity which makes them unacceptable to the majority of Twentieth Century American readers"—strongly suggesting the remaining ninety-five tales contained no such obscenity. Delving into the Czech literary past, and also situating the tales alongside such ostensibly contemporaneous works as Chaucer's *Canterbury Tales* or Boccaccio's *Decameron*, the Woollcott essay posed as history lesson but cleverly worked as covert legal argument, insisting on the book's nonprurience.

The actual tales were a bawdy bunch indeed, 350 pages worth of short ribald stories with sexual punch lines, staffed with maidens, peasants, wives, husbands, and religious figures, all driven primarily by lust. Presented as stories told to the pregnant Queen Barbota as she retires to a "sequestered suite in the palace" surrounded only by her ladies of the court, a typical *Waggish Tale* involved a "slothful youth" named Cherep who feigns blindness to avoid military service. To test the claim, an officer brings the "pretty, buxom wench who was Cherep's sweetheart" before him and undresses her. As Cherep insists he sees nothing, the officer pulls the youth's pants off and laughs, "I know of a surety that you can see more than you claim, quite plainly in fact. Your *indicator* shows that you do!"

So they went: several further erection jokes, a good portion of premature ejaculations, copulation based on mistaken identity, all sorts of tricks and subterfuges used by travelers to share beds with farmers' daughters, and more. The actual province of the stories frequently fell into unavoidable doubt, with a reference to a "new-fangled rubber device" and a few lapses into stereotypical black American dialect most glaring, but altogether the *Waggish Tales* retained the spirit of its purported contemporaries. Although the stories and humor stayed almost monolithically sexual in nature, the book meticulously avoided overt eroticism or graphic content; a stray line about "the one tit which was lying right next to me" was as vulgar as it got. Anyone carefully following the law of obscenity in 1948 would probably have bet on *Waggish Tales of the Czechs* passing through the mail unperturbed.

Certainly Roth himself took that bet in publishing it. It was yet another bet he lost. This time the Post Office shifted tactics. Instead of honing in on the advertising, it went back to the book itself, declaring *Waggish Tales* obscene in early 1948. At an administrative hearing in March, Roth's friend and onetime mentor Shaemus O'Sheel, a well-published journalist, attempted to defend him. When the postal inspector asked whether he would call a story obscene that featured a falling hat suspended in midair because it rested on a naked man's erection, Shaemus insisted, "I do not call it an indecent joke." Cutting to the heart of obscenity law's role in policing sexual mores, the inspector demanded, "are there not many stories that deal with relations between men and women of a sexual or erotic nature which do not relate to normal coitus?" When a bemused Shaemus simply responded in the negative, the inspector struck back with a three-page tale of a man listening through a hotel room wall to a woman "protest shrilly, indignantly" against her male companion's request. When she finally submits to her partner's prodding, the story concludes with her "speaking thickly, with a gagging kind of intonation as though her tongue had swollen to inordinate proportions": "*Now* do you believe that I really love you, Benedikt?"

The coercive masculine sexuality in the story was not, of course, the target of postal complaint. That aspect fell well within long-established literary and cultural custom. The intimation of oral sex, however, was a different matter, and not part of "normal coitus." Though the subsequent official legal paper trail of Roth's case as it percolated up through the court system never once returned with any specificity to that moment in the hearing, almost entirely speaking of the *Waggish Tales* in general collective terms, the 1948 hearing provided a rare peek at the precise bureaucratic calculus used to determine the "normalcy" on which legitimate sexual representation hinged. When the Post Office confirmed the obscenity of the book the next month, it was no surprise.

Ironically, the postal proceedings transpired at the precise moment of publication of *Sexual Behavior in the Human Male*, better known as the first Kinsey Report. Indiana University biologist Alfred Kinsey and his team had spent years interrogating, classifying, and quantifying actual human sexual activity, and their overwhelming conclusion was that Americans preached one sexual doctrine and practiced another. Not only was premarital, extramarital, and autoerotic sexual behavior widespread and statistically "normal" (a word Kinsey rejected, precisely for its easy slide into enforced norms), but so were same-sex activity and, indeed, oral sex.

The Kinsey Report (a volume on female sexual behavior followed five years later in 1953) sparked much outrage, but more importantly, forced a national dialogue over sexuality. As the country confronted Kinsey's explicit sexual content, the salacious circulars for *Bumarap* or folksy idiom of *Waggish Tales* could but take on a quaint quality. Against this backdrop, Roth mounted a challenge to the postal authorities. The federal district court for southern New York denied Roth's request for an injunction against postal suppression from New York postmaster Albert Goldman, so he appealed higher. In his petition for a writ of certiorari to the Second Circuit U.S. Court of Appeals, Roth denied that his merchandise promised or delivered anything obscene. Returning to the character of *Waggish Tales'* humor that he had highlighted in the book's introduction, Roth's brief cited "the most authoritative modern psychologists such as Hall and Freud" to argue that the tendency of their sexual humor was "to sublimate the feeling of desire into the more social expression of laughter"—hardly an affront to normalcy.

Roth also accused the Post Office of a "wholly arbitrary and illegal misinterpretation of the book," and of "stretching bureaucratic zeal to the utmost." The Post Office "interfered with my constitutional right to circulate literature through the mails and has ruined my business without due process of law," Roth insisted. His lawyer Harry Rappaport, hoping the court would take heed of liberalizing tendencies in recent decades, defined obscenity as that which "has a tendency to excite the sensual desires of the average reader." The *Waggish Tales*, with their "Chaucerian literary quality," simply did not match that standard.

Roth's case — *Roth v. Goldman* — caught the court's attention, and, responding to both the climate of the day and the ongoing crisis in obscenity doctrine, it took the case. The three-judge panel assigned offered hope. Augustus N. Hand had played a significant role in the modernization of obscenity law, while Jerome Frank had introduced the phrase "legal realism" in his 1930 book *Law and the Modern Mind*, helping spearhead an intellectual movement dedicated to rethinking the foundations of law. Frank's book frequently adopted psychoanalytic and sociological approaches, sharing affinities with Roth's brief. And while Charles Clark sparred with Frank personally, he too came from a legal realist background as a Yale law professor. A more sympathetic panel would be hard to imagine.

Whatever hopes the personnel on the bench gave Roth were quickly dashed when the court issued a terse per curiam (unsigned) opinion in February 1949. In a mere two paragraphs, the court reviewed the charges and concluded there could be "little doubt" of the fraudulency of the circulars. As to the obscenity of *Waggish Tales*, the court noted the "many doubts now held as to the feasibility" of obscenity law, but nonetheless went on to call the book "obscene or offensive enough by any refined standards," a remarkably conservative legal standard for such a progressive group of jurists (the average reader Roth's brief cited made no claims to refinement). Using curiously hesitant language, the court went on to assert, "within limits it perhaps is not unreasonable to stifle compositions that clearly have little excuse for being beyond their provocative obscenity and to allow those of literary distinction to survive." As if to apologize for backtracking from the federal courts' general trajectory of liberalization, the opinion finished by noting that "judicial review channeled within the confines of a plea for an injunction should not be overextensive," suggesting that if it had been a criminal case with Roth facing imprisonment the court might have been less complacent.

All three judges endorsed the brief opinion. Yet behind the scenes each expressed profound ambivalence. In their private correspondence, the judges wavered. Charles Clark, the third judge, disliked *Waggish Tales* immensely. "I hate all this stuff," he wrote, blaming the Post Office for essentially giving it free advertising. Calling the stories "dull," he found it "hard to see how they can incite to lust." Clark even offered to take a strong stand against the Post Office: "I am not too averse to a crusade if you gents want to indulge." But adhering to "principles of administrative responsibility," it was "hard to see clear legal error." He concluded his memorandum, "Tentatively, I vote to affirm."

Augustus Hand, meanwhile, had allowed imported contraceptives and *Ulysses* into the country in the 1930s. But *Waggish Tales* bore no such medical or literary weight. He brushed aside Roth's challenge to the fraud orders as insubstantial, but acknowledged that had he been postmaster, he would not have targeted the book. Yet in examining it, Hand saw only "repeated salacious barroom stories." The architect of sexual liberalism had carved out space for legitimate heterosexual pleasures, but the waggish tale that stood out to Hand was "one that I think undoubtedly dealt with unnatural practices," presumably returning to the implied oral sex the postal inspector had highlighted at the hearing. "With some doubt," Hand voted to affirm the postmaster's ruling.

Finally, Jerome Frank expressed the greatest doubt. "If we are to rely on contemporary mores as a test," he wrote to his colleagues, "then this book is not obscene." Willing to uphold the *Bumarap* circular's fraudulence, Frank voted to reverse on *Waggish Tales*' obscenity. He prepared a lengthy dissent.

Sometime between the late-January conference and the early-February announcement of the court's opinion, Jerome Frank underwent a change of heart. He joined the opinion ruling against Roth on every point. Having prepared his dissent, however, he could not quite relinquish it, and in an unusual move appended a revised version as a concurrence. In the course of nearly 3,500 words, Frank argued against his own acquiescence, in one of the strongest critiques of obscenity law ever issued by a sitting judge.

Frank issued his concurrence as an overt plea for the Supreme Court to weigh in on the case, "thus dissipating the fogs which surround this subject." The censoring of *Waggish Tales*, he suggested, constituted "no great loss" to art or culture, but he warned that it "may put in peril other writings, of a higher order of excellence." From there, the rhetoric escalated. The court's ruling allowed great censorial leeway in "one fallible man," the postmaster, making him "an almost despotic arbiter of literary products." Frank's next paragraph cut to the chase: "Such a condition is compatible with the ideologies of

Hitlers, Czars and Commissars. It does not accord with democratic ideals which repudiate thought-control."

Aligning himself with the clear and present danger test, Frank claimed "no sane man thinks socially dangerous the arousing of normal sexual desires." Nodding to the ongoing broader social discussion, he suggested that even links to "socially harmful sexual conduct" would need to be proven with evidence "at least as extensive and intensive as the Kinsey Report." In the absence of any such proof, the circulars themselves tended to "show that a considerable number of the reading public, and especially those who would buy and would probably read *Waggish Tales*, want books like it." In other words, social mores at the ground level revealed a widespread — thus "normal" — demand for precisely the materials that social mores in the abstract would allegedly preclude.

As obscenity doctrine collapsed into itself under Frank's skewering depiction of its pointlessness, the judge went on to contrast *Waggish Tales* to Balzac's *Droll Stories*, the very comparison with which Roth had begun the book. Having just reread the Balzac volume "within the past few days," Frank could not see, "nor understand how anyone else could see, anything in that book less obscene than in *Waggish Tales* which the Postmaster General has suppressed." The only difference was age, which afforded Balzac "Classic" status and consigned Roth to the role of smut peddler. Balzac's stories were every bit as leering, lusty, and crude. Honing in on the court opinion's reference to "literary distinction," Frank wondered if the postmaster general would need to become a literary critic. "Jurisprudence would merge with aesthetics," he mused; "I cannot believe Congress had anything so grotesque in mind."

In such haste had Frank revised his dissent into a concurrence that at times, as when he declared himself "disturbed by the way my colleagues' ruling runs counter" to democratic ideals, he seemed to forget that he too had agreed to the per curiam opinion. Ultimately, though, his intellectual evisceration of the ruling notwithstanding, he did concede. Citing his "judicial inexperience," he "yielded" to his colleagues — "But I do so with much puzzlement," he added.

Surely disappointed by the outcome of the case, Roth also recognized the legal ammunition Frank had deliberately provided by attaching his concurrence. The recalcitrant publisher refused to bend to postal will, and even as the appellate court handed down its ruling, he continued his old tricks. *Tina and Jimmy Learn How They Were Born* arrived in early 1949 from Boar's Head, another Roth imprint. Written by "Marie Lorenz" (Roth's daughter Adelaide was actually featured in the dust-jacket "author" photo), it told the story of two suburban siblings nervous about the newest addition to their family, as their mother's pregnancy reaches delivery. Most of the book features the family maid, Sweetie, explaining reproduction to them through fables. "Before you and Jimmy and your new sister were born you were such tiny eggs inside of your mother," she explains. "Then your father came, the way the Good Giant came over the fields and woods in the story, smiled at your mother, and comforted her, and made the eggs come to life."

Intended for children, the book featured nothing graphic or sexual, and drew some good reviews, with a Wisconsin newspaper calling it "quite the best of its kind." So far, nothing controversial. But Roth's advertising circular for it seemed to represent an entirely different book. "Sex crimes against children usually begin at home," it began, before invoking the Kinsey Report— "a shock to the prurient as well as to the prudish who unconsciously think of children as not very different from the dolls they play with." Going on, the circular chided such moralists: "But to masturbate—why, that's degenerate, to say nothing of downright sinful."

Roth was right that Kinsey had identified a sexuality in children that society had yet to recognize or admit. What any of this had to do with the benign, indeed banal, *Tina and Jimmy* was anyone's guess, and legalities notwithstanding, the circular was spurious enough to qualify as fraudulent in the everyday sense of the term. The Post Office did nothing, and indeed, despite its recent legal victory it took a more subdued approach to Roth in the wake of Frank's powerhouse concurrence. With the case presumably bound for Supreme Court review, postal censors trod carefully, wary of providing any further evidence of their overreach.

It was, for instance, perhaps inevitable that Roth would capitalize on the Kinsey Report. Norman Lockridge's *Sexual Conduct of Men and Women* followed it closely, with a whimsically anthropological bent on human desire that could have come directly off the pages of Roth's *Beau* two decades earlier. "By no stretch of the imagination," initially found the postal inspector, could the book be "be classified as 'serious instruction regarding sex matters.' " Instead, it "degraded" the "dignity of sex" to "the state of prurient sensationalism." The book itself, a not entirely unclever string of observations, gave the authorities material to work with in its singular fixation on courting rituals, harems, adultery, impotence, and other topics centered on sexual behavior, but Roth exercised caution in its contents; one particularly law-conscious section on the marriage night contained a section cheekily titled "The Unmailable Details." A half century after Ida Craddock's marital manuals, Roth's book remained distinctly less explicit. Rather than pursue the book, postal solicitor Frank Delany dismissed the case against it in April 1949.

Postal agents even apparently came to an informal agreement with Roth in the spring of 1949, something they had previously refused. In a letter to one agent, Roth called himself "deeply grateful" for "making it possible for me to come to an understanding with the post office department." Roth allowed the office to block orders for five new books, but outlined an arrangement in which postal monitors would "let me know whenever a circular of mine happens to fall short of postal standards, and give me an opportunity to revise, making it unnecessary to continue these time- and money-wasting legal processes." In return, Roth promised that his subsequent circulars would abandon "suggestive art work" and that he would "confine myself to a full, factual presentation of whatever books I offer for sale."

The otherwise undocumented agreement appeared viable, at least in the short run. Roth was able to resend his books, and he toned down the advertising. *Forlorn Sunset*, one of the previously recalled books, was sent with a circular that only obliquely called it "the sort of book that every reader hugs in his privacy." Roth did attempt to capitalize on the initial suppression, noting that he had been called to Washington, D.C., to show why the book should not be barred as obscene — another tactic that hearkened all the way back to his early efforts in *Beau* to cull from the threat of obscenity an allure for his text.

Fragile truce notwithstanding, Roth had no intention of abandoning *Waggish Tales of the Czechs* to postal decree. Even as he reached his informal deal with the gatekeepers of the mails, he could hardly ignore the gauntlet that Jerome Frank had thrown down. Appealing the case to the Supreme Court, Roth asked the highest court in the nation to step into the obscenity fray and clarify it at last. Circumstances in 1949 were as contingent as they had ever been. The Court had repeatedly signaled its endorsement of a strong First Amendment, at least for political speech, but frequently modulated its opinions in ways that left obscenity a legal gray area – the "fog" Jerome Frank had described. Roth's case could potentially play a major role in clarifying obscenity doctrine, if the Court chose to use it as a platform for such intervention.

Waggish Tales of the Court

The Supreme Court to which Samuel Roth appealed had been completely reshaped by Franklin Roosevelt and his successor Harry Truman, who together repopulated virtually the entire Court between the late 1930s and the 1940s. The single overriding factor in the two presidents' nominations was support for the New Deal – and later, Truman's extensions of it in his Fair Deal. All else was secondary. Matters of racial inequality, church and state, and freedom of speech played little role in Roosevelt's or Truman's decisions. Nonetheless, by the late 1940s a general trajectory of Court support for civil liberties could be ascertained, heralded by Justice Harlan Fiske Stone's famous fourth footnote in the otherwise unexceptional 1938 *Carolene Products* opinion, in a case that dealt with federal milk regulations. In the footnote, Stone called for a heightened standard of judicial scrutiny toward laws that discriminated against "discrete and insular minorities," such as those that targeted racial, religious, or national groups for separate treatment. This signaled an important shift away from reviewing federal economic regulations (as the Court had been doing up until the mid-1930s, generally with hostility) and toward securing rights and liberties for the socially marginalized. Though the Court in the 1940s was not yet willing to overturn the grievously unjust 1896 *Plessy v. Ferguson* opinion that had paved the way for "separate but equal" racial segregation, it had begun to chip away at Jim Crow by finally demanding some semblance of that promised equality.

Since none of the justices was chosen for his First Amendment views, it made sense that many would view free speech through the dual lens of the New Deal and the horrors of World War II and the Holocaust. Thus former Michigan governor and U.S. attorney general Frank Murphy, for instance, wrote his very first opinion (*Thornhill v. Alabama*) in 1940 overturning an Alabama statute against picketing, securing an important victory for organized labor, a major New Deal constituency. This reflected an expanding conceptualization of what the "speech" in free speech entailed; where earlier Courts had suppressed labor speech because it was linked to action, Murphy defended *actions* because they were a part of expression. His vision of free speech was not unlimited, though. The constitution, he wrote, guaranteed "at the least the liberty to discuss publicly and truthfully all matters of public concern, without previous restraint or fear of subsequent punishment." To even the very liberal Murphy, that amounted to political speech, necessary for a robust democracy. Neither Murphy nor any of the justices included sexual politics within their understandings of the political sphere.

By the mid-1940s the Court was splintered into factions, both doctrinal and personal. Felix Frankfurter dominated one side. An Austrian Jewish immigrant who had grown up on New York City's Lower East Side, catapulting himself through sheer force of will and intellect into Harvard Law School and the national political elite, Frankfurter shared something of a personal trajectory with Samuel Roth, albeit to very different ends. He had taken radical stances as a law professor, supporting labor rights, the NAACP's fight for civil rights, and allegedly murderous anarchists Sacco and Vanzetti, among other causes. Appointed to the Court by Franklin Roosevelt in 1939, though, Frankfurter surprised many with his philosophy of judicial restraint, taking a very deferential stance toward legislative and executive action.

On the bench, Frankfurter quickly revealed his First Amendment doctrine in a 1940 case involving mandatory flag salutes for public elementary school students. *Minersville School District v. Gobitis* involved Jehovah's Witnesses who took religious exception to the salute. Writing for the Court, Frankfurter rejected their claims decisively. Recognizing the "conflicting claims of liberty and authority," Frankfurter sided with the latter. "National unity is the basis of national security," he explained, bowing to the building nationalist sentiment as the nation moved toward war. Subsequent opinions consistently extended this deference to government action against forms of speech outside the mainstream.

Over the course of the decade, in famously lengthy, pedantic opinions, Frankfurter would support contempt of court charges for newspaper editorials and labor-activist statements critical of active judges, injunctions against union picketing when the union was allegedly involved in violence, and local ordinances against sound trucks that drove around delivering amplified messages. A "wise accommodation between liberty and order" was how he described his free-speech perspective.

Samuel Roth could take more hope in the opposing wing of the Court, led by Hugo Black and William O. Douglas. Former Alabama senator Black was appointed by Roosevelt so casually in 1937 that his early association with the Ku Klux Klan had not even been vetted by the administration. Whatever baggage Black's past carried, though, as a justice he worshipped at the altar of the Bill of Rights. To Black, the First Amendment did "not speak equivocally," as he put it in 1941. Embracing the clear and present danger test, Black emphasized that "the substantive evil must be extremely serious and the degree of imminence extremely high before utterances can be punished." Few examples met this standard. That same year when he dissented against Frankfurter's opinion on the union picketing injunction, Black called the First Amendment "the foundation upon which our governmental structure rests and without which it could not continue to endure as conceived and planned." This was not a justice likely to give postal censors much ground.

By mid-decade William O. Douglas had joined Black as the Court's most vocal defender of unfettered expression. Like Black, Douglas came from a background that evidenced little interest in civil liberties; in his case, expertise in business law had led him into the New Deal inner circle through his leadership of the Securities Exchange Commission. Once on the bench, however, Douglas began indicating his agreement with Black's position, and he delivered a powerful opinion in early 1946 that finally resolved the postal suppression of *Esquire* in favor of the magazine, ridiculing authoritarian censorship. Wiley Rutledge, a justice given to less memorable or eloquent opinions than the bold First Amendment–defending duo, aligned himself with them as well, forming a clear free-speech judicial bloc.

The tensions between Frankfurter and the Black/Douglas team went beyond doctrinal disputes. Fervently elitist, Frankfurter looked down upon Black as a southern rube. Even after his impression was disproved through Black's sharp intellect, Frankfurter maintained his disdain. Toward Douglas, he felt nothing but personal scorn, considering him petty and manipulative. The bad feelings infected the whole Court, creating a toxic environment in the 1940s. In one notorious 1946 episode, Robert Jackson, another New Deal appointee, went so far as to issue a public condemnation of Black, a virtually unprecedented breach of Court etiquette. The divisions on the Court left two polarized camps, Frankfurter's judicial deference and Black and Douglas's vehement free-speech support, with several other justices caught in the middle.

Frank Murphy and Robert Jackson, for instance, believed in the democratic necessity of free speech, but within limits. Murphy's opinion for a unanimous Court in *Chaplinsky v. New Hampshire* (1942) upheld the conviction of a Jehovah's Witness who called a police officer "a God damned racketeer" and "a damned Fascist," on the grounds that such "fighting words" could rightly be criminalized as "epithets likely to provoke the average person to retaliation, and thereby cause a breach of the peace." Meanwhile, Jackson wrote a stirring opinion against a West Virginia mandatory school flag salute in 1943. While technically centering on freedom of religion, the case carried clear free-speech implications. "If there is any fixed star in our constitutional constellation," he wrote, it was that no official could "prescribe what shall be orthodox in politics, nationalism, religion, or other matters of opinion." By the decade's end, though, horrified by the atrocities of Nazism and European fascism, Jackson had no problem with letting Chicago declare a racist, anti-Semitic speaker guilty of a breach of peace when an angry crowd outside the auditorium where he spoke began to riot. Extending the First Amendment to cover such deliberate provocations, he contended, might "convert the Bill of Rights into a suicide pact."

Roth could likely count on Jackson, Murphy, and Frankfurter rejecting his arguments. Newly appointed Chief Justice Fred Vinson showed few free-speech proclivities at all. He had been on the Court of Appeals that heard the *Parmalee* case freeing a nudist book in 1940, and had written a dissent registering discontent with his colleagues' liberal attitude — and that was for a book whose "purity" of authorial motive Vinson conceded. Roth could hardly count on even that.

By the mid-1940s it had been a half century since the Court had substantively weighed in on obscenity. Even as the twentieth century had witnessed the ascent of the First Amendment to its preferred position, *never* had the Court suggested anything *but* that obscenity remained outside the definition of free speech. Its scope as a legal concept had been sharply curtailed by sexual liberalism, but its acceptance as a criminalized matter had not been challenged anywhere within mainstream legal currents. Murphy lumped obscenity with "fighting words" in *Chaplinsky*, and even free-speech advocate Douglas had mentioned "the validity of obscenity laws" in his *Esquire* opinion.

In two cases shortly before Roth's, the Court tentatively began to examine the obscenity question, but without delivering clear results. Both came out of New York state and, if anything, added to the fog. Murray Winters's case came first. As noted above, the magazine dealer had been convicted for selling such crime-themed pulp as *Headquarters Detective*, with lurid and gruesome tales of police and criminals. Though he also sold racy magazines like *The Model Poses*, the state had made clear in its repeated victories in the New York legal system that it was the crime material at stake.

Busted through the efforts of the intransigent New York Society for the Suppression of Vice, the longtime dealer of questionable publications bore some resemblance in his career to Samuel Roth. But while Roth had alienated the literary community with his book-pirating, Winters was able to enlist them, appealing to the Supreme Court armed with amicus curiae — "friend of the court" — briefs from the Authors' League of America and the ACLU. Their briefs on behalf of Winters spoke the Court's language. They invoked the First Amendment's freedom of the press, the preferred position free speech occupied among constitutional liberties, and the clear and present danger test as the only acceptable criteria for suppression. Any such measure needed to be narrowly tailored, but the New York obscenity statute under which Winters was convicted, they argued, was vague and overbroad.

Nonetheless, when the Court first heard Winters's case, it deadlocked 4–4, with Robert Jackson absent to preside over the Nuremberg trials. When the Court splits evenly, the lower court decision is affirmed. For Winters, this meant his conviction stood. But with Chief Justice Harlan Fiske Stone's death and the appointment of Fred Vinson as his replacement, the Court ordered a reargument later that year. Again, things came close. William O. Douglas's conference notes recorded another 4–4 split—but this time with himself passing (Rutledge's notes record Douglas calling the case "close"). Frankfurter, Stanley Reed, Jackson, and the new chief justice voted to affirm, and recent Truman appointee Harold Burton joined them, showing little interest in the debate. Douglas's handwritten notes marked Burton as simply calling it a "workable statute," which was enough.

Whatever the reason for Douglas's wavering, his eventual position was fairly assured. In the meantime, both Vinson and Reed swung around, creating a strong majority for reversal. Writing for the majority, Reed walked carefully. In the original conference, he had voted to affirm the conviction, apparently based on aesthetic grounds. According to Douglas's notes, Reed would have decided otherwise if the case had centered on something of merit, like Theodore Dreiser's *An American Tragedy*. For Winters's publications, full of "deeds of lust and evil," he instead sided with the state's right to "protect its citizens." Reed's change of mind hinged on the narrow grounds of the statute's vagueness, not on any broad endorsement of the right to publish filth.

In his opinion, Reed began by recognizing "the importance of the exercise of a state's police power to minimize all incentives to crime, particularly in the field of sanguinary or salacious publications with their stimulation of juvenile delinquency." Nonetheless, Reed found the state court's construction of the statute too vague, particularly its belabored attempt to define obscenity and indecency in what it called "a different manner" from the general understanding of obscenity as a matter of "sexual impurity." This different manner, including depictions of crime, created sweeping standards that made it impossible for publishers to draw the "line between the allowable and the forbidden" in advance, thus constituting a violation of free speech and press.

Winters v. New York, finally delivered in early 1948, was the Court's most substantive return to obscenity law since the 1890s. Murray Winters could celebrate, but the opinion held little consolation for someone like Samuel Roth. Justice Reed made painstakingly clear that New York's error was in lumping poorly defined "indecent" works about "criminal deeds of bloodshed or lust" with strictly *obscene* materials. Reed concluded his opinion with a direct assertion that it carried "no implication" that a state "may not punish circulation of objectionable printed matter, assuming that it is not protected by the principles of the First Amendment."

The Court's only other direct engagement with obscenity was, if anything, even more disappointing. When New York City prosecutors charged Doubleday & Company for publishing Edmund Wilson's *Memoirs of Hecate County* in 1946, they drew the ire of the entire literary community. Unlike Winters, Roth, or other purveyors of work associated with lowbrow culture, Wilson was a respected author and critic (except perhaps to NYSSV agent Harry Kahan, who led this bust as well as Winters's), and the case outraged the literati, who saw it as a pathetic last gasp of outdated Victorian mores. Prosecutors met them on this turf, from a different angle. In local court, they somewhat surprisingly argued directly for the *Hicklin* test of tendency to deprave and corrupt youth, calling it "so well established in this state that it should not now be changed except by legislative action," the past three decades of federal court action deemed immaterial.

Wilson's book satirized the middle-class suburban New York world in a series of stories, and one, "The Princess with the Golden Hair," came to dominate the trial. Called to the defense, Columbia University professor Lionel Trilling termed the book a "rather Swiftian representation of manner," to which an irate judge replied, "not everybody is a professor," wondering how relevant such lofty analysis was to the average reader. More to the point, prosecutors honed in on the "rather precise and literal account of a woman's sexual parts in the sexual act" in the key story, which graphically detailed the emotionally hollow seductions of a would-be Casanova. The three-judge panel found the book obscene, with one dissenting member calling the story "honestly concerned with the complex influences of sex and of class consciousness on man's relentless search for happiness." While the prevailing judges left no written opinion, clearly the explicit sex alone sufficed, regardless of motive or role in the greater textual constellation of the book.

Doubleday spent 1947 appealing its way through the New York court system with neither any luck nor even so much as a written opinion giving it material to challenge. The *Columbia Law Review* criticized the absence of written opinions and called the obscenity ruling a "retrogression in judicial attitude toward genuine literary endeavors" that "should be specifically repudiated by higher New York Courts on review," but it was not to be. Reaching the top of the New York courts without satisfaction, the publishing firm looked to the Supreme Court. The moment was ripe for such a case. With obscenity doctrine clearly a mess, New York courts contrasted to federal ones, and the incorporated First Amendment still untested with regard to obscenity, *Doubleday v. New York* seemingly promised resolution.

The competing briefs at the Supreme Court read like entirely different cases, so divergently did they frame the issues. To the state, it was and remained a state issue, one already settled by New York's obscenity statute. The brief contented itself with listing a vast number of state obscenity laws and chronicling Wilson's graphic sexual depictions — "more than fifteen assorted sexual acts are described or suggested," it carefully counted, plus "three frustrated attempts at intercourse."

Doubleday, on the other hand, called the *Hicklin* test "thoroughly discredited," and repeatedly distinguished *Memoirs of Hecate County* from "cheap pornography" by filling its briefs with reviews from highbrow publications. Descriptions of sex, it noted, were not an exception to the clear and present danger test, and New York had failed to specify exactly what dangers Wilson's book posed to the reading public. Joining in with an amicus brief, the ACLU added an angle of sexual modernism, asserting, "today sex is not even an 'unconventional' subject" and citing the Kinsey report as evidence. It situated *Memoirs* within a broader social liberalization toward sexuality, undermining any sense of danger around the book's admittedly highly explicit scenes. "Here, for the first time, is presented to this Court an opportunity to determine the limits of free expression," the ACLU concluded.

Not everyone at the Supreme Court was impressed. Chief Justice Vinson read the book and voted to affirm without further comment at conference. Harold Burton revealed a moralistic streak, reminding his brethren that although the family was the basic "unit of living," as Douglas's notes recorded it, the "disregard of adultery is evident in the book." Robert Jackson, on the other hand, showed some personal doubt about the book's harmful qualities, but argued that the Court "must pay some respect to state courts" and joined in affirming, as did Reed, whose ambivalence had been clear even as he went the other direction in *Winters*.

This made a solid block of four justices against Doubleday, perfectly balanced against four dedicated to its right to publish. Black and Douglas, of course, were joined by Wiley Rutledge and the quiet Frank Murphy, who said little at conference. This left the case squarely in the hands of Felix Frankfurter. Hardly a free-speech crusader, Frankfurter had shown a general pattern of deference to state courts on First Amendment matters, emphasizing always what he called "vigilant judicial self-restraint" over personal beliefs or politics. Even when he sided with free speech, as in *Esquire*'s case against the postmaster general, he inserted a concurrence in the unanimous opinion mostly to insist the case "lies within very narrow confines" of postal authority. Yet Frankfurter was also an unrepentant elitist, unperturbed by the suppression of crime magazines, raucous sound trucks, or other social blights but surely concerned over governmental censorship of a book by a reputable, renowned author.

What decided Frankfurter's actions in the case, ultimately, was not his judicial philosophy, but rather his warm personal friendship with Edmund Wilson. Frankfurter recused himself. A 4–4 split meant the New York courts were affirmed. *Memoirs of Hecate County* remained obscene in the state, and the Supreme Court's first direct confrontation with obscenity since the 1890s was a frustratingly inconclusive nonprecedent, useless to all.

This left Samuel Roth on extremely unsure legal footing and without the resources of Winters or Doubleday. While the ACLU had supported both these cases with powerful briefs, it left Roth to fend for himself. "We are considering the possibility of filing a short brief," ACLU attorney Herbert Monte Levy wrote Roth in early 1949, but nothing came of it. While neither the records of the ACLU nor Roth's personal papers contain further material clarifying why ACLU interest trickled off, the group's policy remained one of choosing only cases in which the material had merit. "The book is a serious work of literature," the group had written of *Memoirs of Hecate County* in its defense of that book, with an author who "has had a distinguished career as editor, writer and critic." Few would say the same of *Waggish Tales of the Czechs*, or of Samuel Roth.

Left to his own devices, Roth filed a petition for a writ of certiorari, asking the Supreme Court to hear his case. He filed *in pro per*, writing his petition on his own (though the historical record is unclear as to why, Roth's stormy history with lawyers provides one possible hint). The solitary effort showed Roth was a shrewd man, aware through personal experience of the bureaucratic machinery of obscenity law, but he was no lawyer, and his petition reflected this. It began effectively, rightly calling Jerome Frank's lengthy appellate opinion "as close to a dissenting opinion as a concurring opinion can get." From there, Roth took a scattershot approach. The postmaster denied him due process of law in his arbitrary order, Roth contended, before invoking the Fourth Amendment's protection against search and seizure. Only briefly did he allude to the First Amendment. Roth called the case "a dangerous departure" from the Court's standards in the *Esquire* case, but otherwise grounded the petition only superficially in recent trends in obscenity doctrine.

Some of Roth's petition made effective rhetorical points, but as a legal document it was far from compelling. Roth seemed to think his property-rights argument for selling the book was compelling, but it floated in a curious disconnect from the entire history of free-speech debates. The keywords of "clear and present danger," and other phrases that carried currency in the debate, were nowhere to be found.

The government's responding brief was no masterpiece of legal argumentation, but it spoke the right language, even delivering one clever argument in claiming the "literary style" of *Waggish Tales* was "spurious," wearing off "like the 'black lamp' smudge that could be erased from the indecent pictures in *Rosen v. United States*," the long-ago 1896 case where the Supreme Court had made its last substantive decision on the topic. The brief's governmental authors barely addressed Roth's more irrelevant arguments, but cited a roster of cases defending their key points that the postmaster's actions had not been arbitrary, and that the federal obscenity law lacked either vagueness or subjectivity.

In this form, the petition to hear the case went to the Supreme Court. Roth's greatest asset was the *Esquire* precedent. In it, Douglas had described the magazine as full of "smoking-room type of humor, featuring, in the main, sex," which some witnesses had considered "salacious and indecent," others "only racy and risqué," while still more "condemned them as being merely in poor taste." Surely the same could be said of *Waggish Tales*.

Little documentation remains from the Court's consideration of the case, consisting primarily of the certiorari bench memoranda that the justices' clerks prepared for them to summarize cases and help decide whether to hear them. Harold Burton's and Wiley Rutledge's clerks brushed the case aside. William O. Douglas's clerk gave *Roth v. Goldman* the greatest consideration, seeing in it "an important question yet to be resolved." The Court should "place a heavy burden on government when it wishes to ban printed matter for this reason," he wrote. The *Waggish Tales*, however, were "no more than a dirty book"—though neither he nor anyone else at the Supreme Court actually so much as examined the book. Some members of the Court who would support "an attempt at literature" would not be willing to defend "this type of book." His recommendation to Douglas was a very skeptical, "Grant?"

When it came time for the justices to vote on whether to hear the case, Roth's hopes were demolished. On June 17, 1949, Douglas tallied the votes on his docket sheet; he alone had voted to hear the case. First Amendment beliefs certainly determined the decision, though personal relations perhaps played a background role. Douglas had long considered Jerome Frank a close friend, even influencing President Roosevelt to appoint them colleagues at the Securities Exchange Commission during the 1930s, so Douglas surely read Frank's flamboyant concurrence closely. Not even Hugo Black joined him. Black had called it "a prized American privilege to speak one's mind, although not always with perfect good taste, on all public institutions," back in 1941. Voting against Samuel Roth's case several years later, he implied without comment that perhaps sexuality was not yet a public institution.

The justices had no obligation to explain themselves. All Samuel Roth received was the formal declaration on June 20 that his petition was denied. The 1950s would begin with no more clarity on obscenity than the 1940s had shown.

CHAPTER 5

Cold War, Hot Lust

Sexual Politics in the 1950s

When Roth lobbed his appeal at the Supreme Court, it failed to detonate, and obscenity law retained its foggy mist. More literally effective in generating explosions that year was the Soviet Union, whose atomic testing paid off a few months after Roth's loss. Numerous factors generated what history came to know as the Cold War, but Soviet nuclear capacity certainly solidified it. Its ramifications would extend across the globe during decades of geopolitical conflict, but they also coalesced around the body of Samuel Roth, who would end the new decade in a prison cell.

Cold War concerns structured not just American foreign policy in the 1950s, but domestic politics as well. Most famously, McCarthyism spearheaded a broad suppression of dissent. The regulation of sexuality, too, became a national obsession, one deeply intertwined with both external concerns over communism and internal anxieties over "subversion." Indeed, from the start furiously anticommunist Wisconsin Republican senator Joseph McCarthy's ill-founded tirades against purported communists shared both rhetoric and logic with the intense sexual policing of the decade. Noting the pervasive antigay fervor, historian David Johnson has identified a "Lavender Scare" that paralleled and even outlasted McCarthy's Red Scare.

With the federal government wholly committed to building what historian Margot Canaday calls "The Straight State," one that simultaneously excluded homosexuality and carefully policed heterosexuality to produce a dominant "normalcy" that hinged on marital, procreative sex, free speech frequently took a backseat to Cold War concerns. This played out politically in the early 1950s, with jarring Supreme Court opinions that privileged national security over individual First Amendment rights. Politics, sexuality, and law would also converge over obscenity doctrine, as a judicially inhospitable climate developed, encouraged all the while by a resurgent social panic over pornography.

The United States was caught in an ideological bind surrounding the First Amendment. On the one hand, since virtually every aspect of American life was refracted through a Cold War lens, censorship had to be repudiated as something foreign to the American way of life, the province of Soviet totalitarianism—a distinction that also promoted American religiosity as a counterpoint to Soviet atheism (only in the 1950s did "In God We Trust" become the national motto and "under God" join the Pledge of Allegiance). On the other hand, widespread sentiment favored the domestic suppression of both communists and pornography. The solution was to define such suppression seemingly out of existence by framing it as something other than censorship. The framers of the Constitution "never meant the First Amendment to protect filth peddlers who poison minds," explained *Better Homes and Gardens* in 1957. The Supreme Court had already expressed the same idea about communism, and it would ultimately agree with the magazine on smut. Allowing either communist speech or obscene materials was simply not included in what Americans meant when they expressed opposition to censorship.

Samuel Roth observed the development of this lurching national transition from the margins. Perpetually badgered by the postal authorities throughout the decade, he nonetheless managed to avoid both prison and the national eye until prominent figures pulled him back into focus, using him to represent all that was unsavory—and even un-*American*—about the smutmongers who had suddenly become a key national menace. This chapter situates his return to the Supreme Court in its Cold War context, leaving the next chapter to track the precise doctrinal elements of his case that created a baffling but nonetheless enduring precedent.

Varieties of Deviance

Defining words played an important role in the domestic side of the Cold War. Talk of supporting global freedom and democracy rang hollow to the citizens of Guatemala, Iran, Vietnam, and a dizzying array of so-called Third World nations on whom the United States imposed violent, dictatorial puppet governments. At home, though, a complacent media obscured and distorted the stories of such foreign entanglements to bring them in line with the more commendable rhetorical ideals. Much rested on the preservation of this fiction, since every aspect of American life was constantly contrasted to the brutal Soviet domination of its own puppet states.

Other fictions also prevailed, none so fervently as that of sexual normalcy. Again, communist social organization helped structure American norms by counterexample. In place of communal child-rearing, the atomized nuclear family was the key structure. Where Soviet work habits allegedly stripped women of their gender traits, American women knew how to be properly feminine — as then vice president Richard Nixon famously emphasized in his 1959 valorization of consumer abundance and family-oriented technology in the so-called Kitchen Debate with Soviet premier Nikita Khrushchev. American men, too, abided by the patriarchal norms, embodying the strength and virility needed to defend the country.

Holding these gender and sexual norms together was the central institution of heterosexuality. Virulent homophobia reinforced its superiority, with discourse that linked homosexuality and communism in a multitude of ways. A 1950 Senate investigation into the "Employment of Homosexuals and Other Sex Perverts in Government" made pointed use of the phrase "security risk," describing gay and lesbian workers. On the tenuous grounds that such government workers might be susceptible to communist blackmail, President Dwight Eisenhower signed Executive Order 10450 shortly after taking office in 1953. Building off and modifying Harry Truman's loyalty review program, it adopted the Senate recommendation and institutionalized the exclusion of gays and lesbians from federal employment for decades (during which the federal government was the single largest employer in the nation).

Such measures constituted concrete links between foreign policy and sexual politics. What this meant at the ground level was an oppressive decade of police violence, criminalization, cultural misrepresentation, and psychiatric stigmatization for LGBT Americans. At the more abstract level of discourse, homosexuality and communism held symbiotic roles in reinforcing the importance of proper, normal American living. As social fears of porn magnified in the decade, these links would resurface in various ways: sexual deviance was frequently cited to explain political deviance, and vice versa. In a reminder of how deeply Anthony Comstock's idea of *Traps for the Young* had permeated American culture, communism, homosexuality, and pornography were all constantly framed as threats to children — who would otherwise presumably remain pure, heterosexual, and capitalist.

If homosexuality remained the greatest threat to the sexual normalcy on which the American national project relied, it was not alone in its imagined perversity. Heterosexuality, too, had to be disciplined, carefully cultivated and calibrated. By the 1950s, sexual liberalism occupied the mainstream. It was assumed that pleasure was a central component of sexual activity, that many Americans utilized some form of birth control, and that education and knowledge were crucial in helping adolescents adjust to their maturing interests and desires. Yet too *much* pleasure, too *much* distance between sex and procreation, and even too much *knowledge*, threatened to destabilize the nuclear family that so comfortably, and not coincidentally, fit into the housing patterns of the single-family-oriented suburbs that were drawing middle-class white Americans away from the city after the war. Men were to be aggressive, but not *too* aggressive — not wimps, but not psychopaths either. Same for women, still expected to be virgins at marriage, but allowed minor sexual experimentation beforehand. Female norms revolved around the poles of frigidity and nymphomania, terms more ideological than scientific and used to keep women from either rejecting or too eagerly pursuing sex — effectively harnessing them to marital intimacies. Women should be orgasmic, but only in response to their husband's sexual efforts.

Relatively few of these reigning norms corresponded to the actual lived experience of Americans. Alfred Kinsey's *Sexual Behavior in the Human Male* had shown as much of men in 1948, and its follow-up regarding women appeared in 1953, revealing similar truths about the pre- and extramarital, not to mention homosexual and autoerotic, activities of women. Kinsey consistently rejected the idea of sexual normalcy, considering it a myth all too easily used to dictate, and even criminalize, sexual behavior. He also rejected the myth of childhood innocence, noting that children were sexual beings. Such positions placed him outside the mainstream, despite his books' best-selling status. With the Cold War in full swing, Kinsey was unsurprisingly accused by social conservatives of aiding the communist effort to undermine American gender roles, family, and morality. Despite the fact that Kinsey's evidence came from the testimony of women themselves, Democratic Brooklyn representative Louis Hunter asked the Post Office to ban *Sexual Behavior in the Human Female*, calling it "the insult of the century against our mothers, wives, daughters, and sisters."

The Post Office declined to ban the book. Certainly Kinsey's barrage of charts, graphs, and data put the book well within the protected class of nonprurient scientific work, notwithstanding its undeniably titillating uses by readers and the press, always eager to mine it for startling aspects. Samuel Roth would be less lucky. At the same time the postal authorities were clearing Kinsey for the mails, they continued to move aggressively against Roth's publications. The lines of distinction were quite thin. As suggested above, state suppression in the 1950s had to avoid the label of "censorship" to maintain its legitimacy. Material deemed scientific passed muster; material deemed salacious did not. That the categories were hardly exclusive simply added to the confusion.

The national rejection of censorship hinged not on an actual glorious history of untrammeled free expression (which, as previous chapters have shown, simply did not exist), but once again, on juxtaposition against Russian practices. The official state censorship policies of the Soviet Union and its satellites were anathema to American values so, naturally, freedom and democracy demanded resistance to censorship. No less than President Eisenhower urged Americans not to "join the book burners," while the American Bar Association unanimously adopted a resolution affirming the freedom to read in 1956.

Nazi Germany and Stalinist Russia supplied frequent reference points in the decade's public discussion — *those* were the sort of places where censorship flourished. Catholics, too, came under scrutiny. Since the 1930s the Legion of Decency and National Organization for Decent Literature had exerted significant cultural influence with their boycott threats. In Cold War America, such sectarian centralization of power grew increasingly unpopular, and the press turned against Catholic censorship. While filmmakers such as Otto Preminger chafed against the Catholic-initiated Production Code (which had been embraced wholeheartedly by the risk-averse studios), releasing multiple films in the decade without the code's seal to critical acclaim and box-office success, *Harper's* bemoaned the "little band of Catholics" who held such un-American power.

If censorship could be decried in practice, the word still remained murkily defined. One thing it was *not* in the early Cold War years was the suppression of certain dangerous ideologies in the name of national security. Thus the attack on communists mounted by Joseph McCarthy, the House Un-American Activities Committee, or such nongovernmental efforts as the Hollywood blacklist, which rendered movie screens safe for American values by driving leftists out of the film industry, remained other than censorship. So too did the suppression of obscenity. Even as *Redbook* made the usual Hitler allusions in discussing "What Censorship Keeps You from Knowing" in 1951, it added as an aside, "No one, of course, objects to the censorship of obscenity for obscenity's sake." The assertion received no elaboration; it needed none, being understood as uncontroversial. The American Book Publishers Council began a *Censorship Bulletin* in late 1955. It would often cover books *wrongly* accused of obscenity (i.e., books from reputable publishers that had won critical praise), but never object to government action against actual smut.

This left material perceived as smut to fend for itself with very few defenders, at a moment when it could be socially understood only through the same Cold War lens that shaped all national perception. A wave of concern over crime and horror comics that began in the late 1940s set the immediate interpretive template for the antiporn expressions of the 1950s. Beginning with psychiatrist Fredric Wertham's claims that comics contributed to juvenile delinquency and sexual perversions, a national crusade to protect children from such devious influences arose.

Concern over the effect of lurid reading on children dated back to the emergence of affordable printed material in the nineteenth century, but this new chapter situated itself in specifically Cold War anxieties over the production of proper gender and sexual identity, particularly for boys and young men. Wertham worried that the sexualized violence of crime and horror comics could push young readers into perverted identities — "sadists or sissies." Both seemingly opposite poles ultimately collapsed into shared traits, including intimations of homosexuality. This put the comics squarely against American values, and by 1954 the Catholic magazine *America* could speak for a broader consensus in calling them "a cultural and moral menace to our youth." That widespread consensus among social scientists actually considered the effect of comics "quite insignificant," as the *Science News Letter* reported in 1954, mattered quite little.

The Comics Association of America, less interested in the First Amendment than continued profits from its booming business, responded to the outcry by adopting a voluntary code to stave off censorship efforts, much as the film industry had done a few decades earlier. It largely worked, as attention drifted away from comics. Much of this attention was redirected toward pornography. Like "censorship," "pornography" was a somewhat elusive term in the 1950s. Certainly prurient interest was deeply embedded in the consumer economy, from its advertisements to its mass culture. So long as it could be reconciled with dominant values, though, many sexualized items could avoid the dread label. Thus Mickey Spillane's books, which accounted for an astonishing six of the ten best-selling novels of the decade, saturated their pages with strong sex and violence. But his books like *My Gun Is Quick* and *The Big Kill* endorsed Cold War values in stories. Spillane's heroic detective Mike Hammer desired (and "conquered") women, hated (and killed) communists and "queers," and found himself in the mainstream, making Spillane rich and saving him from charges of pornography.

Another massive best seller of 1956, Grace Metalious's *Peyton Place*, likewise brimmed over with sexual intrigue, managing to stay just within the realm of the acceptable, though not without controversy. Even Hugh Hefner's *Playboy*, which debuted in 1953, remained safely "normal." A direct descendant of Roth's 1920s *Beau*, *Playboy* even sounded like Roth: "If you're somebody's sister, wife, or mother-in-law and picked us up by mistake, please pass us along to the man in your life and get back to your *Ladies Home Companion*," wrote Hefner in the first issue, very nearly plagiarizing Roth's circulars of three decades ago. Its naked centerfold of Marilyn Monroe and subsequent "playmates" went further than *Beau* had, but the smart, sophisticated *Playboy* published freely, endorsing the expanding consumer culture and in the process becoming an integral part of it.

Despite their blatant appeal to erotic interests, Spillane, Metalious, and Hefner avoided being classified as pornographers. Too popular, too suave, or simply too normal for such a label, they all fell within the parameters sexual liberalism had staked out. Social space existed for *desire*, so long as it refrained from *prurience* — another elusive term, but always understood with hints of perversion. Men desiring women, or the morally inflected feminine gossip networks through which the drama of *Peyton Place* unfolded, toed this line.

Less fortunate was Samuel Roth: too shadowy, too perverse, and, not irrelevantly, too *foreign*, he returned to national attention as the pornographer par excellence, a cultural fiend out to deprave and corrupt American children.

Making Monsters

Hot on the heels of the comics crisis, the porn panic followed its logic but developed even more individualized villains. Fear of comics highlighted effects on susceptible children, but rarely emphasized the artists and distributors behind the texts. While antiporn rhetoric would take it cues quite precisely from the comics crusade on matters of effects, it would add a new focus on the "loathsome and lecherous purveyors of pornography," as a 1955 Senate committee called them. It would not take long for Samuel Roth to find himself at the center of this attention.

By 1950, Roth's bid for clarification of obscenity doctrine having been rebuffed by the Supreme Court, his conflict with postal authorities had become something of a routine. They regularly went after his merchandise; he fought their efforts, integrating his victories into his advertisements and cutting his losses when needed to set up new publishing firms not yet considered fraudulent or fictitious. On the whole, he fared well, though it was clear the Post Office carried a vendetta against him.

As the postal inspectors constantly targeted his work, Roth filed a civil suit against acting New York postmaster Harold Riegelman after a translation of Anna Weirauch's German lesbian novel *The Scorpion*, a photo folio simply titled *Nudes*, and Roth's hardbound literary journal *American Aphrodite* were barred from the mails as obscene in 1952. Roth's strongly worded affidavit claimed the order would "damage beyond repair" his publishing business, which he speculated "may perhaps be what is intended." He managed to convince a federal district judge, who granted his injunction against enforcement of the postal order, describing it as "based merely on opinion . . . arbitrary, capricious, and unwarranted in law or in fact."

Roth also beat criminal charges for selling *Beautiful Sinners of New York*, a leering catalog of prostitutes written by "A Flesh Peddler." Charged in early 1951 with mailing obscene matter, Roth faced nine counts based on the book and its advertising circulars. Certainly the material capitalized on reader interest in sex, with shadowy nude sketches and tantalizing details about the "sinners" it chronicled. Of Lilith Andrews, age twenty-three, it noted, "lost virginity to butler at six"; Joanna Bradshaw, it said, found relations with men "satisfying as long as they treated her brutally enough." In a typical Roth move, a foreword by Louis Berg, M.D., called the book "a social document of the first order of importance" because of its window into the minds of the flesh peddler and his "flesh-pots."

Roth's defense lawyer, Nicholas Atlas, had begun his career as a federal attorney, even working on the *Ulysses* case in support of customs efforts to keep James Joyce's novel out of the country. In private practice since 1948, though, he worked for less moralistic clients, making headlines as he defended landlords accused of rent-gouging, patrolmen accused of shakedowns, and extortionists, putting Roth in unseemly company. Atlas did hold progressive ideals, leading efforts from within to integrate the secret society Knights of Pythias in the early 1950s. Most importantly, he knew his obscenity law from experience.

At trial, Atlas moved immediately to dismiss on First Amendment grounds. Judge Edward Weinfeld denied the motion, but allowed Atlas to build his defense around testimony from expert witnesses and comparisons to other best sellers. One sharp-tongued literary critic even defined a best seller as "a book of 900 pages that has a great deal of sex in it." When a surprised judge Weinfeld asked, "Is that your serious answer?" the critic affirmed and noted Norman Mailer's *The Naked and the Dead* and James Jones's *From Here to Eternity*, two gargantuan war novels with plenty of sexual content. The critic compared *Beautiful Sinners* to the Kinsey report, a rather tenuous comparison but based on the fundamentally accurate point that both cataloged sexual behavior. In addition, Atlas brought a psychiatrist, who agreed that smut could "only arouse lust in abnormal people." Normal, well-adjusted people could resist its prurient allure.

Charging the jury, the judge reminded them that "if a girl had appeared on a beach in the scanty halter and shorts that is acceptable today" a few decades ago, it would have resulted in indecent exposure charges. The words "venereal disease" had been recently unspeakable, while now "one may read news stories of sexual deviation." Taking the cue, the jurors needed only a half hour to acquit.

As he periodically had since the 1920s, Roth even drew some positive attention in the early 1950s for *My Sister and I*, allegedly a lost work by German philosopher Friedrich Nietzsche. Widely reviewed, and often taken seriously, the book was, of course, spurious, but as a librarian from Columbia University wrote in a measured review for the *Saturday Review*, if forged it was "the most skillful artistic hoax since the Van Meegeren Vermeers." Passing 1952 in successful challenges to postal censors and correspondence with Princeton philosophy professors over his Nietzsche book, Roth temporarily avoided the growing storm over pornography.

The clouds became visible that year, in the form of a House of Representatives committee on "current pornographic materials." Issuing a report after holding hearings, the committee did not bother to disguise its endorsement of Cold War sexual politics. "It may be that the time has come for the pendulum to swing back again toward decency," the report began. How far back it wanted to swing was suggested by its section on "liberty versus license," language taken directly from the debates of 150 years earlier. Decrying the state of obscenity law — "so elastic that it serves as [an] excuse to print and circulate the filthiest most obscene literature without concurrent literary value to support it, ever known in history" — the House committee asserted that "being granted and guaranteed freedom by no means includes license."

Headed by Ernest Gathings of Arkansas, the House committee did not exactly have its finger to the pulse of smut production in America. Much of its attention focused on the pocket-sized books and lesbian pulp fiction that had recently emerged as growth markets for publishers, so Roth avoided the committee's condemnation. Its suggestions, however, which centered on enhancing the postmaster's powers by exempting him from several current procedural requirements, drew its own condemnation. Bernard DeVoto, still contributing strident anticensorship columns to *Harper's*, wrote of the (quite poorly composed) report that "surely such half-illiterate writing is a greater danger to thought and morals than all the salacious literature ever printed in the United States."

Even more moderate news reporting tended to agree—surely in part because the committee did as weak a job of defining "pornography" as the courts had with "obscenity." In contrast to the stag films that circulated underground, the "art model" nude films and photos that advertised freely, or even the openly eroticized men's magazines with nude pictures that predated *Playboy* but lacked the sophistication that brought it to prominence, lesbian pulp fiction remained a relatively tame genre. While it wallowed in illicit sexuality, its books tread carefully when it came to their suggestive rather than graphic sex scenes. More importantly, as author Marijane Meaker, a pioneer in the field under her pen name Vin Packer, recalled in her memoirs, editors strenuously ensured that the books ended with either death or sudden conversions to heterosexuality, thus ultimately reinforcing antigay social norms after allowing their readers a sexual safari into the forbidden. The Gathings Committee had taken a demonized term with great political potential, but then misused it, failing to generate enough outrage to sustain its censorial recommendations.

Thus Roth stayed safe, for the moment. Moving into the mid-1950s, he stood at the helm of two lucrative periodicals. *Good Times: A Revue of the World of Pleasure* debuted alongside *Playboy* in 1953 and followed a similar, if more tabloid-style, format. Like Hefner's magazine, it placed naked photographs of women at its center, carefully posed to avoid genital display. *Good Times* took a more lowbrow approach than *Playboy*'s emphasis on "Picasso, Nietzsche, jazz, sex," as Hefner famously wrote in outlining the topics of conversation his ideal playboy would choose; for Roth's readers, articles like "Breasts Awake" discussed, indeed, "the varieties of the female breast" — "in word and picture," as an advertising circular rushed to promise. Articles on the romantic lives of such celebrities as Rita Hayworth and Zsa Zsa Gabor ran next to what Roth called "unbelievably frank and beautiful tales of marital and extra-marital relationships" and "reviews of the sexiest books, plays, and pictures, every item illustrated with sensationally lovely nudes." In the magazine, excuses to show images of naked women ran from classical paintings to articles on showgirls with back-stage photographs.

Meanwhile, *American Aphrodite*, billing itself as the "first and only privately published periodical in the United States," had begun a few years earlier. If *Good Times* was Roth's return to his 1920s' *Beau*, *Aphrodite* was its *Casanova Jr.'s Tales*, taking a more literary angle on similarly sexual matters. Roth garnished his advertising circulars for *American Aphrodite* with topless photographs and sensationalistic descriptions, but its actual contents paralleled quite closely his 1920s magazines, interspersed only with mild sketch images. "We live in an apocalyptic age, a time of infinite trembling," Roth began the first issue. In his two-page editorial statement he managed to invoke Socrates, Jesus, the Buddha, Yeats, Plato, Descartes, and more. His central thesis seemed to be that modern war had created a "social and aesthetic vacuum," and his magazine sought to fill it by reviving "love in all its marvelous manifestations, especially in the realm of the erotic," which had been "aggravated" by the "Comstocks of our time."

If that was a high aspiration, the first story hardly measured up. Rhys Davies's "Way of a Man with a Wife" mostly chronicled the efforts of a workingman to see his wife naked. Socrates, it was not — though Davies had written the "Bed of Feathers" story that had gotten Roth in legal trouble a decade ago, a reminder of both Roth's recycling tendencies and those of the law. "To See and Touch a Naked Body" was the next story, clearly marking a thematic path. Other content ranged from stories, essays, and poetry by Roth himself to recycled material from T. E. Lawrence, Dante, and plenty more Davies. While sex occupied center stage in *American Aphrodite*, so pseudo-highbrow was the periodical that an essay on the "Laureate of the Obscene" in the third issue discussed the notoriously libertine John Wilmot, earl of Rochester, without conveying any real sense of his crass, lusty poetry. By the fourteenth issue, in 1954, a collection of "Uncensored Passages from English Classical Literature" grew no more risqué than Daniel Defoe's eighteenth-century Moll Flanders recalling, "I made no more resistance to him, but let him do just what he pleased, and as often as he pleased."

If dedicating publications to the celebration (if not quite textual achievement) of sexual pleasure was now a three-decade-long constant in Roth's life and career, so too were exposés capitalizing on the private lives of famous people, from Valentino to Herbert Hoover to Nietzsche. Publishing Lyle Stuart's *The Secret Life of Walter Winchell* in 1953 fit this pattern, but also solidified for Roth an influential enemy. Winchell made a point of attacking Roth in his syndicated newspaper column, making sneering references to "scummy Samuel Roth, the King of Pornography." Police raided Roth's office in early 1954, arresting him and Pauline on obscenity charges, as well as third-degree assault charges for Sam, who allegedly began a scuffle with a policeman.

Though the charges were dismissed the next year on the grounds of a faulty warrant, Roth considered Winchell responsible for the arrest. Despite the paranoia he'd shown before, Roth was not irrational in this belief. Indeed, Winchell was passing information on Roth to the FBI, including assertions that the publisher "has been making derogatory remarks concerning the Director [J. Edgar Hoover], Winchell, and Senator McCarthy." When the FBI looked into Roth, a New York postal inspector explained that he "always seemed to stay enough within the law to keep from distributing the obscene material upon which prosecution might be successful." While FBI head Hoover was militantly committed to pursuing obscenity cases, a reluctant FBI ultimately had to conclude that it had "no subversive information" on Roth.

Whatever backstage machinations the venal Winchell was engaged in (and they were many), the publicity he brought coincided disastrously for Roth with that bestowed by Senator Estes Kefauver. Keenly attuned to the workings of media and technology, Kefauver, with an ambitious eye toward the presidency, had early realized that combining senatorial investigations with the booming television broadcasting field could result in useful national publicity. And so Kefauver spent the early 1950s investigating, first organized crime and then comics. Again sharp in his cultural assessment, Kefauver saw the comics panic passing at mid-decade and quickly turned his attention to pornography. More than any other single figure, the Tennessee Democrat brought pornography into the public eye, in the process manufacturing a new crisis that would ultimately devour Roth whole.

Part of the appeal of hearings for Kefauver was the opportunity to confront vilified opponents and engage in a bit of grandstanding political theater. He had done this very effectively with the mob bosses and comics publishers he had faced, so he was eager to repeat the tactic with purported pornographers. He carefully stacked the deck against them, bringing in medical and scientific experts to attest to the harmful qualities of smut. Several proved willing to comply. As Dr. Benjamin Karpman, chief psychotherapist at St. Elizabeth's Hospital in Washington, D.C., testified, "There is a very direct relationship between juvenile delinquency, sex life, and pornographic literature."

Other witnesses carried less scientific weight, but expressed similarly heightened anxieties about smut. A Catholic priest blamed pornography for generating a "guilt complex" among teens, who were inspired to "acts of masturbation, acts of self-abuse, acts of unnatural things between fellows and girls" when they fell afoul of its debasing influence. Inspector Roy Blick from the Washington, D.C., Morals Division called smut "more dangerous than narcotics," since "you inject narcotics [in]to an individual and it is over with. These pamphlets, these booklets," he continued, "can be passed from one to another. It is the same as a prostitute that can infect an army of men if she is permitted to hang around the camp." When Kefauver asked Blick whether there was "any doubt in your mind that a lot of sex crimes that we have had — that is, criminal assault, rape, and other kinds of sex crimes, are the direct result of this pornographic literature," Blick expressed none. Pornography, he averred, caused "kids who are just at the age that they should know right from wrong to become perverts and homosexuals."

It was comics redux: exposure to porn could cause anything from frigidity to homosexuality to psychopathic behavior in children and adolescents. It was, of course, in many ways also Comstock redux, as these reiterated the central arguments of his own Victorian treatises. Kefauver put great effort into distancing himself from Comstockian connotations, frequently invoking the need for sex education to bring himself in line with the tenets of modern sexual liberalism and show himself not a retrograde prude. Still, what he added to the Victorian mind-set was more surface gloss than fundamental challenge.

With the social dangers of smut thus established, Kefauver and his allies also emphasized its pervasiveness. Calling it a "$500 million-a-year racket" (albeit without much evidence — "we estimate," the committee's report simply explained), Kefauver's report claimed much of this smut wound up in the hands of children. James Bobo, Kefauver's chief counsel at the hearings, brought sensationalistic detail to this aspect, being sure to spell out "dildoes" for the record as he noted that such items were "going out in the mails to youngsters as young as 12 and 13."

A main attraction of the Kefauver hearings was his confrontations with those he deemed pornographers. Such key figures in the semi-underground national distributional network as Edward Mishkin and Abraham Rubin were delivered subpoenas, but most refused to cooperate, pleading the Fifth Amendment's protection against self-incrimination. Kefauver used these moments as opportunities to rail against the alleged pornographers, but they gave him little else to work with. Samuel Roth, however, decided to speak; the hearings provided a rare national forum in which to vindicate his name, something he had been fixated on since the *Ulysses* "booklegging" scandal decades ago. From the start, on May 31, 1955, the third day of hearings, he miscalculated badly. Even in explaining his willingness to speak, he defended the Fifth Amendment but added, "I know that it will be at least 50 years before an honest man will be able to plead it without being misunderstood." If his goal was to reclaim his reputation, beginning with a statement that would be read to a national audience as being in sympathy with communists and fellow travelers was hardly the way to go.

Under questioning, Roth counted the names on his mailing lists at 400,000. "I have never published or advertised a book an adolescent would bother to read," Roth claimed; "I have never offered books to juveniles, and refused to serve them whenever they were so identified in my mails." This was exactly what Kefauver was waiting for. One of his investigators immediately confronted Roth with evidence that his circulars had indeed reached children. "What do you say about all of this?" the counsel demanded. Roth first tried to explain how he bought his lists from other companies, which gave "the best assurance you can possibly get" that no minors were included, but he conceded, "there is no point in my disputing" that the assurances had not been met.

The line of defense Roth then adopted took little account of dominant Cold War sexual politics. "My real point," he explained, attempting to shift the focus, "is that if they reached minors they couldn't possibly have any bad influence on them, and they would disregard them." The language in the circulars, he insisted, "may mean something to a Senator, may mean something to a mature adult, but cannot mean anything to a boy or a girl." Given the "battery of females that any child sees on any morning in a ride through the subway, in a walk through a street" Roth said, child protection was "ridiculous as an argument against my business."

Roth reflected the worldview of a working-class immigrant whose formative years transpired on the crowded streets of the Lower East Side, a world where the boundaries between public and private, between child and adult knowledge, were far more permeable than the domestic ideal of the rapidly suburbanizing 1950s. That there was "certainly nothing that would be new to children whose eyes are wide open wherever they walk" was almost surely true; that it directly conflicted with powerful ideological impulses to believe otherwise was even more true. Roth seemed to think he was making his case against blissful childhood innocence in a forum governed by detached objectivity. It was yet another tactical mistake.

Kefauver continued to hammer at the theme, asking Roth where on any of his literature he asked customers' ages before sending it. When Roth vaguely suggested his initial mailing contacts with recipients included this, Kefauver was again prepared, with a large collection of Roth's mailings showing "no inquiry about the age on any of them." A clearly flummoxed Roth could only sputter, "I am not making a perfect explanation, because there is no perfect explanation." The best he could offer was to note that his customers had to spend at least $1.98, which suggested "they were mature people."

As a senator, Estes Kefauver represented racial liberalism, and was one of the very few southern politicians who would refuse to sign the 1956 Southern Manifesto decrying racial integration. He was not, however, above a bit of immigrant-baiting, playing off Cold War nativist fears of foreigners next in pressing Roth about his citizenship status. Roth fumbled this, too, first affirming his naturalization, then admitting under further questioning, "I am not a naturalized citizen. Forgive me. I became a citizen on my father's papers, and that must have been when my father became a citizen in 1915. On the other hand, in 1940, or 1939, I went to the Immigration Department and demanded a certificate, certifying that I was a citizen on my father's papers, and I have that certificate." Kefauver continued to request clarifications. With the unspoken subtext at the hearings that many of the alleged filth merchants were Jews, the effect was simply to call attention to the various layers of perceived un-Americanness folded into the smut trade.

At the end of Roth's questioning, Kefauver had the last word. "Mr. Roth, we appreciate your coming here and talking very freely," he began, before shifting into a more confrontational mode. Kefauver knew of no one, he claimed, "who doesn't feel that the kind of slime that you have been sending through the mails is highly deleterious to our young people, and damaging to their morals." The committee had received "many, many more complaints" about Roth's mailings than any other mail-order dealer. "Personally," Kefauver concluded, "I think it is very reprehensible. Thank you, Mr. Roth."

The attack continued when the Kefauver Committee issued its report in 1956. Reaching a foregone conclusion, it found that "the impulses which spur people to sex crimes unquestionably are intensi- fied by reading and seeing pornographic materials." It charged Samuel Roth as "one of the most notorious of the violators of Federal and State laws pertaining to the production and distribution of indecent literature." Media coverage was extensive and supportive, with the *New York Times* headline reading "Smut Held Cause of Delinquency." *America*, having already taken its cues from Kefauver the past summer, regularly called "pornography peddlers" "as dangerous to society as dope peddlers" and also guilty of "a form of subversion to which even Communists do not stoop."

That last comment returned the issue to its ever-present context. Kefauver, who began his career as an ardent New Dealer, was no red- baiter, but his entire antiporn effort hinged on that unspoken back- drop, as indicated by his interrogation of Roth's citizenship status. The evidence to support his analysis, after all, was strikingly slim, and never more than anecdotal. The *Science News Letter* had already asserted in 1953 that "pornographic literature does not lead to sex crimes, does not create juvenile delinquents," accurately calling this "the opinion of most leading psychiatrists and psychologists." Nothing had changed since then in terms of new research discoveries, so Kefau- ver had simply selected sympathetic experts and disregarded this less popular assertion.

If Kefauver's conclusions carried little scientific weight, they still made sense to Americans immersed in Cold War anxieties. Pornog- raphy shared qualities with communism, as forces that destabilized and undermined the American family. Slipping from one to the other flowed naturally. As McCarthyism receded at mid-decade after the leading anticommunist bit off more than he could chew with unfounded accusations against the military that turned sentiment against him, some McCarthyites simply shifted gears from commies to smut. Pennsylvania judge William Cercone, for instance, had made his mark as a red-busting prosecutor in Pittsburgh. Appointed (and later elected) local judge in 1956, Cercone replaced the communist threat with porn. "Of all the causes of child delinquency, the most menacing danger," he asserted, "is the great avalanche of obscene magazines now descending upon us, with their pornographic pictures and licentious articles." The exacerbated concern over smut could be seen in the state and local bodies that began springing up around the nation: the Georgia State Literature Commission, the Rhode Island Commission to Encourage Morality in Youth, the Youth Protection Committee in Salt Lake City, and dozens more, all products of the 1950s.

Kefauver himself refrained from directly asserting concrete links between communists and smut, but others were less circumspect. Pennsylvania Representative Kathryn Granahan held regular hearings on obscene mailed matter throughout the late 1950s, airing the outlandish claims of witnesses who claimed direct communist-smut links. The head of the Hungarian Catholic League of America, for instance, told Granahan's committee that America's smut supply was "fed by the Communists to reduce morals over a period of time that sort of softens the people." Such believers often cited a purported, though transparently phony, communist pamphlet on "Rules for Bringing about Revolution," which advised to "corrupt the young, get them away from religion, get them interested in sex." What Kinsey had shown widespread, these anticommunists considered un-American; the tension between these two worldviews was what sustained the very meaning of the elusive *prurience* — lewd, perverse interest in sex that went against healthy American desire.

Samuel Roth found himself further drawn into this political/sexual nexus when he cropped up as a demonized reference point in 1956 congressional hearings on the scope of Soviet activity in the United States. An indictment against Roth had mentioned business dealings with labor historian Philip Foner, and Foner was called to testify. An avowed Marxist, Foner wrote numerous important historical books on class struggle in American history. As a result, he had been hounded out of his teaching job at the City College of New York in an anticommunist purge of the early 1940s. To make ends meet, he helped run the Citadel Press, which published a combination of radical leftist and sexually suggestive material, ranging from Communist Party member Herbert Aptheker's gargantuan *Documentary History of the Negro People in the United States* to less momentous works like *The Sexually Adequate Male.*

Much of Foner's testimony consisted of investigators grilling him about his connection to Samuel Roth. Has Citadel published any "obscene and pornographic" material, he was asked. What was his connection to Roth's Remainder Book Company? To the magazine *Good Times*? The experienced Foner calmly pleaded the Fifth Amendment to all questions, refusing to answer.

Not much came of this particular investigation, though the committee inserted into the record an article from the right-wing magazine *Counterattack* using the Roth-Foner link to blame communists for pornographic moral corruption. The episode served to highlight the omnipresent Cold War backdrop that formed the subtext of all Roth's 1950s experiences. Without any conclusive evidence, or even direct assertion, it helped raise questions about Roth's motives and connections. Most important to Roth himself, it brought up the issue of his latest legal case, the one that was headed toward the most punitive outcome he would experience in his life. Whatever preferred position the First Amendment had obtained during the 1940s was called severely into question by the doctrinal developments of the 1950s, and Roth was forced to navigate choppy legal waters whose currents bore a Cold War undertow openly hostile to a man socially defined as a dubiously American, communist-affiliated pornographer.

Chilling the First Amendment

The very phrase "Cold War" was something of a misnomer, suggesting a conflict between the United States and the Soviet Union that never descended into actual military warfare. In fact, if the two superpowers never went directly to war, they still generated a massive body count, fighting by proxy in Korea, southeast Asia, and numerous African and Latin American nations.

It was at home, ironically, that the Cold War took more literal form, putting a discernible chill on civil liberties. Nothing the U.S. government did approached the sweeping and brutal totalitarianism of Russia's Stalinist iron fist, to be sure. But a clear civil liberties contraction occurred in the 1950s, directly and overtly influenced by the Cold War. The First Amendment ramifications were profound, and Roth's case would be decided in this frosty climate.

Changes at the Court did not bode well for First Amendment protection. Chief Justice Fred Vinson minced no words and entertained little ambivalence when it came to the growing national security state. The deaths of Frank Murphy and Wiley Rutledge in 1949 switched the balance of power in the Court. Where those two justices had reliably sided with Black and Douglas on First Amendment cases, with a fifth vote often plucked from the remaining brethren to give them a majority, President Truman replaced them with his attorney general, Tom Clark, and Indiana senator Sherman Minton, in what critics saw as political cronyism. Like Roosevelt, Truman's main concern was for his Fair Deal, which built off the New Deal, and civil liberties among his Supreme Court appointees came as a distant afterthought. Unlike Roosevelt's nominees, who fortuitously coalesced around progressive positions on that front, Truman's showed less enthusiasm (though Clark's views would eventually grow more progressive). Minton and Clark frequently joined the chief justice in approaching the First Amendment through a Cold War vantage point.

If any single case reflected the chill placed on the First Amendment by the Court, it was surely 1951's *Dennis v. United States*. In that case, involving Eugene Dennis and several other leaders of the Communist Party of the United States, Vinson laid down a sweeping reinterpretation of clear and present danger itself that left much of First Amendment jurisprudence in question. Dennis and his colleagues had been tried and convicted under the 1940 Smith Act, which criminalized the teaching and advocacy of the overthrow of the U.S. government or the organization of any group so committed. The act had been clearly directed at communists; Dennis and his allies were certainly that. The stage was set for a major constitutional challenge: could the government criminalize mere teaching and advocacy (both of which Dennis had openly engaged in), as opposed to more tangible forms of insurrectionary activity?

Vinson's opinion was pure, unadulterated Cold War formula, openly admitting that "the inflammable nature of world conditions" shaped its reasoning. Free speech, to Vinson, was not an "unlimited, unqualified right," but something that "must, on occasion, be subordinated to other values and considerations." He endorsed the clear and present danger test, but then adjusted its meaning in light of the national security state's needs, adopting the standards Learned Hand had set out when *Dennis* was at the lower federal court: "whether the gravity of the 'evil,' discounted by its improbability, justifies such invasion of free speech as is necessary to avoid the danger." If Supreme Court doctrines are generally balancing tests of competing constitutional interests, Vinson stripped the clear and present danger of much of its weight and left the scales to be set by the legislative and administrative branches.

The chief justice showed little concern for scholarly analysis of the Frankfurtian sort. "To those who would paralyze our Government in the face of impending threat by encasing it in a semantic straitjacket," he wrote dismissively, "we must reply that all concepts are relative." Yet another fuming Black dissent ensued, accusing the Court of sustaining "virulent censorship." Declaring the Smith Act unconstitutional on its face, Black kept his dissent deliberately terse, simply offering hope that "in calmer times, when present pressures, passions and fears subside, this or some later Court will restore the First Amendment liberties to the high preferred place where they belong in a free society." If the 1940s had witnessed an expanding understanding of "speech," especially as it pertained to actions, *Dennis* suggested the 1950s would deliver a retraction.

Such cases boded poorly for any liberalization of obscenity doctrine in the 1950s. By the end of the previous decade, many assumed the clear and present danger test could apply to obscenity. Justice Wiley Rutledge suggested as much at oral arguments in the *Doubleday* case. Doubters disputed this analysis, though, with none less than Zechariah Chafee himself, a quarter century after helping build modern civil libertarianism, weighing in, calling it "very hard to fit" obscenity into the test. Were it necessary to do so, Chafee reasoned in his 1947 book *Government and Mass Communications*, "serious shock to the sensibilities" of readers might itself constitute an actionable danger—quite a low bar for prosecution.

The legal trajectory of the early 1950s pushed that bar ever downward. After Vinson's dilution of clear and present danger in *Dennis* (which allowed the federal government to prosecute over one hundred Communist Party officials under the Smith Act), the *Columbia Law Review* noted that clear and present danger "has never been law." While enshrined in legal and political ideals since its devising by Oliver Wendell Holmes in 1920, and used numerous times in landmark Supreme Court cases, technically it had never commanded more than four members of the bench at any one time.

As if to drive home the point, the Court delivered yet another constriction of free speech in 1952, as Felix Frankfurter's opinion in *Beauharnais v. Illinois* upheld a state law against group libel. None of the justices endorsed the racist drivel disseminated in leaflets passed out on Chicago streets by Joseph Beauharnais, president of the pro-segregationist White Circle League of America, which warned of the "rapes, robberies, knives, guns and marijuana of the negro" sure to follow any integration. The willingness of Frankfurter, with the assistance of Truman's four appointees, to allow Illinois to criminalize publications subjecting "the citizens of any race, color, creed or religion to contempt, derision, or obloquy" was seemingly unprecedented in legal history. Predictably, Black and Douglas objected vigorously, noting that antiracist laws in Illinois might well be met with pro-racist laws in the South that used similar language to suppress civil rights discourse. Frankfurter simply responded that libel had never been protected speech, so group libel merely extended the concept.

In a brief aside at his opinion's end, Frankfurter both dispensed with the clear and present danger standard and also set the course for obscenity doctrine. Since libel had never been protected speech, consideration of clear and present danger was "unnecessary." "Certainly no one would contend that obscene speech," he added as an example, "may be punished only upon a showing of such circumstances." Not even Black or Douglas argued with this point. For that matter, Douglas himself had cited obscenity as a legitimate area of government action in his *Dennis* dissent, as an example that "freedom to speak is not absolute." Listing "the teaching of methods of terror and other seditious conduct" as things that "should be beyond the pale," Douglas gratuitously continued, "along with obscenity and immorality."

Not even the rare free-speech victories of the early 1950s challenged this. In *Burstyn v. Wilson* (1952), the Court finally bestowed First Amendment protection on movies, nearly forty years after first rejecting it. Written by Tom Clark, the opinion hewed close to the facts of the case, involving Italian filmmaker Roberto Rossellini's *The Miracle*, a pointed religious satire that had outraged the Catholic infrastructure of New York. Reversing the state censor body's ban of the film, Clark asserted that "sacrilege" was not a legitimate ground for suppression. Obscenity, he suggested, could still be targeted by state censor boards—thus the case simultaneously seemed to end film censorship even as it also allowed its continuation.

As even the extreme free-speech wing of the Court showed casual unconcern, obscenity law lay adrift in the lower courts. With the clear and present danger test in tatters, the First Amendment on the defensive, and a pervasive backlash against perversion, obscenity law itself became a clear and present danger—to those accused of violating it.

Confusion Is Sex

The lower courts of the 1950s acted without guidance, as they had since the 1890s. By the Cold War, however, the structural pressures of this indeterminacy had compounded into a doctrinal crisis. The Supreme Court had dodged it in the 1940s, but as the chaos grew ever more egregious, the avoidance grew harder to sustain. At every level from the local to the state to the federal, courts devised ad hoc, inconsistent obscenity rulings that demanded clarification.

Even in New York City, local courts showed a disregard for federal precedent. When the commissioner of licenses demanded newsdealers remove nudist magazines from their racks in late 1951, a local court upheld the order in *Sunshine Book Company v. McCaffrey*, denying it constituted a prior restraint of free speech. When the dealers cited the 1940 federal *Parmalee* decision that had allowed *Nudism in Modern Life* through customs, the New York court agreed that *Parmalee* supported their case. "Insofar as it does," however, "it is rejected as unsound." Reflecting the Cold War anxieties of the time, the court noted without citation that the magazines were "bound to add to the already burdensome problem of juvenile delinquency."

Such cases spent little time analyzing Supreme Court precedent, partly since there was so little available to discuss. This was a nationwide tendency, and the 1954 Missouri Supreme Court case *State v. Becker* serves as a representative example. Harold Becker was convicted in St. Louis for selling *Sunshine & Health* and other nudist magazines. When the state supreme court affirmed his conviction, the only Supreme Court precedent it substantively discussed was *Winters v. New York*, which had stricken New York's ban on crime-themed publications but upheld its obscenity law. With only that minimal guidance from the high court, the Missouri Supreme Court felt free to fall back on *Hicklin* as governing. It noted the more liberal federal opinions of the past two decades, but simply declared that it declined to follow them. Such cases, explained the court, had not "considered certain basic concepts and teachings which we deem important." After all, "we live today in a clothed civilization."

Viewed from the larger trajectory of the prior decades spent modernizing obscenity law, a case like *Becker* seemed a reactionary travesty. But technically speaking, the Missouri court was well within its rights to dismiss the more liberal eastern federal courts, whose jurisdiction ended well short of St. Louis. And even if the Missouri court had wanted to seek closer guidance from the Supreme Court, it had little to go on. *Hicklin* was dead out east, but the high court had never seen fit to send its official funeral notice; not to mention, the legal fate of nudism in New York City showed that *Hicklin* was perhaps as capable as Mark Twain of surviving notice of its own passing anyway.

If obscenity was a mess in local and state courts, it was no less so at the federal level. When the Ninth Circuit Court of Appeals in California affirmed the obscenity of the booklet *Arabian Love Manual* in 1953, it hardly spoke with confidence when it called the 1896 Supreme Court *Rosen* precedent "probably the leading case" in determining the outcome.

Gay-themed texts, from male physique magazines to queer underground avant-garde films, remained frequent targets of obscenity prosecutions in the Cold War era, and the federal courts often allowed for such efforts. The federal district court for Maryland, for instance, in early 1955 examined a German portfolio of prints depicting ancient Greek, Roman, Etruscan, and Egyptian vases. Reflecting the concerns of the times, the court explained that "many of them show acts of sodomy and other forms of perverted practice," placing them outside the acceptable sphere of Cold War sexuality. The court found the portfolio obscene.

Again, the Supreme Court's absence was glaring. The Maryland court even invoked Vinson's 1940 *Parmalee* dissent, a fairly undistinguished citation, hinting that it was guessing at the current Court's disposition by looking back to the chief justice's earlier position from his years on the D.C. appellate court. As the Kefauver-led crusade against smut heated up in 1955, clarity inside the courtroom continued to deteriorate. Perhaps the absolute nadir came in the federal district court for the District of Columbia, as it assessed a group of nudist magazines, including *Sunshine & Health*. Ransacking the entire corpus of obscenity case law for anything useful, Judge James Kirkland could find nothing from the Supreme Court in the twentieth century. He compiled the various federal rulings of recent years. Definitions of obscenity and its synonyms descended into a parade of verbal horribles: disgusting, filthy, foul, abominable, "offensive to chastity and modesty," licentious, "having a tendency to excite lustful thoughts," polluted, and many, many more terms filled the opinion.

Since the terminological torrent did little to actually flush out a doctrine, Kirkland resorted to a protracted case-by-case examination of the nudist images. "Posterior views of nudes" were not obscene. Children "photographed in a frontal view which reveals the diminutive and undeveloped genitalia": not obscene either. A "young girl in her early twenties" eight to ten feet from the camera, "in a frontal view showing the clear detail of the pubic area," as well as a "mixed group" including a man whose "genitals are clearly shown," did meet his bar. Ultimately, the inclusion of the obscene images rendered the magazines unmailable. The case, *Sunshine Book Company v. Summerfield*, thus favored the postmaster general. The opinion itself dissolved obscenity into a case-by-case basis where some combination of aesthetic, sexual, moral, and judicial reasoning replaced any meaningful doctrine whatsoever. Lest Kirkland's determinations be reduced to banning the erotic, he took particular exception to a woman with "large thighs" whose "matted varicose veins cause her to be grotesque, vile, [and] an object of scorn."

With the court system so clearly unequipped to bring basic rationality, much less consistency, to obscenity, scholars attempted to intervene. The scholarly journal *Law and Contemporary Problems* dedicated its autumn 1955 issue to the question of obscenity, with every article essentially agreeing on the fundamental point that the law had not effectively absorbed or defined the notion of obscenity. An anthropologist noted that obscenity was a cross-cultural phenomenon that denoted something taboo, though what that something was varied across cultures. A psychoanalyst, meanwhile, discussed the obscene's ties to shame and filth, links internalized during childhood. As to how such diffuse origins translated into law, none could effectively say; law school professors William Lockhart and Robert McClure dismissed most definitions of obscenity as mere "strings of synonyms," reading between the lines of the existing case law to excavate its internal logic.

What Lockhart and McClure found was mostly an *absence* of logic. Judges, they concluded, had failed to clarify what was at stake in obscenity cases, actual behavior or simply impure thoughts, and they had disguised this ambiguity in the loose rhetoric of corrupting and depraving "morals" — that is, the *Hicklin* standard. Brushing aside the arguments connecting smut to antisocial conduct as "bare conjecture," the professors instead argued that whatever harm might result from obscene materials was "relatively harmless."

Lockhart and McClure quickly emerged as the most prominent scholars of the obscenity debate in the 1950s. Their *Law and Contemporary Problems* article built off their much longer "Literature, the Law of Obscenity, and the Constitution," published a year earlier in the *Minnesota Law Review*. In that article, the most influential of the decade, they set out to prove that "literature dealing with sex is entitled to the same freedom of expression as literature dealing with any other significant social problem." Castigating the Supreme Court for its persistent evasiveness, Lockhart and McClure contended that sex formed precisely the sort of "problem of society" that labor and economic issues had during the 1930s, and that the Court was obligated to interpret discussion of sex in a manner akin to the way it had unionization efforts, as something protected under the First Amendment. Turning the tables on the censors, Lockhart and McClure suggested *they* were the ones bearing pathologies: "often an emotionally disturbed and intemperate person with a paranoid personality" was their character-ization of the censorious.

In devising their constitutional obscenity framework, Lockhart and McClure picked and chose from the most liberal court opinions of the past several decades: the book had to be taken as a whole, not just its most salacious parts; the proper barometer was the average person, not children or the mentally unbalanced; and the knowledge of the seller had to be established before any prosecution could ensue.

This analysis represented the apex of the sexual liberalism that had been slowly surfacing as the dominant trend of twentieth-century American culture. Yet in a reflection of how even Lockhart and McClure's progressive vision remained enmeshed in Cold War belief structures, the authors still allowed for the suppression of pornography. While they had thoroughly eviscerated the implicit underpin-nings of obscenity law, leaving little rational basis for it, of "typical under-the-counter pornography" they simply wrote, "which is, of course, not entitled to constitutional protection." A few times in the course of the article's hundred pages, they returned to "pornography," and the closest they came to a definition was "designed to stimulate sexual appetites, contributes nothing to the expression of ideas, and is without literary merit."

The problem was, these were exactly the phrases directed by numerous courts over the years at D. H. Lawrence's *Lady Chatterley's Lover*, Henry Miller's *Tropic of Cancer*, and other "serious" works of literary sexuality that Lockhart and McClure sought to protect. What they offered was a thoughtfully restrictive, and highly influential, interpretation of the constitutional boundaries of obscenity—but *not* an escape from the cycle of subjective semantics that had burdened the concept since its origin. The authors hinted at the latent aesthetic hierarchy contained in their notion of social value. They had obvi-ously read and admired such respected but "obscene" works as *Ulysses* and *Memoirs of Hecate County*. In a brief reference to Samuel Roth, though, they dismissively mentioned "dirty books that, lacking wit, are dull or even repulsive," and that "repel rather than attract the nor-mal reader." "Such a book, apparently," they wrote, making clear they had not bothered to read it, "is *Waggish Tales of the Czechs*."

No figure of Theodore Schroeder's stature would emerge in the

1950s to offer a libertarian rejection of obscenity law per se. Instead, ACLU attorney Herbert Monte Levy continued the case-by-case approach that took interest only in cases with claims to cultural legitimacy. Lowbrow, tawdry, sleazy merchandise found little sympathy from Levy. When a quack doctor found his pamphlets advocating the stimulation of the brain through nonclimactic masturbation barred from the mails as obscene in 1952, Levy found the case unworthy of ACLU attention. Likewise for nude photos sent through the mail, and mildly bawdy cartoon postcards as well. Even Henry Miller's notoriously sexually explicit — though critically celebrated — novels Levy rejected as mere "dirt for dirt's sake" in 1953. An official 1954 ACLU publication told readers the group had "no quarrel whatsoever with appropriate laws which punish obscenity," though it left deliberately vague what it deemed appropriate.

Even the most aggressive defender of American civil liberties, then, committed itself to expanding freedoms *within* the structure of obscenity law, rather than working to dismantle that structure in the name of unfettered free expression. This left outsiders like Samuel Roth in precarious positions. Permanently consigned to a vicious cycle of cultural disrepute that had begun with his pirated *Ulysses* and then spun further as his exclusion from literary circles pushed him into the smut trade, Roth held little hope of receiving validation under the guise of "social value." That his books had for three decades served on the front lines of sexual liberalism, not to mention addressing Jewish and immigrant identity and other such social issues, meant nothing without the imprimatur of *some* cultural power brokers. None stepped forward.

Roth on Trial

As the obscenity debate grew ever more stagnant in the mid-1950s, Roth remained, unwillingly, at its center. His earlier case had fallen short of convincing the Supreme Court to step in. The Kefauver Committee had offered him to the American people as a child-corrupting, smut-peddler monster. And, like clockwork, he found himself back in court, caught in the crosshairs of Cold War politics, free-speech debates, and the "recrudescence of Puritanism" that Lockhart and McClure called "epidemic" in their 1955 article. Roth had dodged the local obscenity charges he believed instigated by Walter Winchell in May 1955. Two months after that—and one month after his Kefauver testimony—he was walloped by a new charge, this one federal, carrying twenty-six counts.

This was not the rote bureaucratic nuisance of arguing with the Post Office over which books could be mailed. These were criminal charges, bearing severe prison sentences, delivered in the least opportune social climate in decades. Named in the indictment were both items and their circulars: *Wallet Nudes*, *French Nudes at Play*, *2 Undraped Stars*, *Photo and Body*, and other such nude-photo collections, as well as Roth's "real" publications, *Good Times* and *American Aphrodite*. Listing the various counts, the indictment took note of addresses to which Roth's circulars had been sent, the Uhlich Children's Home in Chicago among them.

Roth's lawyer, Nicholas Atlas, tried to get the case dismissed in September 1955. In a memorandum of law, Atlas raised three points. First, the charges were vague, applying to both circulars and materials themselves without much clarity over, for instance, which issues of the magazines were at stake. Second, the materials were not, by law, obscene. The test Atlas offered was "only that is obscene which offends the sense of shame of the community as, at the time, constituted." In determining that sense, Atlas insisted that experts—sociologists, psychologists, statisticians, and anthropologists—were "not to be ignored in this process." Finally, Roth's material posed no clear and present danger, and was thus protected by the First Amendment. The motion to dismiss failed, but it did outline Atlas's strategy at trial.

Awaiting the trial, Atlas attempted to draw Alfred Kinsey in as an expert witness. Controversial as he remained, Kinsey certainly carried the full weight of authority as America's foremost, and best recognized, sexual expert. Atlas used some flattery in a letter to Kinsey, but received only a coldly formal notice back from his secretary that the sex researcher was away on business. Roth would have to face a jury with lesser-known experts testifying.

When the trial began in late January 1956, before Judge John Cashin, the government showed it had learned from its last serious contest with Roth, over *Beautiful Sinners of New York* a half decade before. In that trial the prosecution had let the book speak for itself, while Atlas had called a succession of experts to undermine the charges. Atlas clearly planned the same approach, but this time his experts would be countered with ordinary citizens affronted by Roth's mailings. Aggrieved moral indignation versus dispassionate social science analysis: these would be the terms of the trial. Recently appointed Judge Cashin was no stranger to the intersection of law and morality, dating back to his investigations as a federal attorney in the 1920s enforcing Prohibition, but he allowed both the government and the defense to take their diverging approaches to the question of obscenity.

The prosecution's witnesses came first. New Yorker Symphorosa Livermore opened the testimony, declaring of a Roth circular, "I only looked at the outside page and was so disgusted that I didn't look at anything more." Others came from as far as Ohio and Michigan, all reiterating the same message: they had received Roth's mailings, they were offended, they experienced concern over their children receiving the sleazy circulars. As Roth's defender, Atlas had little to work with, but handled it poorly, badgering the witnesses in a way that came off as surly and condescending. To Livermore, he asked if she understood the Greek and Roman references on the mailings; to another, he inquired, "Are you a collegian?" When one concerned woman affirmed that she let her son read the Bible, Atlas pestered her, "Did you realize, Mrs. Kloviski, that according to the Bible, Lot's daughters got him drunk and lay with their father in order to have offspring? Did you realize that? It is in the Bible. Did you realize it?" Whatever intellectual points he intended to make, Atlas failed to consider that his belligerence might alienate a jury that identified with these ordinary citizens.

Midway through the trial, the story "Venus and Tannhauser" took center stage in the government's case. It was an odd emphasis. Though included in the third issue of *American Aphrodite*, Roth had actually included it in *Casanova Jr.'s Tales* all the way back in 1928, without incident. Written at the turn of the century by British author and sketch artist Aubrey Beardsley, but left unfinished and unpublished at his early death in 1898, the story celebrated the grotesque, offering a fantastical cavalcade of perversion in the form of a fable about the Chevalier Tannhauser entering the Hill of Venus and encountering a profusion of decadent spectacles. While the story wallowed in graphic and transgressive sex, it did so in such rarefied, pretentious prose that the average person's most likely response would be to reach for a thesaurus. As Tannhauser is bathed by a "troop of serving boys," for instance, he "chased the prettiest of them and bit his fesses, and kissed him on the perineum till the dear fellow banded like a Carmelite, and its little bald top-knot looked like a great pink pearl under the water." That something perverse was transpiring was clear; what exactly it was, was perhaps less so. When Tannhauser's paramour Venus undertakes an erotic encounter with her pet unicorn, the prose again lifted into a register that many readers might not have even understood.

More than the specific content, the overall air of depravity made "Venus and Tannhauser" a target. Other material in the third issue of *American Aphrodite* fit a more conventional model of prurient interest, from a leering poem called "Tit-illations: An Ode" to "Maiden's Fury," a "short novel on the attempted seduction of an ugly woman," but nothing else so defiantly celebrated its own deviance. Prosecuting assistant U.S. attorney George Leisure asked the judge if he could "point out to the jury the specific parts that the Government does contend are obscene"; they were to take works as wholes, but the suggestion came "in the interests of saving time." In response, Atlas moved for a mistrial, on the ground that recent press coverage in the wake of the Kefauver Committee's work had created a climate that barred a fair trial (typical press accounts of Roth included headlines like "Exposed: The King of the Pornography Racket," in the tabloid *Top Secret*). Denied, he again moved to dismiss on the absence of a clear and present danger. That, too, Judge Cashin denied.

So Atlas moved into his defense, which hinged on a succession of expert witnesses. First, psychologist Albert Ellis. While no Kinsey, Ellis carried sterling credentials, having taught at Rutgers and New York University, served as former president of the New York Society of Clinical Psychologists, and written five books including *The American Sexual Tragedy*, all of which railed against the ignorance and hypocrisy of current standards and norms. Recent decades had seen "significant changes in treatment of women, sex, marriage, and so on," Ellis explained; greater liberalization meant changing standards of obscenity. This increasingly sexualized culture bore no relation to youth crime, he asserted. The desire to look at nude photographs such as the ones in Roth's publications was "perfectly natural."

On cross-examination, Ellis conceded, "I cannot think of anything that I would consider obscene." In case jurors thought they could, Atlas dismantled legal obscenity from another angle too, bringing further psychiatrists and psychologists, including Irving Lorge, creator of the Lorge-Thorndyke Semantic Count, a statistical measure of language whose main conclusion was, as Lorge put it, "There is no person who is an average man." Finally, Atlas made sure to read portions of contemporary best sellers, such as Norman Mailer's *Deer Park*, to the jury to remind them of how sexualized mainstream culture had become — another tactic that had worked well in the *Beautiful Sinners* trial of 1951. His basic message to the jury before the defense rested was to trust experts over individual citizens; it was the experts who knew more.

In contrast, prosecutor Leisure gave the jury a different framework: "Can you imagine the audacity of that man, mailing that envelope to the Uhlich Children's Home?" Highlighting Atlas's condescension toward the government witnesses, Leisure said of one, "I don't think she was so uneducated or so stupid." In much the way President Eisenhower would go on to beat his intellectual "egghead" challenger Adlai Stevenson with down-home folksy wisdom in the election later that year, Leisure disputed the statistically inclined psychologist's refutation of the average person. To find such a being, he told the jury, they "wouldn't do badly at all to look at those people" who testified against Roth. Psychologist Ellis had doubted that true obscenity existed; "I will take the plumber from Alliance, Ohio," Leisure declared. And in case the jurors wondered what importance the case held, Leisure reminded them: "Acquit him, and I can assure you that the sewers will open."

Judge Cashin's charge to the jury reflected the 1956 state of obscenity law in federal courts. The material should be evaluated as a whole, by its impact on the average person — whether or not such an entity existed. Cashin defined obscenity as "that form of immorality which has relation to sexual impurity and has a tendency to excite lustful thoughts." Finally, the jury should judge by the "common conscience" of the community as a whole, not their own prejudices or opinions. This returned to Atlas's earlier emphasis on community standards, but the judge rejected his attempt to define the community through expert knowledge. The community, as Cashin outlined it, included "religious and irreligious, men, women, and children."

Sent to deliberate, the jurors expressed some confusion about the charges, which involved both advertising circulars and the advertised material itself. Could they find a circular obscene, but not the item it advertised? Vice versa? Judge Cashin said yes, and though the jurors seemed a bit uncertain still, they retired to discuss. They needed only ten hours. Returning to the court, they signaled that they had reached a verdict.

On most of the charges, Samuel Roth was acquitted. The jury had not found *Wallet Nudes*, *Stereoptic Nude Show*, or *Chicago Sex-Dimensional* or their circulars obscene. On four counts, though, they convicted: three circulars for *Good Times* and *American Aphrodite*, and then the issue of *Aphrodite* itself that contained "Venus and Tannhauser." Four of twenty-three might seem a decent ratio for Roth, but the proportion meant less than the sentence. Judge Cashin cut to the chase. He sentenced Roth to five years in prison and a $5,000 fine. Atlas requested bail pending the inevitable appeal, promising Roth would move into merchandising razor blades, publishing religious classics, and reopening his school for English language training from the 1920s. An unimpressed Cashin refused. Samuel Roth could appeal his most stringent sentence yet, but he would do so from a prison cell.

CHAPTER 6

Anatomy of a Case

In mid-1956, *Roth v. U.S.* (as it was retitled now that Samuel Roth was the appellant) had yet to take on major significance as a case. Roth was a longtime offender, as Judge Cashin noted in sentencing him, and this was simply one more episode in a history dating back three decades.

It might easily have remained that way, sliding into the middle of a law-review footnote and out of historical memory, had outside circumstances not intervened. On appeal, Roth's case reached the same court that had ruled against him in 1949, but this time federal appellate judge Jerome Frank wrote an even more impassioned opinion — albeit yet again in perversely concurring form. The Frank concurrence bestowed visibility on *Roth v. United States*, at the precise moment that the Supreme Court finally acknowledged it could no longer sit out the obscenity debate. While the *facts* of *Roth* were fairly unexceptional, its constitutional issues, as a federal case that directly challenged the Comstock Act, gave it an importance the other state-level obscenity cases the Court also took on lacked. It was *Roth* that would define the relationship of obscenity to the First Amendment.

This chapter traces the anatomy of the case as it took shape through Roth's legal arguments, the appellate court's response, and the briefs, oral arguments, and internal deliberations of the Supreme Court. Though Samuel Roth's fate is sealed by this chapter's end, chapter seven goes on to examine the obscenity doctrine that emanated out of his case.

Speaking Frankly

Roth's appeal reached the Second Circuit Appellate Court in June 1956. On appeal, the nature of the case shifted from such trial concerns as witness testimony to matters of constitutionality and procedural integrity, but nothing in his legal brief stood out as particularly innovative: Judge Cashin had improperly distinguished "filth" (which aroused "disgust and revulsion") from obscenity (which hinged on lust and lasciviousness); the government had established no clear and present danger in Roth's mailings; some of the evidence had been obtained through forgery, ordered by government agents under fake names; the prosecutor's comments to the jury had been inflammatory; the jurors had shown confusion about the charges; and Roth had not received a fair trial. The government's brief responded in kind with its own pro forma rebuttal, simply brushing aside many of Roth's claims, with an accurate claim that mail orders under fake names had long been upheld by the courts.

Though the court took three months to hand down its decision, Judge Charles Clark clearly did not spend that time carefully composing the court's opinion. In leaden, boilerplate prose, Clark affirmed the conviction, declining to "initiate a new and uncharted course" by overturning the federal obscenity statute that Roth considered unconstitutional. The Comstock law, after all, was "long regarded of vital social importance and a public policy of wide general support."

To Roth's supporting arguments – that the trial judge had included the word "filthy" in his charge to the jury, and that federal agents had committed entrapment by ordering his publications – Clark paid only nominal attention. He considered it a "serious problem" when "real literature is censored," but since Roth's wares were "only salable pornography," no closer review was necessary. After all, Clark noted, the "strongly held views of those with competence in the premises" linked smut to juvenile delinquency. For an "old hand" at sending "such lurid pictures and material," no cause for judicial sympathy existed. As a weary Clark concluded, "indeed this case and our discussion somewhat duplicate his earlier appearance in *Roth v. Goldman*."

While the *Waggish Tales of the Czechs* case of eight years earlier had been civil rather than criminal, Clark was correct in many ways. And with a bland opinion representing a technically unanimous court, Roth's latest challenge might have ended there, without much substantive ground for a further appeal, save for yet another bizarre concurrence by Jerome Frank. Once again, Frank wrote a lengthy, impassioned essay that read as a dissent, and a rather polemical one at that, only to wind itself back up into a concurrence.

Frank's actual opinion was short and pointed, beginning with a confrontational questioning of Clark's reference to juvenile delinquency. Obscenity, Frank reminded his colleague, was to be evaluated by its effect on "average, normal, adult persons," not children. Since no actual link to smut-generated behavior among average adults had been shown by anyone, obscenity law bore the "troublesome aspect" of criminalizing the mere provoking of "undesirable sexual thoughts." Even with the clear and present danger test "somewhat watered down" by *Dennis*, this seemed to fall short of the Supreme Court's own standard for the suppression of speech. This left an "exquisitely vague" law, which, Frank noted, the high court had only alluded to in passing. Never had the Court substantively revisited obscenity in the years since the First Amendment had risen to its preferred position among constitutional liberties.

Nonetheless, Frank agreed with Clark that the Court had declared obscenity law valid, and inferior courts were bound by this. Frank's 1948 concurrence in the earlier Roth case had read like an invitation for the Supreme Court to mount a full review, and it had failed. This time, he took a more brazen approach. After a sweeping statement that such intellectual luminaries as John Milton, Thomas Jefferson, James Madison, and John Stuart Mill all "pointed out that that any paternalistic guardianship by government of the thoughts of grown-up citizens enervates their spirit, keeps them immature," and threatens further censorship beyond just sexual matters, Frank nudged the Supreme Court even more directly, in a lengthy appendix to his opinion, outlining "factors which I think deserve consideration" from the Court.

Frank's appendix began with an extensive survey of free speech in American history, from the framing of the First Amendment through the Cold War. As the savvy jurist pointed out, it was difficult to situate the Comstock Act within the original meaning and intent of the framers, since conservative Victorian morality developed only well *after* the more open bawdiness of such late-eighteenth-century figures as Benjamin Franklin. Though densely footnoted and expansively researched, Frank's appendix never even feigned neutrality. At one point it sarcastically noted that even if obscene materials *did* stimulate actual behavior, it might not be a terrible thing so long as it avoided "anti-social" sexual expression. "Without such behavior," the judge wrote with a distinct smirk, "the human race would soon disappear."

Other lines of argument extended the attack. Judges have made an arbitrary and irrational exception for "classics"; obscenity law itself functionally operates as a prior restraint in the chilling effect it imposes on those who might otherwise publish challenges to sexual orthodoxy: these were two of Frank's most potent angles. Even the average-person test fell beneath his rhetorical sword as "far too vague" to justify an exception to the First Amendment. Brushing aside such red herrings as juvenile delinquency, Frank described what he saw as the implicit logic of obscenity as nakedly as possible: "it would seem that its validity must rest on this ground: Congress, by statute, may constitutionally provide punishment for the mailing of books evoking mere thoughts or feelings about sex, if Congress considers them socially dangerous, even in the absence of any satisfactory evidence that those thoughts or feelings will tend to bring about socially harmful deeds." His contempt for that notion needed no explicit elucidation.

Frank's rather daring experiment drew the ire of his colleagues on the Second Circuit. Charles Clark, perhaps chafing over a section in which Frank debunked theories of juvenile delinquency and sexual deviance caused by smut, sent him a note beginning with praise over his "quite amazing intellectual and emotional tour de force, with real Kinseyian overtones." Clark quickly qualified, "I think this fine for an essay or monograph, but really quite out of place for an inferior court." Chiding Frank for ignoring Fredric Wertham's *Seduction of the Innocent*, as well as going on an "intellectual joyride," Clark betrayed his own prejudice against Samuel Roth, calling it "particularly unfortunate to do so for this admitted leech — an old and detestable hand at the salacious (and not literary) trade."

Outside the courtroom, Frank's appendix drew the attention it sought. The ACLU Censorship Panel took inspiration from it, calling on the organization to reexamine its position on obscenity. Some soul-searching ensued. At a November 1956 meeting, Censorship Panel member Harriet Pilpel "expressed concern that some of our previous public statements might imply that we conceded exemption from the First Amendment to obscenity laws." This, of course, drastically understated the case, as affirmation for obscenity laws had been the overtly expressed position of the ACLU for decades. Acknowledging the inconsistency in the group's standards, which defended political radicals who posed no clear and present danger but allowed for the prosecution of publishers, the panel approved two resolutions. One asserted that the constitutional guarantee of free speech was universal, with "no special category of obscenity or pornography to which different constitutional tests apply." The other required any obscenity statute to hinge on the material in question representing a "clear and present danger of normally inducing behavior which validly has been made criminal by statute."

These were strong statements, but they masked some hesitation. When one member proposed a resolution asserting that the ACLU "should oppose any obscenity law even if it meets the constitutional test," it failed 5–4. Herbert Monte Levy claimed "most psychologists" agreed that pornography held a causal connection to "anti-social behavior," while Pilpel expressed concern over "protection of the young." Dan Lacy, from the American Book Publishers Council, was more worried about private vigilante action, which might escalate in the absence of a law. In short, Jerome Frank had prodded the ACLU toward a stronger stance, but not quite categorical opposition to obscenity law.

Another response to Frank's appendix came from University of Chicago law professor Harry Kalven, who reviewed it for the *Library Quarterly*. Although faulting the appendix for being "too unsystematic and too short-winded to persuade," Kalven credited it for forcing the Supreme Court's hand. Predicting that the Court would uphold the federal obscenity law, he wrote, "the difficulty is in understanding why this should be so." In trying to decipher the furtive logic of obscenity law, Kalven suggested, "the real concern here is with something everyone is too reticent to mention—masturbation" (which, to be sure, along with homosexual activity remained a criminalized act—neither of which the ACLU had yet challenged, thus technically meeting its clear and present danger test). In other words, obscenity law remained grounded in obsolete Victorian anxieties that *should* have been displaced by sexual liberalism—yet proved strangely resistant to change. Had he read Kalven's piece, Roth would surely have agreed with the sentiments but found little solace in Kalven's expectations.

Framing the Case

The Supreme Court was Roth's next logical step, and his petition for a writ of certiorari presented him as an important figure in the fight to modernize literature, listing his previous convictions for such now-reputable works as *Ulysses* and Richard Burton's translation of *The Perfumed Garden*, while sidestepping sleazier episodes such as the pornographic *Memories of an Hotel Man* that had sent him to prison in 1936. Legally, the brief made three central arguments. First, obscenity laws should exist only at the state level and be "only civil not penal in nature." The case for this rested on a reading of the First Amendment in conjunction with the Ninth and Tenth Amendments, which respectively reserved rights to the people and the states on issues not directly determined by the Constitution. Those reservations created an "unqualifiedly absolute bar to federal authority over utterances allegedly obscene," Roth's legal team contended. His new set of attorneys included O. John Rogge, a former radical who had been excommunicated from the political left for criticizing the Soviet Union, helping the government's case against accused spies Ethel and Julius Rosenberg, and testifying against civil rights leader W. E. B. Du Bois after his late conversion to communism. As a fellow outcast from his own chosen community, Rogge presumably felt some affinity for Roth—and his presence served as reminder of the Cold War backdrop.

Though Roth's brief cited copious evidence from the 1787 Constitutional Convention, noting that founding father Roger Sherman had considered a declaration of press liberty unnecessary because "the power of Congress does not extend to the press," the constitutional analysis was also rather dated. The brief offered a powerful example of the first federal effort to regulate the press, when President Andrew Jackson tried to suppress mailed abolitionist literature in the 1830s and even southern politicians opposed it for fear of expanded federal power, but no acknowledgment was given of the profound shift in the meaning of American federalism that followed the ascension of the national government in the decades after the Civil War. The Ninth and Tenth Amendment argument thus seemed rooted in an obsolete historical era.

Roth's second argument cut closer to the chase, declaring the federal obscenity statute in direct violation of the First Amendment. A lingering consequence of "that feverish Puritan, Anthony Comstock," the obscenity law failed to meet the various standards the Court had set for suppression of speech. Here, the brief moved into the modern era, detailing the various tests the Court had set out, from breach of peace to overthrow of government to clear and present danger. Obscenity met none of them.

Finally, Roth suggested the obscenity law was vague and overbroad, thus violating the Fifth Amendment's due-process clause. Making effective use of Jerome Frank's appendix, it found "nothing constant" about obscenity doctrine "except its changeability." The brief was officially filed on December 17, 1956.

Unsurprisingly, the government vigorously disagreed. With Solicitor General J. Lee Rankin and Assistant Attorney General Warren Olney III as its lead authors, the lengthy response brief articulated the official national positions. "Certain kinds of speech," it began, "such as opinions in the realm of politics, economics and religion, have a greater social value than other kinds." Within this hierarchy, obscene publications "have a negligible social value."

Whatever its merits, this argument sounded more plausible in the abstract than in the specific, and the brief wavered between the admission that "no rigid or arbitrary scale of values can be stated" and the assertion that "there does exist some comparative scale of value." The scale, when presented in its particulars, appeared rather muddled. Political, religious, economic, and scientific speech came first, but then "general news and information," "social and historical commentary," literature, art, entertainment, and music followed, in descending order, without any explanation. Most curiously, the bottom three categories were obscenity, profanity, and then finally commercial pornography, a truly inexplicable ordering that distinguished obscenity from pornography and also ranked it higher than profanity, which had at the very least a strong and compelling claim to First Amendment protection.

Also oddly, the governmental brief broke nonmailable obscenity into three categories. "Hard core pornography," it claimed, comprised over 90 percent of the materials confiscated. A minuscule amount of "borderline material" — "the sort with which the petitioner in this case has been associated over the years" — also fell in, and then finally novels with "serious literary intent" but graphic descriptions of sex, which the government assured amounted to no more than 2 percent of all obscenity cases. With no evidence cited to justify the figures, they seemed designed to assure the justices that obscenity targeted only worthless, perverse works.

Betting (correctly) that the Court would find Roth's Ninth and Tenth Amendment argument frivolous, the government brief spent little time on them, also glossing over the vagueness charge. "There is a solid core of material," it contended, "which, within the common law and under the statutes, is known to be obscene without doubt. This includes those matters which explicitly and purposefully deal with sex conduct in a degrading or perverted way, with no artistic aspect whatever." It was a somewhat disingenuous phrasing, since the definition *included* those matters but was clearly not *limited* to them, by the government's own admission of the serious novels that did carry artistic worth, but again, Rankin and Olney knew the First Amendment argument would occupy center stage, so did not belabor the vagueness charge.

At its heart, then, the government's brief could not avoid moving the discussion into the realm of public morality. The history of obscenity doctrine left no choice; there was simply no way to defend it without invoking the moral policing that had animated Anthony Comstock to begin with. Yet in an era of Kinsey reports, *Peyton Place*, and Mickey Spillane, how could one defend a paternalistic governmental authoritarianism over people's reading practices that seemed to chafe against the public sentiment in support of free speech? Rankin and Olney were careful not to hinge their argument on any factors that might change. The clear and present danger test was mentioned, in its watered-down post-*Dennis* form, as necessitating only that a "social interest is in substantial danger of being injured," but it was too fluid a concept to anchor their case. The effects of pornography, too, were too susceptible to social scientists and their empirical skepticism, so the brief also declined to mount its case on that front — though in a circular touch, it did note "that existing delinquency has not primarily been caused by pornography speaks as much for the effectiveness of the existing restraints as anything else."

Instead, the government based its case on a single fundamental claim: "No idea of any value is denied a hearing by the barring of obscenity." Given that First Amendment claims depended on "a weighing of competing interests" — a stance that had indeed carried a Court majority ever since the advent of the modern First Amendment — this meant that interest in "the maintenance of public morality" outweighed private rights to publish obscene material, given its worthlessness. After all, William Lockhart's and Robert McClure's law articles on obscenity had been cited by Jerome Frank and Roth's lawyers, and were clearly intended to combat obscenity prosecutions — yet the law professors themselves had declared pornography of negligible value, and its suppression as socially insignificant, so the government could also cite them for its argument.

Immediately upon making this argument, the government conceded that there *was* one possible idea contained in obscene material, namely, "that there is pleasure in sexual gratification by any and every means, without regard to religious or moral teachings, legal prohibitions, the requirements of sound mental and physical health or the proprieties of a civilized society." The social value of these notions "is, of course, nil." Since there was no avoiding the fact that this position was nakedly and incontrovertibly one of prescribing sexual norms, the brief folded that aspect into the very idea of "public morality," which it called "more than a set of manners or even a code of unrelated rules. It is the element of 'ought' that lies behind the laws and rules of an organized society."

The public interest, then, went beyond mere social science questions of individual response and behavior. Rather, it reached the much larger "risk of breaking down the existing moral restraint and leading to prohibited conduct over a period of time" through the normalization of otherwise proscribed sexual desires and behaviors. While the brief avoided directly Comstockian language, it repackaged the ideas in Cold War rhetoric. "Just as in the *Dennis* case, the feared conduct may be the result of repeated indoctrination," this time not by communists but smutmongers.

Proper obscenity law enforcement, however, would "aid parents in keeping the home free from the forced invasion of agencies which will tend to destroy and subvert that training" (in good morals). Even though the government agreed that the average person had become the proper barometer, it was not above invoking anxieties over child protection to score points. The brief even cited then senator Hugo

Black supporting obscenity trials in 1937. Surely Olney and Rankin knew they would never win Black's vote, but highlighting his own complicity in obscenity only two decades earlier served to emphasize that his and Douglas's free-speech absolutism was out of keeping with historical trends.

Of course, sexual nonconvention *was* an idea, one whose immense social importance had factored into debates over everything from birth control to divorce to homosexuality — precisely the sort of topics that had historically been targeted by obscenity law. By conflating "obscenity" with "pornography" (even as it seemingly distinguished the two), the government's brief obscured that history and instead painted obscene materials with the least flattering brush possible — even as it acknowledged Roth's own circulars and publications did not fall into the "hard core" category it so leaned upon to justify suppression. On none of these fronts was the government's brief a masterpiece of argumentation. If it were to succeed, it would have to be on the First Amendment balancing test tipping toward the Court's belief in "public morality."

A flurry of amicus curiae — "friend of the court" — briefs poured in from interested parties, all on Roth's side. The ACLU reflected its emerging stance, arguing, "Absent evidence that the publications will probably and immediately cause anti-social conduct, the conviction violates the First Amendment." The Authors' League of America took a different tack, replacing the clear and present danger approach with an emphasis on privacy; display in public places should be the focus of governmental regulation, not private reading practices. "We respectfully submit that the problems of prohibiting the 'obscene' have been overly complicated by a reluctance to trust the judgment of individual members of the community," the League added.

Morris Ernst, filing individually, took on the thankless task of fleshing out Roth's Ninth and Tenth Amendment arguments, perhaps because the ACLU itself had not bothered. In private correspondence earlier that year, ACLU staff counsel Rowland Watts had declared himself "not impressed" with the Tenth Amendment argument, which would allow great leeway in state censorship. The Ninth Amendment argument of powers reserved to the people he found "personally attractive," but would be "much surprised if the Court gave it any consideration as it practically never has in the whole history of the Constitution." (He would be right, until the 1965 *Griswold v. Connecticut* case, involving contraception for married partners.) Finally, the publishing companies of men's magazines *Playboy* and *Rogue* filed a brief. Echoing the various other arguments, it made little impact on the case and would only rise to importance a decade later, after its lead author Abe Fortas was appointed to the Supreme Court.

Once the initial briefs were filed, each side had a chance to offer replies. The government had little to add, but Roth's team took the government to task on a few points, particularly its blurring of "obscenity" and "pornography" for effect. Since the obscenity statute "is not confined, nor does it even refer" to "hard core" material, Roth lawyer David von G. Albrecht disputed the relevance of the government's discussion. He also took exception to the "varying values" placed on different forms of speech "like price-tags on cuts of meat." Finding no "substantive evil" ascribed to obscenity, Albrecht called the government arguments about public morality "the sort of nonsense that we finally arrive at when the government decides to go into the business of censorship"—using an effectively demonized term as counterweight to the governmental reference to protecting families and children.

The Roth response brief also marshaled quotes from Jefferson and Madison to bolster its Tenth Amendment claim, but the most personally important addition made in the reply briefs was Roth's claim that the Court "certainly has a right to inspect all the publications to see whether as a matter of law they are not obscene." Lost in the adjudications over obscenity doctrine was the fact that Samuel Roth faced five years in prison. That made the Court's overturning the obscenity statute an all-or-nothing proposition for Roth. Unless the justices found it unconstitutional, incarceration awaited. Calling on the Court to review the materials offered another out, a way to reverse his conviction without necessarily taking the ultimate step. In a purely doctrinal sense, it was clearly corollary to the main claims; for Roth himself, it was essential.

The Supreme Court declined to take Roth's bait on that issue. In mid-January 1957, it granted certiorari, meaning it would hear the case, but limited the scope to the original three constitutional questions. It would be Roth or Comstock triumphant, with no middle ground.

A Constellation of Obscene
Questions

The Supreme Court Roth's case reached was a dramatically different entity from the 1949 Court that had refused his last attempt to catch its eye. Both personnel changes and the pressure building up from the confused and conflicted lower courts had profound effects behind the bench. On the former front, the death of Fred Vinson in 1953 resulted in the appointment of Earl Warren as chief justice. Several of the brethren were hardly sorry to see Vinson go. The acerbic Felix Frankfurter privately called his death "the first indication that I have ever had that there was a God." Not only would Warren bring a healthier dynamic to the explosive personal tensions within the Court, he would also shift it into a more progressive trajectory, witnessed most dramatically in the 1954 *Brown v. Board of Education* decision that at long last overturned six decades of Court-sanctioned racial segregation in public schools. While the Vinson Court had chipped away at segregation, it had been unwilling to directly reject the doctrine of separate but equal. In only his first year on the Court, Warren had miraculously managed to gather a unanimous Court.

Three years after Warren took his seat, he was joined by William Brennan. Replacing the undistinguished Sherman Minton, Brennan emerged from the New Jersey Supreme Court with little fanfare. President Dwight Eisenhower mostly just wanted a Catholic justice for political reasons, and Brennan fit the bill. Attorney General Herbert Brownell did most of the minimal vetting. For Ike's sake, Brennan was supposed to provide good public relations; his relative youth signaled vitality, and his membership in the Democratic Party was to reflect Eisenhower's nonpartisanship. From this inauspicious appointment, he would grow into not only the Court's chief obscenity architect, but also its primary liberal driving force. Two other Eisenhower appointees, John Marshall Harlan and Charles Evans Whittaker, were culled from federal appellate courts on the basis of their moderate conservatism, but neither would prove doctrinaire upon ascending to the high court.

Meanwhile, the Court had begun to recognize the necessity of intervening into the obscenity debacle. One early and fleeting encounter came in a film censorship case from Kansas, where the state censor board had banned Otto Preminger's *The Moon Is Blue*. Released without the Hollywood Production Code seal in 1953, Preminger's romantic comedy used some mildly frank dialogue, including the word "virgin." In the years immediately after the 1952 *Burstyn* case that gave First Amendment protection to the movies, the Court had overturned a series of censorship actions. Kansas, however, specifically invoked obscenity in the statute that empowered its board of review, and its state supreme court sided with the board, deferring to its judgment on the film's obscenity. This meant the Supreme Court could conceivably enter the obscenity debate. Instead, it issued a perfunctory per curiam opinion, simply declaring "Judgment reversed" with a citation to *Burstyn*, thus lumping it with the various other film censorship cases rather than obscenity doctrine.

By the time *Roth v. U.S.* reached the Court, it had in fact taken on three other obscenity cases, all dealing with more limited questions than Roth's frontal assault on obscenity law. *Butler v. Michigan* emerged out of the Detroit police force's aggressive censorial actions; *Alberts v. California* came to the Court straight from the Beverly Hills municipal court where a Los Angeles smut dealer had been convicted; and *Kingsley Books v. Brown* resulted from a New York practice of obtaining preemptive injunctions against allegedly obscene books. The latter two cases were being held as the Court decided *Butler*, which posed the most specific constitutional question of the bunch. It provided a safe way for the cautious Court to test the obscenity waters before the plunge that *Roth* demanded.

Butler involved the Detroit License and Censor Bureau, run out of the local police force by Inspector Herbert Case. A sort of local smut czar who had risen to some national prominence through his aggressive actions, Case had testified before the Kefauver Committee and appeared regularly as a source in journalistic accounts of the obscenity debate. Journalists could reliably count on him for bold assertions, such as when he told *Better Homes and Gardens* that "there hasn't been a sex murder in the history of our department in which the killer wasn't an avid reader of lewd magazines and books." According to a 1956 ACLU press release, Case's board had banned 192 books by 1954, engaging in "censorship at its unconstitutional worst."

The book that generated a Supreme Court case was a fairly undistinguished one, John Griffin's *The Devil Rides Out*, a lengthy tome following a young American musician in Paris who enters a monastery in the hopes of resisting the "temptations of the flesh" that continually lead him astray. Unsurprisingly, his efforts fail. Case had arrested a seller of the book, under a Michigan statute that embodied the resurgent moral concerns of the 1950s. On the books since the 1830s, the Michigan obscenity statute had been modified at the height of the moral panic over juvenile delinquency in 1953 to criminalize those works with passages "tending to incite minors to violent or depraved or immoral acts, manifestly tending to the corruption of the morals of youth." In both aspects, the reliance on specific passages rather than whole works and the use of children rather than average adults, the revised statute offered a revival of the nineteenth-century standards that had seemingly been superseded by sexual liberalism's modernized obscenity doctrine. The case thus presented a direct showdown between the *Hicklin* and *Ulysses* standards.

Taking up the case after the Michigan high court refused to hear it, the Supreme Court limited its scope to the specific standards of the state obscenity statute, not the validity of obscenity statutes per se. Still, the case was recognized as momentous, being the first time in the century that the Court would directly rule on obscenity. Certainly, it would serve as a beacon of doctrinal developments to come.

Preparing for the case, several justices sent their clerks out to read *The Devil Rides Out*. Clerks typically prepared a bench memorandum about each case for their justices, summarizing the facts and arguments at hand, and often taking a stand on the case. For *Butler*, the clerks' bench memos disparaged the novel, but Michigan's approach to it more. While a William Brennan clerk noted that the protagonist experienced "some lusty relapses into the sins of the flesh," he suggested the state law was unconstitutional. In a note to the chief justice, a Warren clerk described it as "a serious novel," despite its sleazy qualities. A Douglas clerk told the justice the book contained several "sensual passages," which did not "approach the biological detail" of *Memoirs of Hecate County*. Douglas also had his clerks read other books suppressed under Inspector Case's watch. One noted of John Dos Passos's *Ulysses*-like modernist novel *1919*, the book was "incomprehensible" but clearly "serious writing."

Given the nature of the case, with Michigan's standards a jarringly retrograde effort to return to the days of Comstock, the only real questions were by what count the Court would reverse, and how. The chief justice had brilliantly corralled a unanimous Court in *Brown v. Board*, and clearly a similarly united front would be ideal for the Court's reentry into the muddy and controversial waters of obscenity. At conference, though, two justices voted to affirm Butler's conviction. Tom Clark and Harold Burton had never shown great enthusiasm for the cause of free speech, and still did not. In a smart move, the chief assigned the opinion to the notoriously persuasive (many would say pushy) Felix Frankfurter, himself hardly renowned as a First Amendment progressive because of his philosophy of judicial restraint. Even as recently as 1955, in personal correspondence with Zechariah Chafee, Frankfurter had called unreasonable search and seizure cases more important than free speech, "for the simple reason that the latter has strongly organized forces in its support — the press, the movie interests, publishers, etc."

Frankfurter understood the utility of an undivided Court. In a memorandum to the rest of the brethren, he argued *Butler* "should be decided on a narrow ground on which the whole Court, such is my strong hope, can agree." As such, "I have tried to write as briefly as possible to avoid any intimation, even unintended, on the more or less contentious issues raised by other obscenity statutes." While maintaining rigorous precision in scope kept the case tightly confined to the details of the Michigan law, it also worked to win over the reluctant Clark and Burton. Frankfurter always viewed amassing Court votes as wars of position, and in a gleeful handwritten note to Warren, he exclaimed the dissenters had "given up and have agreed to the opinion I have circulated."

Despite its narrow focus, Frankfurter's opinion did create significant precedent. In it, the normally verbose former professor cut to the chase. By "quarantining the general reading public against books not too rugged for grown men and women in order to shield juvenile innocence," the justice declared, Michigan claimed it was "exercising its power to promote the general welfare." In the quip that came to define *Butler*, Frankfurter scorned the notion: "Surely, this is to burn the house to roast the pig." With the effect being to "reduce the adult population of Michigan to reading only what is fit for children," the statute indeed violated Butler's First Amendment rights.

The Court's first foray back into obscenity doctrine would also be its last unanimous opinion. Frankfurter said nothing about the validity of obscenity laws themselves — for that matter, his record already made clear his endorsement — but did set a clear baseline for judging obscenity. *Hicklin* was finally dead; the *Ulysses* standards were now national. Material charged with obscenity could be evaluated only in the entirety, not in isolated parts. Average adults, emphatically *not* children, were the only legitimate reference point. Because it came from an undivided Court, and because the standards it upheld had been circulating among the lower federal courts for a quarter century, *Butler* proved relatively uncontroversial. It also suggested a cautiously liberal approach to obscenity, one that left Samuel Roth's fate less than certain.

Of the two other cases awaiting resolution as Roth's appeal reached the Court, *Kingsley Books* would reach resolution only after *Roth* and will be discussed in chapter 7. Meanwhile, *Alberts v. California* presented a state-level parallel to *Roth* in many ways. David Alberts arrived at smut through more mundane means than Roth's artistic ambitions and literary exile. Instead, he had gone into business wholesaling food and photographic supplies by mail order in the mid-1940s. With the infrastructure of his Triangle Supply Company in place, erotic books and pictures were simply another market niche to Alberts. Records of Alberts's life and personality are sparse, but by all indications he approached his merchandise with the dispassionate eye of the businessman, with little of Roth's clear personal obsessions commingled with the lucre.

His first arrest came in late 1949, on four misdemeanor counts involving "indecent writings." The *Los Angeles Times* reported that Alberts's "smut factory" resided a mere two blocks from the Hollywood police station and had sent obscene materials to minors. Convicted, Alberts managed to receive a suspended 180-day sentence, though a subsequent 1951 violation left him jailed for two months. To keep his sentence short, Alberts stipulated in writing that he would no longer deal in advertising or selling "any business which involved lewd materials." It was a promise Alberts immediately broke, though in a Roth-like move he incorporated his next venture, Paragon Enterprises, under the ownership of his wife, Violet Stanard (who also went by Violet Alberts), thus providing himself a thin legal shield.

Alberts and Stanard dealt in a lower literary register than Samuel

Roth. While Roth at least attempted to situate his works among the "classics," the Southern California couple rarely bothered with such alibis. Tawdry sensationalism characterized most of their works, with *Memoirs of a Spankee*, *Slaves of the Lash*, and *The Pleasures of the Torture Chamber* filling their catalogs. At a time when the gay panic of the Lavender Scare shaped national policy, they also distributed short books like *Male Homosexuals Tell Their Stories* and *Homosexual Life*, which were remarkably *non*tawdry but inherently controversial in that context. As the Cold War porn crusade coalesced, it was virtually inevitable that Alberts and Stanard would wind up in its dragnet, and sure enough, they were arrested in early 1955, charged with possession and distribution of obscene literature and pictures through the mails.

At trial, in the Municipal Court of Beverly Hills in Los Angeles County, the district attorney broke down the contested merchandise into "degrees of obscenity," ranging from "moderately" to "very" obscene (the works involved all those named above, as well as copies of *Good Times*, Roth's magazine). Further, the trial judge openly admitted not reading the books in their entirety; the transcript includes numerous examples of his references to "the little bits that I read in one of those books." Despite these seeming irregularities, the judge convicted Alberts on two counts, sentencing him to sixty days on one and a $500 fine on the other. Stanard he acquitted, relying on the patriarchal gender norms of the era. Because "she is in the employ and she is his wife," Judge Charles Griffin explained, he questioned "whether she of her own volition is criminally liable."

Not only were some of the procedural aspects of the case dubious, but Judge Griffin never even quite clarified which of Alberts's items had generated the convictions. The books, circulars, and pictures had been grouped into assorted exhibits and approached at that collective level. The result was that nowhere in the legal record were the specific grounds actually named. Alberts's attorney, Stanley Fleishman, saw opportunity in these anomalies. Fleishman had carved out a place as Los Angeles's foremost legal obscenity expert, serving on retainer for several distributors and vetting their merchandise before they sent it. As he testified at trial, he had given Alberts and Stanard the go-ahead for the works that left Alberts convicted, so he had something of a stake in the matter. After a local appeal to the Los Angeles appellate court failed, Fleishman took bold action in appealing straight to the Supreme Court. The Jerome Frank *Roth* appendix and the docketing of *Butler* alerted him to the fact that the Court was now effectively compelled to take on obscenity cases, and *Alberts v. California* posed fresh new constitutional questions.

In his brief for Alberts, Fleishman mentioned all of the troubling courtroom moments, but also launched a full-scale assault on the law of obscenity. In a constitutional sense, *Alberts* paralleled *Roth* but raised a technically distinct question. Whereas *Roth*, as a federal case, directly invoked the First Amendment, *Alberts*, being a state case, relied on the Fourteenth Amendment's incorporation of the First Amendment. As Roth's lawyers had, Fleishman also added a fairly weak federalism argument, this time from the opposite angle; Roth's team contended obscenity was a state issue, while Fleishman argued that state regulation of the mails infringed on federal law, which covered the whole field of obscenity in the mails. In both cases, these points came as transparent afterthoughts, with the crux of the matter being the legitimacy of governmental suppression of obscene materials. On this front, Fleishman's brief took a more radical stance than the Roth team. The latter had worked hard to distinguish Roth's "borderline" material from the "hard core" filth with which the government sought to conflate it. In contrast, Fleishman refused to dodge the "hard core" tag and unambiguously demanded First Amendment protection even for such material that claimed no redeeming value beyond interest in the erotic.

Hitting at every possible weak point in the doctrine of obscenity, Fleishman reminded the justices of its origin in religious principles. He surveyed the history of offhand references the Court had made to obscenity, finding an unexamined "vast constitutional abyss" between the exceptions the Court had made for various forms of speech that related to conduct ("fighting words," "loud and raucous" noise, etc.) and texts such as Alberts's, which did "no more than incite thoughts and arouse desires." And following that logic, Fleishman linked obscenity law to censorship and the specter of a governmental thought-police, in effectively Cold War–tinged language. "The censorship of books which allegedly stimulate 'sexual impure' ideas," he wrote, "is basically a desire to maintain the status quo in sex attitudes, while recognizing that different convictions, tastes, and judgments exist. The attempt is to coerce unanimity of opinion by authority."

Refusing to concede that "hard core" was even a meaningful category, Fleishman instead called it something defined through " 'knowing look' and 'sly wink' to assert that 'we are all certain' that there are some 'obscene and indecent' books which are worthy of the bonfire only." Declaring it "impossible to determine what 'anti-social conduct' a State normally would seek to prevent," Fleishman grounded his brief on the question, "How certain can we be that an idea has 'no social value'?" Missing no opportunity to build rhetorical power, he even situated *Alberts* alongside the Court's recent advances against segregation, citing *Brown v. Board of Education* to show how "the Constitution has been upheld even against 'old' abuses." Like the Jim Crow South, the Comstock Act was an obsolete product of a time now passed.

In response, the State of California delivered an uninspired brief largely consisting of lengthy quotations from various cases. Its fundamental argument was that the state had the right to "protect its citizens' health, general welfare, and morals," a phrasing based on the conceptions of state police powers that had emerged in the nineteenth century. "Pandering to the warped, the neurotic, the emotionally disturbed and distorted individual, by the exploitation for profit of the most vicious of human aberrations," the state legal team contended, "seems a far cry from the matters intended by the authors of the First Amendment" to be protected. Disputing Fleishman's righteousness, the state attributed David Alberts's "zeal" less to a crusade for freedom than "an avaricious desire to continue the flow of profits from the pennies of perverts and the dollars of the depraved."

The *Alberts* case drew much less attention than *Roth*. At the ACLU, Herbert Monte Levy continued his conservative approach, dismissing *Alberts*. "Pure eroticism without any ideational content should not occupy our time," he wrote to a colleague. In a moment revealing the motivations that drove organizational policy, he added, "This was a kind of sexy comeon advertising for sexy stuff, which is bad public relations to defend." Historian Judy Kutulas has argued that state and regional branches of the ACLU often took more hard-line stances than the national body, and *Alberts* bears out her analysis. While Levy rejected the case, the Southern California ACLU did contribute a brief. It took a strong clear and present danger stance and declared "the state can claim no legitimate interest in matters of taste." Beyond the Southern California branch, no other parties filed amicus briefs in *Alberts*.

When the Supreme Court agreed to hear the case, it initially held it pending resolution of *Butler*. Fleishman found this dangerous, since Butler's lawyers had challenged only the details of Michigan's law, not the validity of obscenity law per se, so hinging *Alberts* on *Butler* made no sense. Fleishman petitioned to have the cases consolidated, but the Court refused. By then *Roth* had been taken up, so instead *Alberts* and it were bound together. The Court would determine the constitutional status of state and federal obscenity law in one fell swoop.

Before the Bench

Oral arguments provide the only visibly dynamic exchange in Supreme Court cases, where everything else is handled through briefs or behind closed doors among the justices. The arguments allow attorneys the chance to flesh out or clarify their cases, and the justices to press them on various points. *Roth* and *Alberts* came before the Court on the same day, April 22, 1957, in sequential hourlong rounds. Neither round of oral arguments added great new substance to the cases, often serving instead as an opportunity for Felix Frankfurter to harangue most of the lawyers before him, but each did bring a few significant details to light.

Roth went first, and Roth's attorney, David von G. Albrecht, got off to a rocky start, even after the chief justice began the hearing by misidentifying him. Beginning with the contention that the government had conceded Roth's publications were "borderline entertainment" but focused their argument on "commercial black market pornography," he attempted to highlight the discrepancy, but found himself interrupted repeatedly by the justices asking for clarification. Frankfurter struck the most aggressive posture, especially when it came to the scope of the Court's inquiry. When Albrecht doubted the jury's having even read Roth's works, Frankfurter asked, "Are any of those questions open here?" before lecturing him on the narrow scope of the Court's review, which emphatically did not pertain to the facts of Roth's case, but only the abstract constitutional questions. Traditionally, the Court extends its review only to the specific questions it has granted in the writ of certiorari, and in *Roth* this did not include things like the behavior of the jury—or even the actual nature of Roth's texts. Albrecht attempted to argue that "consideration of the constitutionality of this statute not only applies to the statute on its face, but also as applied." To that, Frankfurter dripped with condescension, chiding Albrecht, "You can't just swim in the midst of the Pacific Ocean in these matters. You've got to get some footing on some terra cotta, terra firma."

Aside from Frankfurter's prodding, the other justices gave little response to Albrecht's presentation—and thus little indication of their stances. None of them commented on the attorney's complaint that the government had sent "sealed exhibits" to the justices, apparently containing examples of pornography at its worst, which was never shared with Roth's team. This practice was unusual, at the very least, but whatever impact it had on the justices' thinking went entirely unremarked, and no records remain of the secret exhibits' content. When Albrecht's strenuous efforts to distinguish Roth's merchandise from this unrelated smut went unappreciated by the justices, he no doubt read it as a bad sign.

Roger Fisher, arguing the government's case, faced less intrusive questioning. At one point in his presentation, he spoke for over five uninterrupted minutes, a grace period never allowed Albrecht. Primarily, he repeated key points from the briefs, reminding the Court that 90 percent of obscenity cases fell into "the blackmarket, hardcore pornography sort." When Justice Douglas pressed Fisher on definitions and whether obscenity posed any clear and present dangers, Fisher mentioned both "immediate conduct" and "long-range conduct induced by a breaking down of morals." A clearly hostile Douglas responded, "This sounds more like Mr. Comstock." Attempting to respond in a more clearly twentieth-century style than Comstock's feverish denunciations, Fisher described the "psychological harm of the housewife who opens the morning mail and finds one of Mr. Roth's circulars." Assuming his hypothetical housewife would feel "strongly" about being "hit in the face with dirty pictures and debasing discussion of sex at home in the morning mail," Fisher considered his point proved.

Little else of great interest marked the *Roth* hearings, and *Alberts* offered more of the same, with Frankfurter now badgering defense attorney Stanley Fleishman. Again, an irritated Douglas in turn grilled the government representative to no particular end. Only Justice Brennan took up the government's breakdown of categories ranging from "moderately" to "very" obscene, leading assistant district attorney Fred Whichello to resort to insisting, "Every man in the street knows what obscenity is." When asked which of David Alberts's books was most obscene, Whichello chose *Questions and Answers about Oral-Genital Contacts.*

While Stanley Fleishman was easily the best orator of the whole round of hearings, ultimately they added quite little to the briefs already filed. Frankfurter had shown evident skepticism toward the defense attorneys, and Douglas dismissiveness toward the government lawyers, but most of the justices had not broadcast their inclinations. The questions of federalism presented in opposing ways by *Roth* and *Alberts* had taken up minimal time, so clearly both cases would hinge not on those side questions but on the relation of obscenity to the First Amendment.

Four days after oral argument, the justices met to discuss the cases in conference. Held privately, with no outsiders or even clerks present, the conference provides the justices an open environment to air their thoughts. Douglas's jotted notes leave the best available evidence to reconstruct the conference discussion of *Roth* and *Alberts*. According to tradition, the chief justice spoke first. As Earl Warren saw it, neither of the convictions violated the First Amendment, nor were the obscenity statutes vague. "State and federal government should be able to protect themselves against depravity," he explained.

Hugo Black had already well established his First Amendment stance and had little to add: reverse on both cases, he said. With the discussion proceeding in descending order of seniority, that left Frankfurter to weigh in next. Notorious among the justices for his long, pompous lectures at conference, Frankfurter presented a core message that "obscenity is an adequate standard." If free speech were absolute, he warned, "you can't protect even children." Douglas, predictably, disagreed, following Black in cutting to the chase in favor of reversals.

This brought the discussion to the remaining Truman appointees, Harold Burton and Tom Clark. Neither was recognized for his support of free speech, or for adding much to conference discussions.

"We have here the hard core of obscenity," declared Burton: affirm. Without additional comment, Clark agreed.

Eisenhower's second appointment after Warren, John Marshall Harlan, mused at greater length. States should have a "wider field in defining obscenity" than the federal government, he thought; since the problem was local in nature, states deserved more "leeway" in confronting it. Further, though Frankfurter had snarled at Roth's lawyer for raising the issue, Harlan was troubled by the facts of Roth's case, which, he responded to Burton, had "nothing approaching the hard core of obscenity." Affirming Alberts's conviction, Harlan voted to reverse Roth's.

This left recent appointees William Brennan and Charles Evans Whittaker. Brennan believed obscenity laws did not violate the First Amendment, nor were they vague. Likewise, Whittaker thought state and federal law had the "power to eliminate smut." An irritated Douglas found such proclamations severely lacking in analytical rigor. In a "P.S." to his conference notes, he scribbled. "This was a most annoying discussion." Those in favor of affirming the convictions, he believed, "never mentioned once what the standard for obscenity is." Instead, they "merely stated that smut could be suppressed."

For Douglas, this did not suffice. What mattered at this point, however, was not analysis but numbers. At the end of conference discussion, the justices voted, and the results were decisive. On *Alberts*, all voted to affirm except Black and Douglas. On *Roth*, Harlan joined the dissenting duo, making it a 6–3 victory for the federal government. State and federal statutes were constitutional, and Samuel Roth and David Alberts were bound for imprisonment. All that remained was for the Supreme Court to articulate its obscenity doctrine in a written opinion.

CHAPTER 7

Writing *Roth*
The Court Opines

As the first substantive Supreme Court obscenity decision of the twentieth century, *Roth v. United States* faced high expectations, not to mention inescapably intense scrutiny from all angles. Because the chief justice was on the side of the majority, he held the job of assigning the opinion (had he not been, the task would fall on the senior majority justice). Warren himself couldn't take it, though with the majority, he had reached his position through logic to which he alone subscribed (outlined in his concurrence, discussed below). That still left five other justices, but the quintet offered no cornucopia of good options.

Neither Tom Clark nor Harold Burton held much stature among Court watchers, and given the duo's frosty attitude toward free speech, Warren could hardly count on either of them to modernize obscenity doctrine. Clark had seemed begrudging enough in allowing films to claim First Amendment protection in 1952. John Marshall Harlan, on the other hand, was dissenting in *Alberts*, which was attached to *Roth*, putting him out of sync with the rest of the strong majority on both cases. This left Frankfurter and Brennan. Frankfurter clearly found the issue engaging, as witnessed in his lively performance at the oral hearings, and no doubt had both intellect and temperament to deliver a learned disquisition, a judicial opinion in the form of a scholarly monograph, as was his wont.

The chief justice chose Brennan. The decision made sense; the freshly appointed justice carried little of Frankfurter's baggage, lacking the reputation of pedantic domineering that his elder deservedly held. Yet because Brennan had studied under Frankfurter years earlier as a Harvard Law student, his selection appeased the cantankerous former professor. *Roth* marked Brennan's entrée onto the obscenity stage — and however much of a cameo he intended it to be, it cast him as primary architect of Court obscenity doctrine for the next fifteen years.

Brennan's majority opinion attempted two overall things. First, it kept obscenity outside the First Amendment's province, definitively asserting that obscene material lacked claim to free-speech protections and that it could be criminalized by state and federal governments. Second, it brought obscenity doctrine into line with the advances of the federal courts over the previous few decades, solidifying the centrality of sexual liberalism as dominant state policy and tightly restricting the scope of obscenity prosecutions.

It attempted these things, but achieved only faltering success. Brennan distinguished sex from obscenity, but also separated obscene material from the realm of ideas and politics, distinctions that fell short of resolving the protracted obscenity quagmire. *Roth* was intended to bring clarity, regularity, and most of all *finality* to a confused and unstable topic. Instead, with two concurrences from Warren and Harlan, and a scathing dissent from Douglas, it revealed a fractured Court unable to agree on a basis for obscenity laws. The Court had avoided obscenity for six decades, but once caught back in its web, it would remain enmeshed for decades. *Roth* merely began the prolonged debacle.

———

The Brennan Doctrine

Having recently arrived on the Court from a rather meteoric rise to the New Jersey Supreme Court, Brennan lacked a deep background in First Amendment jurisprudence. His own father, a city commissioner in Newark, had tried to ban the sex-hygiene film *The Naked Truth* in 1926, and lost in court. Brennan himself had cited the case from the high New Jersey bench in his most substantive judicial statement on the topic, a 1953 case involving burlesque shows, also in Newark. Careful observers could have seen foreshadowing of his *Roth* opinion in *Adams Theatre Co. v. Keenan*, where Brennan affirmed a trial court's order to the city to issue the stage and film theater an operating license on free-speech grounds. Describing a "universal agreement" that "outrightly lewd and indecent" material lacked First Amendment protection, Brennan nevertheless warned of the "amorphous" quality of that label. It carried the "danger that censorship upon that ground is merely the expression of the censor's own highly subjective view of morality."

Did "every reference to motherhood, birth or the sex relationship ipso facto classify the presentation as lewd and indecent?" Brennan wondered. His answer was negative. The "mere fact that sexual life is the theme . . . or that characters portray a seamy side of life and play coarse scenes or use vulgar language," he ruled, "does not constitute the presentation per se lewd and indecent." Instead, Brennan insisted on a "dominant effect" test in which the work as a whole amounted to "erotic allurement 'tending to incite lustful and lecherous desire,' dirt for dirt's sake only, smut and inartistic filth, with no evident purpose but 'to counsel or invite to vice or voluptuousness.'" While he would polish this formulation a bit for *Roth*, it did contain the seed of his thinking.

Meanwhile, despite Brennan's accomplishments prior to reaching the Court, Frankfurter continued treating him like a student, seeing in him a protégé. In a familiar pattern that had already sprawled across decades, Brennan at first proved receptive to this mentoring, only gradually coming to resent it as manipulative interference rather than honest advice born of wisdom and goodwill. As Brennan drafted his opinion, Frankfurter sent a memorandum in May suggesting "all there is wisely to be said regarding the proper construction of obscenity statutes" had been said in three earlier cases: the 1913 *Kennerley*, its update two decades later in *Ulysses*, and the 1936 *Levine* case (all discussed in earlier chapters).

While all three cases would inform Brennan's thinking, the younger justice also recognized, as Frankfurter did not, that more needed saying. Liberalizing as those cases were, they neither individually nor collectively laid out a sustainable doctrine. Brennan's aspirations went further; he sought to bring the discussion to a close. Obscenity followed Brennan from his very appointment. His first full oral argument upon being seated had been *Butler v. Michigan. Roth* would be his effort at a definitive statement that consolidated the previous ideas, but also wrapped them up firmly in what the earlier opinions mostly took for granted: *why* obscene materials were not included in the First Amendment. In preparation, he had his clerk draw up a memorandum summarizing every nook and cranny of the relevant case law, immersing himself in a mountain of precedent.

Though Brennan's opinion would go through several drafts, its basic components appeared intact from the start, with a working version circulating among the justices by early June 1957. Hoping brevity would provide clarity, Brennan minced no words, keeping *Roth* taut as could be. He would write not in Frankfurter's encyclopedic manner, canvassing the history of the topic and displaying his mastery. Instead, Brennan attempted to write *decisively*. *Roth* would be a proclamation, not a history lesson. After four terse paragraphs laying out the facts of *Roth* and *Alberts*, Brennan cut to the chase.

The first, and primary, dispositive question arrived without rhetorical flourish. As to whether obscenity "is utterance within the area of protected speech and press," Brennan cited ten cases from *Ex Parte Jackson* in 1877 through *Beauharnais v. Illinois* in 1952 to show that "this Court has always assumed that obscenity is not protected." From there, he moved into a minimalist history lesson, spending four sentences establishing the eighteenth-century origins of obscenity alongside blasphemy and profanity, all under the legal header of libel. After mentioning it once, Brennan downplayed blasphemy, dropping it out of the equation to note, "Thus, profanity and obscenity were related offenses."

Frankfurter's influence on this section shone through brightly. That preconstitutional understandings of freedom of speech at the state level "gave no absolute protection for every utterance" was a Frankfurtian observation, and to drive the thought home, Brennan returned to it in the next paragraph, summarizing his exposition thus far: "It is apparent that the unconditional phrasing of the First Amendment was not intended to protect every utterance." Eager to move past the history lesson, Brennan simply cited Frankfurter's *Beauharnais* opinion as the governing precedent. His only direct reference to the national founding era was a 1774 letter from the Continental Congress to the people of Quebec, which outlined the "importance" of freedom of the press as consisting, "besides the advancement of truth, science, morality, and arts in general," primarily in its "ready communication of thoughts between subjects."

As Brennan read the letter's implications, freedom of speech and press "was fashioned to assure unfettered interchange of ideas for the bringing about of political and social changes desired by the people." Even more than "political and social changes," the *ideas* occupied the core of Brennan's thought and formed the dividing line between protected and unprotected expression. In the next paragraph, Brennan delivered the statement that defined his obscenity doctrine. "All ideas having even the slightest redeeming social importance – unorthodox ideas, controversial ideas, even ideas hateful to the prevailing climate of opinion," he wrote, "have the full protection" of the First Amendment. But "implicit in the history of the First Amendment" – a history he had not, in any meaningful way, established – "is the rejection of obscenity as utterly without redeeming social importance." As such, "We hold that obscenity is not within the area of constitutionally protected speech or press."

Those assertions, the heart of *Roth*, locked into place with an almost syllogistic logic. Brennan wanted a legal algorithm, one with a neutral rubric through which alleged obscenity could be assessed, and at least in the abstract, he had it. Yet this sleek rhetorical surface smoothed over serious semantic stumbling blocks. *Ideas* were an odd peg on which to hang such importance, especially since only a decade ago the Court had explicitly declared, "We do not accede to . . . suggestion that the constitutional protection for a free press applies only to the exposition of ideas" in *Winters v. New York*. Even if obscenity did lack what scholars would call "ideational content," it remained unclear why a mere lack of social importance would be worse than "hateful" ideas that did have that content.

Further, Brennan clearly linked the "redeeming social importance" to the "bringing about of political and social changes desired by the people" that he had found described in the 1774 Continental Congress letter. Yet for decades Samuel Roth's books had called for social changes that would legitimize various sexual desires and behaviors; even the government's own briefs had acknowledged that "pornography" could cause social change. And that these ideas were "desired by the people" found no stronger evidence than Roth's three decades of financial sustenance. Clearly, Americans wanted access to these materials, as witnessed in their continuous purchasing of them, which spoke louder than any verbal declarations of morality.

None of this found traction with Brennan, who maintained an austere legal formalism in his opinion. To this point, precisely the halfway mark, *Roth* reeked of outcome-based reasoning, justifying the exclusion of obscenity from First Amendment protection even if the doctrinal movement had to occur on an abstract plain safely preserved from the messy realm of facts. In a further mark of apparent conservatism, not to mention indebtedness to Frankfurter, Brennan dispensed with the clear and present danger test in a remarkably offhanded manner. Evidence linking obscenity to "anti-social conduct" was moot, since "obscenity is not protected speech." Without further ado, Brennan simply brushed aside a major and carefully developed civil libertarian argument, again quoting Frankfurter's *Beauharnais* opinion for authority.

For all this, Brennan had no intention of facilitating censorship and suppression. He fashioned himself a liberal, and in the second half of *Roth* he set out to ensure that the very constitutional framework he had just outlined would remain restrictive and careful in its application, preventing any future Comstocks from asserting power. The astute legal historian Lucas Powe notes of Brennan's jurisprudence that he often "embraced a technique of conceding in principle to the government's power to pursue its objective, while simultaneously making it extraordinarily difficult for the government to do so." *Roth* certainly fit this mold.

If the first half of *Roth* was hasty and conservative, the second, liberal half announced itself boldly. "However," Brennan began, pausing briefly after having vanquished the clear and present danger test, "sex and obscenity are not synonymous. . . . The portrayal of sex, *e.g.*, in art, literature, and scientific works, is not sufficient reason to deny material the constitutional protection of freedom of speech and press."

What Brennan here invoked was presumably the expanded heterosexual pleasures that had been legitimized by sexual liberalism's half-century-long movement into the mainstream. Calling sex "a great and mysterious motive force in human life," he noted that it "has indisputably been a subject of absorbing interest to mankind through the ages; it is one of the vital problems of human interest and public concern." The phrasing of "public concern" put Brennan's opinion in line with the 1940 *Thornhill v. Alabama* precedent, where Frank Murphy had used that language to ground his powerful First Amendment defense of labor activism; considering that not even Hugo Black had seemed to think sexual matters qualified as holding public significance when Roth appealed to the Court in 1949, this acknowledgment of sex as a public concern showed the modern, progressive spin Brennan put on obscenity doctrine. Sexual discourse was unambiguously included in freedom of speech.

Yet at a time when Alfred Kinsey's influential work fought so hard to demystify sex, Brennan's retreat to the poetic language of "mystery" operated as an evasion, a refusal to confront the overt advocacy of obscenity law as a form of sexual policing the government had offered in its briefs. In *Roth*, the links between sex and morality, as Brennan saw them, would remain obscure. Brennan subsumed this tension into the phrase "prurient interest," which became his boundary for where depictions of sex shaded into obscenity. Exactly what prurient interest was, Brennan did not quite say. His early drafts of *Roth* simply took its definition for granted. Later, he added a footnote, reading, "I.e., material having a tendency to excite lustful thoughts." The footnote went on to quote *Webster's New International Dictionary*, which declared prurience to include "itching; longing; uneasy with desire or longing; of persons, having itching, morbid, or lascivious longings," with "lewd" also appended. Brennan then equated this with the American Law Institute's recently devised Model Penal Code definition of obscenity, where prurient interest was comprised of "a shameful or morbid interest in nudity, sex, or excretion."

Visible between the lines of this thicket of verbiage was Brennan's earnest desire to standardize obscenity through some formal test that would displace obscenity from the realm of the moralists and situate it in a manner more akin to the social sciences, with objective, neutral criteria. But footnote 20, with its wide-ranging, open-ended definition of "prurient interest," belied these aspirations, its references to lustfulness, morbidity, shame, and "itching" coming quite literally out of Anthony Comstock's lexicon. By banishing this all to a footnote, Brennan could downplay this lineage, but the ghost of Comstock haunted *Roth*.

Nonetheless, Brennan persisted in his embrace of liberalization. His constitutional borderline secured, he at last offered the newly official Supreme Court test for obscenity: "whether, to the average person, applying contemporary community standards, the dominant theme of the material, taken as a whole, appeals to prurient interest." Material that met this standard could safely be declared devoid of socially redeeming value. That this built off the important lower-court opinions of the past quarter century he acknowledged in a plump footnote whose citations included, ironically enough, Jerome Frank's concurrence in the 1949 *Roth v. Goldman* case that the Court had refused to take up. If *Butler*'s undermining of the old *Hicklin* test had not been obvious enough, Brennan added for effect that it "must be rejected as unconstitutionally restrictive" of free speech.

With this, a new doctrine was born — or, more accurately, a long-standing doctrine of the federal courts was belatedly ratified. The final section of *Roth* addressed the other constitutional issues, such as vagueness and the Tenth Amendment, raised by Roth's and Alberts's attorneys, giving only glancing attention before Brennan arrived at his curt conclusion: "The judgments are affirmed."

Justices typically circulate working drafts of opinions within the Court to solicit feedback and, more to the point, to negotiate content and phrasing to form and keep majorities. Brennan ran a tight ship on *Roth*, and his records reflect fairly minimal assistance from the other justices. In a memorandum to Brennan five days before the final draft, Harold Burton suggested cutting a gratuitous eight-page appendix from a British case and added, "I agree with your opinion" — a telling sign of its doctrinal positioning. For, while Brennan saw himself carefully balancing long-held understandings of obscene materials as outside the law with the modernizing imperatives of sexual liberalism, the constituency of his five-justice coalition told a different story. Burton, Tom Clark, Charles Whittaker, and Felix Frankfurter gave Brennan his majority, and collectively they unquestionably represented the conservative wing of the Court on First Amendment issues (Warren concurred separately). Brennan could dress his opinion in liberal rhetoric, but in a doctrinal sense, *Roth* offered a clear victory to the Court's conservative wing.

Did that make Felix Frankfurter the invisible force behind *Roth*? The elder justice was rightly famous for his manipulative machinations, and while relations between him and Brennan would shortly sour as Brennan recognized such efforts, in his early terms on the bench the new justice remained somewhat under Frankfurter's spell. Frankfurter had gone after the clear and present danger test at oral arguments, and Brennan fulfilled his goal of disposing of it. Frankfurter's influence was also reflected in Brennan's citations of his opinions as precedents. Yet Brennan had brushed aside Frankfurter's suggestion that obscenity doctrine was already satisfactory as it stood, and *Roth* suggested a wider swath for sexual expression than Frank-furter had ever advocated. A more powerful force than Frankfurter was the backdrop of Cold War sexual politics, which so deeply satu-rated American life that it took on an ambient, invisible quality. That sexual expression was awash in ideas, and inherently political, both the governmental briefs and the entire decade's state policies made unde-niably clear. But if democracy rested on a "marketplace of ideas," dis-sident, "deviant" sexuality was simply not to be afforded access to that marketplace — and in the process, it was thus defined out of existence.

Fifteen years before the feminist movement would assert that the personal was political, the Cold War state had clearly assumed it, but then concealed that assumption in a set of loaded words designed to force an apparent cleavage between the personal and the perverted. "Prurience" was William Brennan's contribution to that lexicon, join-ing such companions as *degeneracy*, *lasciviousness*, *morbidity*, and their companions in performing the invisible ideological labor of sexual regulation. Nothing prurient could contain an idea, the doctrine declared — at least, not a socially important one. In this belief, Bren-nan stood in good liberal company. "Social importance," after all, had been ACLU member and intellectual free-speech theorist Alexander Meiklejohn's criterion in the 1940s, so Brennan was hardly at odds with the liberal establishment. The Supreme Court rarely ventures too far beyond prevailing opinion, and *Roth* provides one clear exam-ple of its desire to remain within social consensus.

The most bitter irony of Brennan's opinion, though, was that it devised a test for obscenity under which Samuel Roth, had it been used at the trial court level, would almost surely have been exoner-ated — and then refused on procedural grounds to apply it. Whatever condemnations might be delivered of *American Aphrodite* or *Good Times*, neither could accurately be called completely lacking in redeeming social importance, and even the government had distin-guished their "borderline" qualities from "hard core" pornography. Similar arguments could be made for David Alberts, but at least he received the consolation of a mere two-month sentence; with no fur-ther recourse within the judicial system, Roth's five-year sentence was now a certainty.

Diverging Angles on Obscenity:
The Concurrences

With its solid five-justice bloc, Brennan's majority opinion in *Roth* became binding doctrine. Not every justice agreed with its logic, though, and Chief Justice Warren and Associate Justice Harlan offered concurrences based on alternative groundings for obscenity law. Warren's took a more conservative tack that shifted focus from the texts themselves to the actions of the accused. It carried little immediate influence in 1957 but would return to wider Court favor a decade later. Harlan, on the other hand, as the only justice to give substantive attention to distinctions between state and federal laws, delved into questions Brennan clearly preferred to avoid.

As chief justice, Earl Warren lent his name to "the Warren Court," widely (and rightly) renowned as the most progressive assemblage of justices in national history. *Brown v. Board* in 1954 merely gave a taste of the civil liberties revolution to follow, especially in the next decade. Indeed, Dwight Eisenhower famously described his nomination of Warren as "the biggest damn fool thing I ever did," after he selected the career moderate Republican precisely because he expected no waves. On matters of sexual politics, though, Warren's personal conservatism had shaded his politics since his early career as a prosecutor, and this carried into his jurisprudence. He was, as even friend and ally William Brennan later said, a "terrible prude."

Warren wholeheartedly agreed with the majority on excepting obscenity from the First Amendment. In a memo to the brethren, he called obscenity an "abuse of freedom rather than a protected right." Yet, as a former prosecutor, he also showed wariness toward the ways obscenity laws were executed. His brief concurrence restated the facts of the cases, then substantively began by highlighting the "mistakes of the past" in using obscenity laws against "great art or literature, scientific treatises, or works exciting social controversy." The "line dividing the salacious or pornographic from literature or science," he claimed, "is not straight and unwavering."

To reconcile his moralism with this critique, Warren shifted the terrain: "It is not the book that is on trial; it is a person." In his view, the *conduct* of the defendant was the crucial determinant. *Content* was relevant to this, insofar as it provided context, but secondary to *scienter*, a legal term describing action done "knowingly." As Warren noted, the California law in *Alberts* penalized possession and selling done "willfully and lewdly," while in Roth's federal case the judge had instructed the jury that Roth's actions needed to be "calculated" to convict. Both defendants "openly advertised to appeal to the erotic interest of their customers," Warren wrote. Being "plainly engaged in the commercial exploitation of the morbid and shameful craving for materials with prurient effect," both could be constitutionally punished for their conduct without the need for Brennan's obscenity test.

Warren's concurrence found little support in 1957. His opinion ran only five paragraphs and did not outline an actual method for judging obscene conduct. The two key points Warren raised, though—conduct and *scienter*—would reverberate through the obscenity debates of the next decade.

John Marshall Harlan also prefigured certain aspects of much-later developments in his unique opinion. The only justice to take seriously the question of federalism, Harlan resisted facile placement on the liberal/conservative spectrum. Harlan had used his power as a justice to grant Samuel Roth bail in October 1956 after trial judge Cashin had refused, allowing Roth to prepare his case after several months in jail. The act didn't necessarily signal personal sympathy for the publisher of dubious repute, but it did ultimately foretell Harlan's vote. While the other justices saw Roth's federal case, based on the First Amendment, and Alberts's state case, based on the Fourteenth Amendment's incorporation of the First Amendment, as effectively equivalent, Harlan found in them two distinct constitutional questions. Concurring in *Alberts*, he dissented in *Roth*, the only justice to split his vote.

Harlan began with a critique of the generalizations necessitated by creating a distinct class of "obscene" materials without reviewing the materials in question for each case. Juries, he noted, might still find Joyce's *Ulysses* or Boccaccio's *Decameron* obscene, and by the approach utilized in *Roth*, the Court would have upheld the convictions as matters of fact already decided. As well, Brennan's opinion conflated the California state law and the federal law, two distinct statutes, into "one indiscriminate potpourri"; to Harlan, they at least deserved individual consideration.

Moving first into *Alberts*, Harlan strongly concurred. Taking a restrictive stance on the Court's "narrow" role in reviewing state leg-islation under the Fourteenth Amendment, he employed a rational basis test at odds with the general tenor of the Court's valorization of free speech as a "preferred" constitutional liberty—which had been oft expressed and assumed, but never quite solidified as doctrine. It was "not our function" to question the law's wisdom, Harlan wrote, only whether it had a rational basis, suggesting that sexual materials to him were not "essential to a fundamental scheme of ordered lib-erty," the semi-official standard the Court had used since 1937 to deter-mine whether it should apply the more demanding "strict scrutiny" standard of review. To Harlan, not only did the state have a "legiti-mate interest in protecting the privacy of the home against invasion of unsolicited obscenity," but "the domain of sexual morality is pri-marily a matter of state concern." This framework left little hope for Alberts's case, but Harlan went a step beyond the other justices, giv-ing an "independent perusal of the material involved," as he had sug-gested was proper. He found no *ideas* "in any proper sense of that term" in the publications—and with that, gave his assent to *Alberts*.

On *Roth*, however, Harlan took a radically different position. Often considered a moderate conservative, Harlan in *Roth* relied on his fed-eralism to argue boldly against federal obscenity powers altogether. This time, the First Amendment was at stake, presenting to Harlan an issue of "quite a different order" from *Alberts*. Harlan flatly rejected the notion that the Fourteenth Amendment incorporated the First "in any literal sense," meaning that state and federal powers differed. As he had suggested, the then-forty-eight states had broad leeway to act as "experimental social laboratories" on matters of policy. Using *Lady Chatterley's Lover* as an example, he suggested it might not be "wise or desirable" for a state to suppress it, but it was "at least acceptable," pos-ing "no overwhelming danger" to constitutional rights. For the fed-eral government to do so, on the other hand, "seems to me to be intol-erable, and violative of both the letter and spirit of the First Amendment."

In an early draft, Harlan took a sweeping stance, categorically writ-ing, "The federal government has no powers in the area of sexual morality." His final version toned this down, but only slightly. Con-gress had "no substantive power over sexual morality," while "such powers as the federal government has in this field" he termed "but incidental to its other powers." As such, the "federal interest in protecting the Nation against pornography" he labeled "attenuated."

While doctrinally striking, Harlan's opinion was more about the balance of power between state and federal government than about free speech proper. Diminishing federal obscenity policing to virtually nil (though he did cryptically suggest that "hard core" pornography might be properly targeted, without elaborating), Harlan's doctrine would nonetheless have actually *facilitated* censorship, allowing free rein at the state level, which, as witnessed in previous chapters, was almost universally more stringent than the federal level. His notion of turning power back to the states, like Warren's ideas, found no favor at the time, but would await the coalescing of a more conservative court in the 1970s before making something of a return.

————

Free-Speech Absolutism:
Douglas Dissents

The annoyance Douglas had felt at conference carried over into his dissent. With comrade Hugo Black signing on in support, Douglas delivered a robust polemic sparing the Court no criticism of its new doctrine. The core of Douglas and Black's First Amendment doctrine remained a free-speech absolutism rejecting any suppression on expression that fell short of actual criminal action, and they applied this to sexual expression as well.

In the vein of his old friend Jerome Frank, Douglas began with a reminder that "punishment is inflicted for thoughts provoked, not for overt acts nor antisocial conduct." Even the "ill-starred *Dennis* case," he noted, "conceded that speech, to be punishable, must have some relation to action which could be penalized by government." Obscenity lacked even that ostensible logic. The "arousing of sexual thoughts and desires happens every day in normal life in dozens of ways." Why was obscene material so uniquely targeted, as opposed to the numerous other sources of stimulation, from advertising to fashion? Douglas had no answer.

Douglas's dissent hammered at Brennan's opinion, presenting it as unthinking, knee-jerk conservatism that "gives the censor free range over a vast domain" — Brennan's obvious worry, and thus his Achilles' heel. "If we were certain that impurity of sexual thoughts impelled to action," Douglas continued, the Court would be on "less dangerous ground" in criminalizing obscenity. But in the absence of such evidence, sexual materials were singled out in a unique and unconstitutional manner. Would the "common conscience of the community," which Brennan at one point cited, "be an acceptable one if religion, economics, politics or philosophy were involved"? Douglas thought not and wondered, "How does it become a constitutional standard when literature treating sex is concerned?"

Calling Brennan's framework "community censorship in its worst form," Douglas accused it of creating "a regime where, in the battle between the literati and the Philistines, the Philistines are certain to win." He was willing to grant that Congress held power to "proscribe *conduct* on the grounds of good morals," but did not follow Warren in considering the sale of books and pictures as itself actionable conduct. Douglas's examples instead included "nudity in public places, adultery, and other phases of sexual misconduct."

Because they do not bear the burden of elaborating binding doctrine or precedent, dissents are often written with an eye toward the public and in the hope of influencing other justices in the future. Douglas reflected awareness of public sentiment in his revisions. "I can understand (and even at times sympathize) with programs of civic groups and church groups to protect and defend the existing moral standards of the community," he declared, rather insincerely; an earlier version had read, "I can tolerate (though not respect) the activities of busybodies who seek to impose their own morality on others," more indicative of his actual feelings (another deleted sentence, discussing community standards and juries, had tellingly noted, "The more bigoted, the more puritanical, the more perverse the twelve men, the greater the reach of the censor"). The point Douglas wished to make was that such moral activism stood distinct from obscenity law, which enlisted the government on its behalf and thus violated the First Amendment. Moralists still had their right to moralize, he insisted.

As he moved toward his conclusions, Douglas threw in a few last digs at the majority. Calling obscenity "unlike the law of libel" in that "there is no special historical evidence that literature dealing with sex was intended to be treated in a special manner by those who drafted the First Amendment," he hit at two points. First, Brennan's thin historical evidence of its own accord acknowledged that no American obscenity cases could even be located before 1821. Second, the link between obscenity and libel had been "wrongly relied on in *Beauharnais*" — the 1952 opinion by Douglas's longtime adversary Frankfurter, which Brennan had cited repeatedly. For that matter, Brennan had also cited William Lockhart and Robert McClure's article "Literature, the Law of Obscenity, and the Constitution" at Douglas's request, but to different effect. Douglas cited the article to show the foolishness of obscenity law, while Brennan used it to underscore the importance of strict and exacting judicial standards for it (on this, Brennan was unquestionably closer to the spirit of the influential article).

In closing, Douglas reached his own, by now familiar, First Amendment doctrine. The amendment's reach, by its own literal language, was "absolute." Douglas had seen the clear and present danger test watered down, then rejected, and his movement in the opposite direction had taken him to a position slightly beyond that envisioned by Louis Brandeis in the 1920s. Speech, expression, or the press could "be suppressed if, and to the extent that, it is so closely brigaded with illegal action as to be an inseparable part of it." Defending this stance by situating it in an implicitly democratic marketplace of ideas, Douglas concluded, "I have the same confidence in the ability of our people to reject noxious literature as I have in their capacity to sort out the true from the false in theology, economics, politics, or any other field." With this, Douglas also subtly invoked the Cold War context, since the Court had now placed prurience alongside communism as mental terrain apparently too dangerous for unfettered public access.

Roth Received

Two other opinions delivered the same day drew little notice but shed further light on *Roth*. In *Kingsley Books v. Brown*, the Court upheld a New York statute allowing authorities to use a "limited injunctive remedy" against pornography by having a judge find it obscene and then barring sales. This tactic had been used against several volumes of the sexually themed comic *Nights of Horror*, and distributors argued it constituted an unconstitutional prior restraint, citing the 1931 *Near v. Minnesota* as precedent. Writing for a bare majority, Felix Frankfurter found the differences with *Near* "glaring," since that case involved pre-publication bans on nonobscene material. He declared the injunctive relief better for booksellers than criminal prosecution. Delicately dodging the fact that the injunctions allowed for literal state-sponsored book burnings, Frankfurter resorted to dry legalisms, writing, "Section 22-a's provision for the seizure and destruction of the instruments of ascertained wrongdoing expresses resort to a legal remedy sanctioned by the long history of Anglo-American law."

The other companion case involved a burlesque theater in Newark, New Jersey, where the city had implemented a new ordinance in early 1956 against theatrical performances involving either naked bodies or the "illusion of nudeness." A state court had held the ordinance unconstitutionally broad, but it was overturned by the New Jersey Supreme Court, which absorbed the ordinance into an existing obscenity law. Without any comment, the Supreme Court offered a per curiam affirmation, citing *Kingsley Books* and *Roth*.

The *Roth/Alberts/Kingsley/Adams Newark Theater* quartet revealed the gravitational center of the Court's position; though Brennan had written the key doctrinal expression in *Roth*, in fact the five-justice bloc of Frankfurter, Clark, Burton, Whittaker, and Harlan had truly set the parameters, supporting suppression in all cases except Harlan's isolated dissent in *Roth* (which was grounded less in free-speech concerns than in his federalism that reserved expansive censorship powers to the states). Black and Douglas dissented without opinion in *Adams Newark Theater*, with Brennan recusing himself because the case heavily depended on competing interpretations of his own earlier obscenity ruling as a New Jersey Supreme Court justice.

All three, plus Warren, dissented in *Kingsley Books*, with the chief justice calling Frankfurter's bluff on a situation that "savors too much of book burning." Douglas issued a predictably acerbic opinion claiming, "Free speech is not to be regulated like diseased cattle and impure butter," but the critical dissent in *Kingsley* was Brennan's. Frankfurter had happily cited *Roth* in his majority opinion, thus allowing Brennan little leisure time to bask in the illusion that his personal taste for liberalization would necessarily prevail in obscenity cases. His terse dissent hinged on the "fatal defect" of lacking jury trials in the determination of obscenity, but what *Kingsley* really reflected was the almost immediate realignment on the bench that left Brennan siding with his own critics from *Roth*. Exactly what this portended for obscenity doctrine to come remained very unclear in June 1957.

Overshadowing all of the obscenity cases were the series of communism cases handed down a week earlier, which collectively nullified *Dennis* without directly overturning it. The most important case involved fourteen California Communist Party leaders convicted under the Smith Act. Though the circumstances seemed nearly identical to those of *Dennis*, the Court this time reversed their convictions. In a convoluted opinion, Harlan offered a belabored semantic analysis of the verb *organize*, ultimately concluding "advocacy and teaching of forcible overthrow as an abstract principle" was allowable speech. In other cases, the Court reversed contempt convictions for a New Hampshire professor and a labor organizer who had refused to cooperate with a state antisubversive investigation and the House Un-American Activities Committee, respectively.

Dwarfed by the explosive reactions to "Red Monday," as the media dubbed it, press response to *Roth* faded slightly into the background. *Time* devoted a cover story to the Court's "new direction" in the Cold War cases, but ran a shorter, primarily descriptive column on *Roth* the next week. Mainstream opinion of *Roth* generally found little to celebrate. The *Washington Post*, for instance, warned that Brennan's doctrine was "bound to disquiet a great many citizens" and hoped that, "in subsequent opinions, the Supreme Court will define more clearly the point beyond which the wish to protect the weak from bad literature may not trespass upon the normal citizen's right to read what he pleases."

In West Virginia, the *Charleston Daily Mail* ran not one, but two, consecutive editorials on *Roth*. The first time, it disparaged Brennan's distinction between sex and prurience. "The difficulties with this," the paper declared, "we would have thought, would have been apparent to any sophomore in logic." The next day, the paper returned to the topic, finding Cold War confusion in the Court's defense of communist expression but suppression of sexual materials. "Between Propaganda and Trash," the editorial's title ran, "the Court Draws a Line Which is Plain Invisible." Of prurient interest, it mused, "whatever that is."

The warmest reception for *Roth* came from the Catholic press, where Harold Gardiner mused in *America* that it would be "welcomed by those who favor some form of censorship." Straining a bit, he also found "frequent echoes" of canon law in Brennan's opinion, an interpretation the Catholic justice would surely not welcome, given the pressure placed on Catholic public officials to govern, legislate, or rule in nonsectarian ways (a strain witnessed most vividly a few years later during John F. Kennedy's successful presidential campaign).

Indeed, one concerned citizen had written to Justice Harlan to express concern that Brennan "seems to be intent on doing what he thinks is right regardless of what the Constitution says." "I hold no prejudice against Catholics as such," the man assured, but "history strongly indicates that in general they are inclined toward an authoritarianism that is incompatible with democracy." From the reverse angle, a Rhode Island woman from the Newport Citizens' Committee on Literature, a pro-censorship group with ties to the Knights of Columbus and Catholic Daughters of America, wrote to Brennan thanking him. "Most of us were encouraged by the *Roth* decision," she explained, confirming that his effort to distinguish sex from obscenity carried less impact than his distinguishing of obscenity from protected speech.

This was exactly what civil libertarians feared, though they were slow to regroup. *Roth* had demolished the clear and present danger test, leaving free-speech defenders reeling. A Connecticut ACLU member wrote to the *Nation* in September, warning of the "new wave of puritanical moralism" the decision threatened to engender and wondering why it had "slipped by with little comment from the liberal organs of opinion." When the ACLU did issue its annual report for 1957, it bemoaned *Roth*, blaming it for an increase in censorial activity and worrying that one "most unfortunate" outcome might be the necessity of drafting a "geographical atlas of the United States indicating 'obscenity sensitivity,' something along the lines of the annual rainfall index."

Scholarly commentators weighed in more slowly, bound by the delayed publication cycles of academic journals. When they did reach print, their words offered little applause. One of the earliest scholarly assessments to reach print was Henry Foster's *Journal of Criminal Law, Criminology, and Police Science* article in the fall of 1957. Foster delivered an almost unmitigated riposte to Brennan's opinion, calling it "evident that the due process requirement of definiteness is being sacrificed because it is felt that the public interest in suppressing trash is more important than advance notice of what the law permits and condemns." Identifying Felix Frankfurter as the secret "key Justice" of Court obscenity doctrine, Foster called *Roth* an "indulgence in word magic" that would encourage censors. Brennan's social importance test, he wrote, *appeared* liberal but in fact proved useless since much smut "obviously" held *some* social importance. In Foster's eyes, Brennan had merely given a rhetorically liberal gloss to a fundamentally conservative and repressive legal standard.

As the law reviews turned their eye toward *Roth*, the sharpness of the language waned a bit from Foster's aggressive condemnation, but many of his main points continued reverberating. *Duke Law Journal* found that Brennan's opinion "creates some confusion as to just what the standard is," with which the *Vanderbilt Law Review* concurred, also calling *Roth* "somewhat confusing." The latter journal went on to call Douglas's dissent a "convincing argument showing the futility of obscenity laws." *Harvard Law Review* hesitantly offered that the opinion "seems correct in concluding that obscenity is itself so anti-social, or at least is so devoid of any social value, that the legislature does not need a further justification to proscribe it," so long as cases remained limited to "hardcore pornography." But even in that article Brennan could find little refuge, since it went on to downplay his doctrine in favor of the "desirable" suggestions of Warren and Harlan.

Other endorsements likewise couched themselves in trepidation, with *Temple Law Quarterly* arguing Brennan's definition of obscenity "seems to approach acceptability." In the *Ohio State Law Review*, Charles Taylor offered optimism that *Roth* would restrict censors in practice, but acknowledged that "any test which is premised on thoughts provoked, rather than overt acts induced, latently possesses all the seeds of indiscriminate application that had prevailed under the *Hicklin* regime." *Roth* constituted a "progressive step forward," Taylor concluded, but still finished his note with a critique that the "boldest step remains to be taken," with the restoration of the clear and present danger test, the "only standard which adequately protects freedom of expression."

Meanwhile, partisans on both ends of the free-speech spectrum took simultaneous aim at Brennan. In the *Michigan Law Review*, Roth's defense attorney O. John Rogge contributed a lengthy two-part historical essay, built on some of the research from the Roth team's Supreme Court briefs. Linking the obscenity cases to *Dennis* and other suppressive political decisions, Rogge unsurprisingly found the Supreme Court to have acted against the intentions of the Constitution, which bestowed no such federal power. Like Roth's briefs, much of Rogge's argument hinged on episodes that preceded the post–Civil War reconfiguration of federalism, undermining its persuasive power. But Rogge's impressive research base did allow for some effective jabs at Brennan's underwhelming historical evidence. Buried in a footnote, Rogge noted that Brennan's citation of three early obscenity cases included *Knowles v. State*, an 1808 indecency case in which the conviction had actually been reversed on appeal, as well as a 1798 New Jersey statute that "prohibited stage performances but did not deal with obscenity." With clear satisfaction, Rogge wrote of Brennan's historical discussion, "It would thus seem that the Court's statement is somewhat too broad."

From the other end of the aisle, Brooklyn Law School professor Joseph Rubenstein in the *Brooklyn Law Review* took a doctrinaire Catholic stance, declaring that the collected opinions "all seem to miss the nub of the whole matter: morality." Returning to a central theme of the domestic Cold War, he continued, "it is morality that will make or break us, not the stock markets or sputniks." Since Brennan went to such great lengths to distance himself from the overt moralizing of the past, Rubenstein found his stance more similar to than different from Black and Douglas's amoral absolutism, in its carefully rationalized secularity.

Of course, no one was as unsatisfied by *Roth* as its disgruntled appellants. After his Supreme Court loss, Alberts largely vanished from the historical record. One of the very few traces he left behind is a 1964 letter to his lawyer, Stanley Fleishman. Since his case, Alberts wrote, he and his wife had moved into real estate investment and "are no longer connected in any way with mail order business." An attached credit report confirmed the claim.

Samuel Roth was left staring down more dire circumstances in his five-year sentence. Desperate and pathetic, he resorted to contacting the FBI, offering to move to Mexico, infiltrate the leftist expatriate community there, and essentially spy "for the benefit of our national security." Recognizing it as a transparent ruse to obtain freedom, the

FBI ignored Roth's offer. Meanwhile, sent back to the same penitentiary in Lewisburg, Pennsylvania, that had held him for three years in the late 1930s, Roth was deprived of a typewriter, causing him "considerable anguish of mind," as his daughter-in-law wrote to the director of prisons. Finally, in May 1958 he was allowed access to writing materials to compose a book called *My Life with Jesus*, though only upon signing a waiver giving the prison authorities permission to monitor his writing; even behind bars, Roth's publications remained under the eye of the law. His prison correspondence with his wife took on plaintive tones. "I'm in a bad way, Peggy," he wrote in the autumn of 1958, with several years still remaining on his sentence.

Roth focused much of his incarcerated energy on challenging his conviction. Self-composing a lengthy stream of briefs and motions, Roth first blamed his own lawyers, as was his tendency dating back to the *Jews Must Live* debacle of the mid-1930s. He complained of a conspiracy in which they "receded into a line of conduct so perverse that they became blind instruments in the total degradation of the legal process." That Roth abandoned legalistic writing for nearly pulp-like prose did not help his case, nor did the absence of evidence for his multiple conspiracy theories (not terribly removed from, though less anti-Semitic than, the ones he had offered two decades earlier in *Jews Must Live*). Unfortunately for him, this helped obscure some of the more salient points he managed to raise, particularly the borderline status of his publications, which the government itself had acknowledged, as distinct from the "hardcore" category; as well, Roth's charge that his lawyers had failed to call for direct review of his books and circulars themselves in their briefs. This was not a trivial point, given its punitive consequences, and especially considering that the Court was doing just this with other censored books, magazines, and films.

Original trial judge John Cashin reviewed Roth's motions and offered little solace, roundly dismissing them as "wild allegations" in 1959. By that point, obscenity doctrine had moved on, and multiple concurrent readings of *Roth v. U.S.* had begun to shift its meaning in divergent ways. Brennan's worst fears would be realized to the west, where a Catholic lawyer in Cincinnati most brilliantly harnessed *Roth* for its censorial power. Charles Keating had observed the dwindling social influence of the Legion of Decency and National Organization for Decent Literature in the 1950s. Emanating partly out of traditional anti-Catholic prejudice, the shift in cultural positioning more specifically sprang from the sectarian, undemocratic nature of the groups' methods; in a Cold War America desperate to contrast itself to the Russians, boycotts, ban lists, and undue private influence over culture all left the groups looking retrograde. "Obscenity," though, provided a legalistic, constitutional, rational basis for suppressing texts, standing discernibly separate from stuffy old moralism or uncouth group-pressure tactics.

Enforcement of obscenity laws would provide the key platform of Keating's Citizens for Decent Literature, which emerged from the ashes of the fading Catholic groups to extend their substantive missions through extensive grassroots activism over the course of the next decade. At the same time, *Roth* also proved a crucial turning point in what would be labeled "the sexual revolution." Brennan's distinction of sex from obscenity opened the floodgates to a new wave of increasingly graphic sexuality in books, movies, and magazines. Already by 1959, Samuel Roth could angrily write from his prison cell, "I ALONE DID NOT BENEFIT BY THE DECISION IN MY CASE," and he was not wrong.

Much of the 1960s would consist of a protracted fleshing out of the critical tensions of *Roth*. What his critics rarely acknowledged was that William Brennan's conflicted opinion really embodied not so much his own intellectual limitations (beyond, perhaps, being a product of his times), but rather larger, deeper historical tensions within American sexual politics. A green light had been given to punish and suppress obscenity; an equally bright light of the same color gave the go-ahead to ever more direct representations of sex, as long as they carried the critical redeeming social importance to justify themselves. In this sense, Brennan's *Roth* opinion didn't just coincide with the sexual revolution — it helped spawn it and also contain it.

CHAPTER 8

The Two *Roth*s

Liberalization, Regulation, and
the Apparent Paradox of Obscenity in the 1960s

Sending Samuel Roth to prison for five years was a rather inauspicious way to commence the project of obscenity liberalization. Yet this is precisely what *Roth* spearheaded; an opinion that fell well into the conservative range within the spectrum of doctrinal possibilities before the Court in 1957 quickly revealed itself as an instrument of opening culture to a new rush of films, books, and magazines addressing sexual matters in ever more direct manners. From the start, it seemed *Roth* had two faces, a conservative one that drew rebukes from the Court's free-speech wing, and a liberal one that sharply curtailed the deployment of obscenity laws.

On the latter front, *Roth* played a crucial role in setting in motion what general cultural memory recalls as "the sexual revolution." Historians have called that phrase into question, noting the lengthy trajectory of sexual change generated by capitalism, urbanization, and other forces — as well as the limits of the "revolution." The sexual contests of the 1960s did amass into a particularly visceral constellation, though, including everything from the birth control pill to the increasing visibility of the gay and lesbian rights movements. Sexuality at least *seemed* liberated, unbound.

Roth undergirded this framework, providing expanding freedoms but also the borders within which those freedoms were contained. More graphic, more explicit depictions of sex and sexuality were allowable under its tenets, but prurience remained unprotected by the First Amendment — and remained a murky concept applied to those forms of sexual expression that fell outside normalcy. Samuel Roth would not be the last person imprisoned for publishing material officially deemed prurient.

Obscenity doctrine fit well alongside other important Supreme Court cases involving contraceptive access, interracial marriage, and abortion rights, all of which contributed to the sexual revolution while also fixing its parameters. The Court's sexual-rights doctrine, historian Marc Stein writes, was "not broadly libertarian or egalitarian." Instead, it created "special rights and privileges for adult, heterosexual, marital, monogamous, private, and procreative forms of sexual expression." This is exactly what scholars mean when they talk about "heteronormativity," which both equates heterosexuality with normalcy and *also* disciplines heterosexuality to conform to the model Stein describes. In other words, not only heterosexuality, but specific *kinds* of heterosexuality, reign supreme – the non-"prurient" kinds.

The obscenity doctrine William Brennan devised in *Roth* was profoundly heteronormative. The events it set in motion can be told as two separate stories, the two faces of *Roth*. In one narrative, the case spawned what opponents would call a "floodtide of filth," defending all sorts of publications that ranged from nudist magazines to hardcore pornographic films. If that represents the liberal side of *Roth*, it is matched by the conservative *Roth*, which allowed for the continued criminalization of obscene materials. This would send more people to prison and help mobilize a conservative political movement dedicated to rolling back the sexual revolution.

This chapter tells the parallel stories of the two *Roth*s. As paradoxical as they seem, their differences speak to the internal tensions of *Roth* itself. The liberal and the conservative complemented one another in Brennan's opinion, which expanded free speech while reinforcing its boundaries. Some focused on that expansion, others on policing those limits.

The two *Roth*s were, of course, one, reflecting the legacy of the tortured history chronicled in the earlier chapters. History, however, can afford to stay messy; Supreme Court doctrine cannot. *Roth* left a perplexing doctrinal wasteland from which Brennan could not emerge with consistency intact, even after a decade of refinement and revision.

Sex and the Singular Doctrine:
The Liberal *Roth*

If Brennan's 1957 opinion left concerned observers wondering about its implications, the Court wasted little time clarifying with action.

The next term saw a swift series of obscenity conviction reversals that cleared the path for nudist magazines, homosexual publications, and more adult cinema than the Hollywood studios were then producing. *Roth*, it suddenly seemed, promoted free expression after all. The first cases, in late 1957, involved the racy French film *Game of Love*, banned in Chicago, and a set of nudist magazines found obscene in Washington. The Court granted reprieves in per curiam opinions that simply invoked *Roth*, as it did again in early 1958 when it finally cleared *Sunshine and Health* from its years of legal travail.

That same day, January 13, 1958, it even strode onto the most intensely politicized sexual terrain of the decade, homosexuality. After postal inspectors and federal courts had found the pioneering gay-rights magazine *ONE* "obscene and filthy," despite its very self-conscious seriousness and respectability, the Supreme Court wordlessly reversed, again simply citing *Roth*. While the press largely ignored the case or discussed it in the shadows of the nudist magazine case, it was in fact a momentous occasion. *Roth* had been used to support the first gay-rights Supreme Court victory in U.S. history.

This liberal *Roth* could be seen filtering down to the lower courts almost immediately, as well. Only a week after Brennan handed down his opinion, the highest court of New York applied it to the state's film censorship organization, restricting its powers to those films deemed obscene. *Garden of Eden*, a film set at a nudist camp that featured no sex but plenty of undraped bodies (albeit without full-frontal nudity), qualified as *indecent*. It did not, the court ruled, qualify as *obscene*. The state censors' complaints notwithstanding, *Garden of Eden* was cleared for screening in New York, naked bodies and all. The next term, the Supreme Court reversed another New York ban, on a film of *Lady Chatterley's Lover*.

Technically, the Supreme Court plays only a reactive role, taking on cases that have already happened. Yet when it sends clear signals, on issues from school desegregation to economic regulation, it also effectively plays a generative role, structuring the realm of legal possibilities and inviting action. By the late 1950s, obscenity was one of those issues, and *Roth* inspired publishers to take new risks. Most significant among the new literary adventurers was Barney Rosset, whose Grove Press had spent the decade focused on experimental and avant-garde, as well as sexually themed, material. In 1959, with *Roth* very much in mind, Grove published an unexpurgated edition of *Lady Chatterley's Lover*, a bold gesture when even the much tamer film version was still facing its New York ban.

The Post Office predictably seized the book from the mails, but by 1960 Rosset won a decisive victory from a federal appellate court. Over three decades after D. H. Lawrence had written the book — and Samuel Roth had spent time behind bars on its account — American audiences could for the first time (at least, legally) read Lawrence's intended prose, with rugged gamekeeper Mellors telling the searching Constance Chatterley, "we fucked a flame into being." Rarely has a mass audience so flocked to what remained, at its heart, a modernist allegory for the British class system. Recognizing the once-obscene as a lucrative market, Rosset also sent into circulation boundary-pushing work from the past (John Cleland's oft-suppressed 1748 *Fanny Hill*, Henry Miller's 1934 *Tropic of Cancer*) and present (William Burroughs's grotesque surrealist fantasia *Naked Lunch*, full of willfully perverse queer sexuality). While legal battles, often at the local level, would follow Grove Press throughout the decade, the money it spent on lawyers paled in comparison to its highly visible, highly profitable endeavors.

As Grove and others tested the limits of free expression, the Court proved a reliable ally. For nearly a decade after *Roth*, it consistently reversed obscenity convictions, creating a protective legal environment for the harbingers of sexual revolution. *Manual Enterprises v. Day* in 1962 even offered yet another landmark victory for gay publications, clearing male physique magazines with nude photographs akin to those of women in straight-oriented works like *Playboy* for the mails.

By mid-decade, William Brennan had solidified his position as the Court's central architect of obscenity doctrine. *Jacobellis v. Ohio* in 1964 provided his major addendum to *Roth*, returning to its basic premises to expand and clarify upon them. The manager of a Cleveland art-house theater had been convicted of obscenity charges for screening *The Lovers*, directed by French New Wave pioneer Louis Malle. Though the film had won international acclaim, its depiction of extramarital sex went well beyond accepted Hollywood norms, including brief nudity and suggested oral sex. Ohio courts emphatically condemned the film, with the state supreme court memorably calling it "87 minutes of boredom induced by the vapid drivel appearing on screen and three minutes of complete revulsion during the showing of an act of perverted obscenity."

That the Ohio courts would be overturned in *Jacobellis* was a fait accompli, but the road to that end remained less certain. After some internal Court debate, Brennan's June 1964 opinion both reaffirmed and clarified *Roth*. The Court could not simply accept jury verdicts in obscenity cases, Brennan explained. Appealing as the notion was, since it would "lift from our shoulders a difficult, recurring, and unpleasant task," the constitutional stakes were too high to abrogate its duty of review. The Court, he asserted, had no choice but to retain its burden of "making an independent constitutional judgment on the facts of the case" in all First Amendment claims (a luxury it had not afforded Roth).

That the "contemporary community standards" test might refer to "the particular local community from which the case arises," Brennan bluntly disavowed as "an incorrect reading of *Roth*." The proper community should be "society at large." "It is, after all," Brennan wrote, drolly paraphrasing a famous quote from early-nineteenth-century Chief Justice John Marshall, "a national Constitution we are expounding." By those standards, Brennan opined, *The Lovers* fell short of obscenity. He ended with a strong reaffirmation of the *Roth* standards as still governing obscenity doctrine.

Brennan's opinion failed to satisfy everyone. As he had since *Roth*, Harlan continued to endorse wider latitude for states to experiment with obscenity laws. Clark and Warren dissented, as the chief justice broke with Brennan over the nature of community standards. To Warren, they ought to be local rather than national. Balancing this discontent, though, was the surprise movement of Justice Potter Stewart, not a prominent figure in the obscenity debates since his appointment in 1958, toward the Black/Douglas camp. While not quite joining them in complete free-speech absolutism, Stewart went beyond Brennan. In a brief concurrence containing what became his most-quoted line, Stewart restricted obscenity to only "hardcore pornography." "I shall not today attempt to define" the phrase, he added, "and perhaps I could never succeed in intelligibly doing so. But I know it when I see it, and the motion picture involved in this case is not it."

Stewart's quip lacked the searching depth of Brennan's inquiries and doctrines. It was also more honest. In the seven years since *Roth*, Brennan had shown his free-speech sympathies, had made obscenity laws ever more difficult to enforce, but had not succeeded in effectively defining obscenity in a way that proved consistent and predictable — or acknowledged his failure to do so. For those on the margins and borderlines of mainstream culture, every publication remained a gamble, even as the Court delivered another per curiam reversal the same day as *Jacobellis*, making clear that *Tropic of Cancer* could join *Lady Chatterley* on the Grove Press list of legally protected books.

Jacobellis coincided with the apex of what would be remembered as the Warren Court. Though Earl Warren had sat as chief justice since 1953, and though *Brown v. Board* marked a high-water point of mid-century liberalism, it was really with the 1962 appointment of Arthur Goldberg that a solid five-justice bloc of (generally) Warren, Brennan, Black, Douglas, and Goldberg (and then after 1965, his successor Abe Fortas) pushed the Court in a more aggressively liberal direction. In addition to continued support for the African American civil rights movement, the Warren Court heyday included revolutionizing the criminal justice system, expanding the rights of the accused in numerous ways.

Meanwhile, the Court endorsed an aspect of the sexual revolution in striking down a Connecticut anticontraceptive law in 1965. Douglas's lead opinion in *Griswold v. Connecticut* technically applied only to married couples, but it hinted at more expansive freedoms, locating an unenumerated constitutional right to privacy for the first time. "The specific guarantees of the Bill of Rights," Douglas wrote artfully (critics would say obscurely), "have penumbras, formed by emanations from those guarantees that give them life and substance."

The collective impact of the Warren Court's decisions was to put personal rights and liberties on a clear constitutional pedestal. The role of obscenity in this emerging legal and social paradigm remained less than perfectly clear, but as *Roth* approached its decade anniversary, Brennan signaled yet again his determination to reduce the scope of obscenity law to a bare minimum. John Cleland's long-prosecuted novel *Fanny Hill* (*Memoirs of a Woman of Pleasure*, officially) provided a perfect symbolic basis for a sweeping obscenity decision; Massachusetts had banned the book in 1821, and was still after it nearly a century and a half later. In a brief, almost brusque 1966 opinion, Brennan

188   { *Chapter 8* }

paved new ground. "A book cannot be proscribed unless it is found to be utterly without socially redeeming value," he wrote. "This is so even though the book is found to possess the requisite prurient appeal and to be patently offensive." Brennan had not quite overtly adopted Stewart's "hardcore pornography" standard, but his *Memoirs* opinion left little room for the prosecution of much else. A single smidgeon of socially redeeming value could rescue the most patently offensive work, it appeared. It wasn't 1821 anymore.

Indeed, while subsequent doctrinal and cultural directions will be discussed below, the *Memoirs* standards became something of a persistent running joke in sexualized texts, perhaps most iconically in Russ Meyer's graphic soft-core sex comedy *Vixen* (1968), which abruptly shifted gears at the end for a lengthy discussion about racism, Cold War politics, and other pertinent social issues. While *Vixen* actually subtly engages with sexual politics throughout, the structural joke of the final scene was understood by its audience. Film critic Roger Ebert, who thought it "the best film to date in that uniquely American film genre, the skin-flick," noted that it was deliberately "heavy on the redeeming social value department" – "no doubt," he added, "with one eye on the recent Supreme Court decisions that make *Vixen* possible."

Ebert's aside raised an important point. Before *Roth*, a film like *Vixen* could never have been shown in a legitimate movie theater. Even immediately after *Roth*, it would almost surely have met Brennan's criteria for constitutional suppression; Russ Meyer's gleeful prurience went well beyond Louis Malle's tasteful eroticism of *The Lovers*. Only after a decade during which the Court's obvious free-speech sympathies provided legitimization for cultural shifts already in motion could a casual movie review of *Vixen* in a mainstream newspaper even become thinkable. In this sense, the causal imprint of *Roth* on the cultural side of the sexual revolution was obvious, widely understood, and undeniable.

———

The Conservative *Roth* and
Sexual Border Patrol

Roth's liberalization was never complete *liberation*, and its conservative, suppressive side perpetually underscored its more visible public image. *Roth* paved the way for *Vixen*; it also sent Samuel Roth to prison. While culture quickly passed him by, with audiences more interested in the Grove Press's enticing new editions of books he once sold under the table than his own 600-page autobiography about his relationship with Jesus that he composed behind bars, Roth would not be the last person imprisoned for what he published.

It was not only Justice Douglas in dissent who saw *Roth* as bestowing on censors "free range over a vast domain." To Cincinnati lawyer Charles Keating, Brennan's legal formula for obscenity solved two pressing issues. First was the pervasiveness of smut. Even in Keating's conservative hometown, dirty magazines occupied the racks of drugstore and bus stop newsstands, luring readers with their salacious promises. *Roth* delivered a weapon against them. With the Supreme Court itself endorsing the prosecution of obscene materials, no hesitant local officials could claim the legal status of obscenity remained unclear.

But *what* the case did was almost less important than *how* it went about doing it — that is, by providing a new language to cultural conservatives at a moment when their old discourse had eroded. The rise of sexual liberalism had left Anthony Comstock's talk of sin and morality seeming a vestige of Victorian prudery. The postwar years of consumerist affluence had cast suspicion on ethnic or religious groups that didn't assimilate into the new suburban middle class, open to everyone as long as they were white. The boycott tactics of the Catholic Legion of Decency and National Organization for Decent Literature did not fit into a cultural landscape at least ostensibly shaped by consumer desires, where citizens were supposed to vote with their dollars, not with group-pressure tactics. And the Cold War had left *censorship* a dreaded word, something undertaken by totalitarian communist regimes, not freedom-loving Americans. By the mid-1950s an article called "The Harm That Good People Do" was one of the *nicer* descriptions of the Catholic groups' tactics, which involved handing lists of unacceptable books, magazines, and films to local distributors and exhibitors, threatening any who disregarded the lists with a boycott.

By the time *Roth* arrived, Catholic cultural power was visibly on the wane. For a quarter century, Catholic pressure had kept the Hollywood Production Code in place, with the studios more interested in profits than protests. With television increasingly cutting into its market, though, the film industry saw more adult fare as one possible avenue to distinguish itself. This put it in conflict with the Legion of Decency. If the scales began to tilt when *The Moon Is Blue* went out without the Code's seal in 1953, the Legion saw its influence further evaporate in 1956, when Elia Kazan's gleefully sleazy *Baby Doll*, involving a child bride and more sweaty stares of desire than the entire cast's wardrobe could absorb, triumphed over Catholic outrage. The Code technically persisted until 1968, but its final decade was one protracted retreat.

Keating had already begun some local antismut activism when *Roth* came along, but its appearance breathed new life into his efforts. The timing could not have been more perfect; just when Catholic tactics were being viewed with increasing suspicion and derision, a fellow Catholic, Justice Brennan, offered an entirely new framework — and an all-American one of rational, secular, legalistic suppression, at that. Eliminating obscenity, *Roth* showed, was not *censorship*, it was the enactment of constitutional law. A more powerful rhetorical weapon in 1957 would have been difficult to imagine.

Although Brennan's supporting cast of Frankfurter, Burton, Clark, and Whittaker clearly understood the conservatism of the opinion, it remained Keating's unique genius to translate the dry legal doctrine into the stuff of energized activism. This, he accomplished with aplomb. Organizing local supporters under the name Citizens for Decent Literature (CDL), Keating revealed undeniable continuities with the National Organization for Decent Literature, but recast it from a provincial, sectarian group — "a little band of Catholics," one critic had written of the NODL — into a group defined by its very Americanness. As *citizens* eager to support the law, CDL could reach well beyond the Catholicism of its founding cohort and attract the mainline Protestants who still comprised the demographic majority.

CDL made an immediate splash, its antismut message resonating far and wide. Keating parleyed local press coverage into national mobilization almost effortlessly. The shrewd Keating was always prepared for criticism and carefully crafted a public face that downplayed his religion in favor of his youthful swimming championships, World War II military service, career success, and healthy marriage. His tactics perfectly mirrored Hugh Hefner's on the other side of the cultural divide; *Playboy* and CDL, each in its own way, understood the importance of claiming an American identity in the 1950s.

Keating took great pains to distinguish CDL from its repressive forbears, even as he engaged in frequently Comstockian rhetoric. A typical Keating stock speech held its audience's rapt attention with salacious details. "In every malt shop where you and I would go with our friends or dates after school to listen to a juke box and have a coke," high-schoolers could "enter the world of lesbians, homosexuals, sadists, masochists, and other deviates whose names and actions are unknown to most decent people of this country." More tantalizing details followed, from the "appeal to the sodomist" some magazines held to Keating reading passages from a pulp novel in which a character expresses desire to "grab a girl and rip her clothes off and take her." Venereal disease, Keating often reminded, was rising rapidly. Civilization itself was in danger.

None of this sounded much different from Comstock's *Traps for the Young* assessment of the 1880s. But having aroused his audience's attention, Keating led them back to *Roth*. Some called pornography "the price of freedom," he said, but "the Supreme Court of the United States does not agree. This is a nation of laws, and the law is the weapon of decent citizens against the contamination spewing from our magazine racks." Keating's analysis fell short of profundity, claiming a "constitutional right" to "freedom from filth." Brennan would have been horrified to hear that "the test, in short, is whether or not you find this material to be below your level of morality, to be lewd and unclean to your neighbors and friends." It mattered little, though; Keating's legal analysis was never intended as formal lawyerly discourse. The purposes it served were in the rhetorical cultivation of a public image, one that distinguished CDL from the embarrassing censors of the past by situating it in the doctrine of as liberal an institution as the Warren Court.

In this, Keating was again as brilliant as Hefner in utilizing accepted markers (obscenity doctrine and consumerism, respectively) to claim a respectability that neither antismut boycotters nor seedy men's magazines could achieve. It played well in the media, especially with Keating's smart responses in interviews and appearances. He wasn't antisex, he constantly insisted, just anti-*perversion* — a truly twentieth-century smut fighter. CDL units proliferated around the nation – often engaging in precisely the tactics Keating denounced.

In the midst of CDL's ascent, the Court had a less unified front than it appeared. The string of post-*Roth* reversals signaled a heightened scrutiny toward obscenity convictions, but their tight-lipped per curiam nature masked a Court that could not agree on much. Some of this was so invisible it remained unknown for decades. After the homophile magazine *ONE* won its landmark case, it proudly declared the Court had "completely and unanimously reversed the Post Office ban." Only with the opening of William O. Douglas's papers after his death twenty-some years later did it become evident that although the *ONE* case bore no written dissents, it had actually been a bare 5–4 split, eking out for the magazine ever so precarious a victory.

By 1959 the Court's splintered nature grew more visible. In one case, the justices agreed New York could not ban a film of *Lady Chatterley*, but could not agree on an analysis, resulting in six separate opinions, a rather confusing situation. Indeed, *Roth* proved fairly easy to circumvent with a little legal sophistication (or sophistry). After the New York film censors were rebuked for banning indecent films, they simply changed nomenclature, declaring films obscene instead. Though film censors *had* grown generally more relaxed by the late 1950s, they also made use of the Court's new terminology to couch the nature of their bans when necessary. Chicago censors even won a surprising Supreme Court victory in early 1961, when Tom Clark mustered up a bare five-justice majority to uphold a local law requiring mandatory prescreenings of all films for approval by local authorities, over the angry dissent of Warren, Brennan, Black, and Douglas.

Even when enlarging freedoms, the Court drew boundaries. If *Manual Enterprises v. Day* in 1962 opened the mails to gay physique magazines, it hardly constituted a ringing endorsement of queer free expression. By the time of that case, the Court had already denied certiorari in several gay obscenity cases, to the point that Warren's clerk began one summary memorandum for the chief, "This is another homosexual obscenity case," in 1961. Though full frontal nudity was protected in a nonsexual nudist context, when infused with the slightest tinge of homosexual appeal it could land a publisher in prison, as mail-order distributors such as Alfred Heinecke learned the hard way.

While Harlan had declared that gay publications and images "cannot fairly be regarded as more objectionable than many portrayals of the female nude that society tolerates," it remained questionable (in another severely split opinion) just how binding this was.

Brennan recognized the doctrinal disarray, but had no answers. "I have no doubt that we must some day give further thought to the *Roth* test," he wrote to Harlan, but suggested putting it off for the moment. With the Court "hopelessly divided," there appeared "almost no prospect of an agreement of five of us upon anything." The best idea he could devise was to "let the widespread ferment continue a bit longer in legal periodicals and courts over the soundness and meaning of the *Roth* test."

In fact, legal periodicals had remained quite critical of *Roth*. Harry Kalvern delivered a powerful riposte in the 1960 volume of the influential *Supreme Court Review*, returning to the now-abandoned Jerome Frank–like belief that "the evil of arousing revulsion in adults who are a non-captive audience is simply too trivial a predicate for constitutional regulation." Verging on open scorn for Brennan's discussion of sex in *Roth*, Kalvern wrote, "The Court may understand obscenity, but it does not seem to understand sex." The *Minnesota Law Review* concurred in 1962. "The precise function of these laws has never been clear," a team of authors concluded, finding obscenity law reasonable only "as a matter of *Realpolitik*," not logic. Louis Henkin went further the next year in the *Columbia Law Review*, arguing obscenity's only real basis lay in religious dogma and hoping the Court "will begin to disentangle and separate crime from sin in a secular country."

While Brennan in particular kept himself admirably open to criticism, staying abreast of the law-review articles, he remained steadfastly unwilling to reexamine the basic core principle that prurience did not deserve First Amendment protection. Brennan saw the 1964 *Jacobellis* as a liberal intervention to clarify *Roth* and make obscenity laws less arbitrary and provincial. Just as telling, though, was his brief aside that same year in *New York Times v. Sullivan*, where press freedom was supported with the assertion that "freedom of expression upon public questions is secured by the First Amendment." Brennan's citation for this statement was *Roth*; between the lines lay a reinforcement of the belief that prurient interests were entirely separate from public questions—a belief, as William O. Douglas never stopped insisting, belied daily by the advertising industry and most of mass culture. Though sexual politics saturated both cultural expression and state policy, the Court refused to recognize salacious or pornographic expression as taking on inherently political qualities in the ongoing social debate over sexuality. Sex was always and everywhere *already* politicized in the social dialogue that transpired both directly (in public discussions of contraception, for instance) and indirectly (in the Grove Press's catalog, or the ever-more-revealing bikinis on display in teenage beach movies of the early 1960s), but its less savory side remained somehow severed from these discussions, as if politics extended only to the parameters of the permissible, and not an inch or a leer beyond.

Within the mid-1960s cultural debate, the value of prurience was nowhere near as foreclosed as the Court suggested. Hugh Hefner, predictably opposing obscenity laws in his "Playboy Philosophy" column, credited *Roth* with "seriously curtailing the kind of arbitrary censorship that had previously prevailed." Yet he disputed the logic of Brennan's "judicial assumption" that "pure pornography is without any 'redeeming social importance.' " It may, Hefner suggested, "actually have some value as a sublimation and release for pent-up sexual frustration and desires." Radical sociologist Paul Goodman defended pornography in *Commentary*, condemning the Court's logic in *Roth*. "While the liberal court hedges in embarrassment," he wrote, "the police and the administrators lurk to get convictions on any grounds." Goodman called for the Court to "call *not* obscene whatever tends to joy, love, and liveliness, including the stirring of lustful impulses and thoughts."

Such voices remained marginal in the legal arena, however. Of more institutional weight was FBI director J. Edgar Hoover's insistence well into the 1960s that teenage girls could turn to prostitution, hitchhikers could be "subjected to horrifying indecencies," children could be plunged into "wild orgies," and teenage girls horsewhipped by "two young terrorists," all on account of smut. The *University of Pittsburgh Law Review* published his feverish vision in 1964, bestowing it with more credibility than it merited. In fact, by that point social scientists had long since shifted attention from porn because they had found no evidence of harmful effects worth further investigating.

The nation's foremost defender of civil liberties found itself as caught in the crossfire of these debates as the Court did. After *Roth* killed the clear and present danger test's application to obscenity, the ACLU languished without an effective replacement policy. Well into 1959, executive director Patrick Malin Murphy explained in correspondence with the publisher of *Reader's Digest* that the ACLU thought of obscenity as that which "tends to degrade the sexual side of life," a startlingly broad definition. The group's opposition to prior restraint, Malin emphasized, "does not mean we that are opposed to all post-publication governmental action against obscenity."

This Cold War complacency that distinguished sexual nonconformity from civil liberties found itself increasingly challenged within the organization as the 1960s dawned. When the ACLU Censorship Committee canvassed national branch opinions in 1961, the results varied widely. The Arizona branch took a conservative stance, invoking the decline of civilization and arguing that "certain restraints must be recognized." In Southern California, David Alberts's lawyer, Stanley Fleishman, took the opposite position, finding political content in *all* sexual expression. Articulating precisely the perspective the Supreme Court refused to hear, Fleishman argued: "Every writing or representation, no matter how detailed or explicit in matters concerning sex, communicates at least a portion of knowledge and expresses, if nothing more, a belief rebellious against prevailing morality, modesty and prudery, or of need for increased sexual extremes, abnormalities or excesses."

Within the Censorship Committee, fragmentation marked the discussions. One faction called for an absolutist standard against all obscenity laws. Another demanded an exception for "hard core pornography," with Herbert Monte Levy warning of the effects of smut on children. The result was deadlock. When the ACLU finally settled on a new obscenity policy in 1962, it basically rephrased the clear and present danger test, demanding for obscenity cases "proof that the material would cause, in a normal adult, behavior which has validly been made criminal by statute." Later in the decade ACLU positions on sex laws would evolve dramatically, but in 1962 this standard might still include everything from hetero- or homosexual oral sex to solitary masturbation.

If the ACLU found itself in stasis, federal prosecutors did not. When Chief Postal Inspector H. B. Montague sent statistics to an inquiring law professor in late 1965, it showed how little *Roth* had done to stem the tide of obscenity prosecutions. From 201 arrests and 175 convictions in fiscal year 1957, the numbers had risen steadily, to 761 arrests and 637 convictions in 1963, and 874 with 696 convicted in 1965. *Roth* may have made obscenity convictions harder to sustain on appeal, but it clearly had little bearing in the ongoing governmental war on smut at the enforcement level.

A trilogy of cases handed down jointly in 1966 responded to these circumstances. While *Memoirs v. Massachusetts* represented the apex of the liberal aspects of *Roth*, reducing obscenity to that material *utterly* without redeeming social importance, its two companion cases took shockingly regressive directions that left many observers stunned. *Memoirs* itself signaled the shift. In its closing section, Brennan noted it did not "necessarily flow from this reversal that a determination that *Memoirs* is obscene in the constitutional sense would be improper under all circumstances." The "circumstances of production, sale, and publicity" might be relevant, he explained, suggesting that a book "commercially exploited for the sake of prurient appeal" might still be obscene, even if its content did not actually meet the *Roth* test.

Whatever confusion this generated was quickly clarified by *Ginzburg v. U.S.*, handed down the same day. Ralph Ginzburg, a journalist and publisher whose work explored the new terrain opened by the Supreme Court in the 1960s, had attracted the attention of the Justice Department. *The Housewife's Handbook on Selective Promiscuity* offered sex advice to women in autobiographical form from author Rey Anthony, while *EROS* combined sex-themed articles with mild erotic photography in magazine form. Though both flirted with taboos (especially in *EROS*'s photographs of a black man and white woman in a nude embrace), neither went strikingly beyond the pale of other contemporaneous publications. What led to Ginzburg's conviction was his behavior, particularly his smarmy efforts to mail his works from the Pennsylvania towns of Intercourse and Blue Ball. When that failed, he sent them from Middlesex, New Jersey.

At neither the federal district nor appellate court did the judges make a convincing case for Ginzburg's works meeting the *Roth* test. Not even the government itself forcefully denied that the *Housewife's Handbook* had sex-therapeutic value. Instead, the case, and Ginzburg's five-year sentence, came to rest on Ginzburg's advertising techniques, which allegedly *represented* the works as obscene through their tawdry framing.

Ginzburg proved as contentious as any obscenity case the Supreme Court had yet taken on. To Warren, it vindicated the stance he had taken since *Roth*: try the person, not the book. To Douglas and Black, it was yet another no-brainer: reverse, since the First Amendment protected everything, obscenity included. For the other justices, uncertainty prevailed. Though key obscenity architect for a decade, Brennan said nothing during conference discussion. According to Douglas's notes, Potter Stewart declared he did not "understand what *Roth* is" anymore. Liberal recent appointee Abe Fortas said "if he made an independent judgment of this material, he would reverse." Ginzburg seemed to have a good chance of winning reversal. His publications were simply not obscene, and nothing in the Court's decade-long development of obscenity doctrine supported an affirmation.

To widespread shock, the Court affirmed Ginzburg's conviction. Brennan's opinion emphasized Ginzburg's "sordid business of pandering," in which the "leer of the sensualist . . . permeates the advertising." Though advertising tactics had never been part of the *Roth* test, Brennan struggled to reconcile the seeming incongruity. "Where the purveyor's sole emphasis is on the sexually provocative aspects of his publications," he explained, "that fact may be decisive in the determination of obscenity." To justify this, Brennan had to effectively assume all readers had their reading practices determined by Ginzburg's sales pitches: "The deliberate representation of petitioners' publications as erotically arousing, for example, stimulated the reader to accept them as prurient; he looks for titillation, not for saving intellectual content."

By any fair standard, Brennan's opinion was a complete failure. His effort to bring *Ginzburg* in line with *Roth* amounted to asserting that "in close cases evidence of pandering may be probative with respect to the nature of the material in question and thus satisfy the *Roth* test." The dissenting brethren hardly let the matter pass without comment. Though Black and Douglas may have been predictable in the scorn they heaped on Brennan's opinion, more telling was the open anger of the usually polite Harlan and Stewart. Harlan called Brennan's "pandering" an "astonishing piece of judicial improvisation," while an outraged Stewart accused Brennan and the majority of denying

Ginzburg due process of law by convicting him on grounds other than what he was charged with.

In fact, *Ginzburg*'s fragile majority hinged on a secret vote-trade between Brennan and Fortas. When Brennan had wavered on reversing Massachusetts on the obscenity of *Fanny Hill*, Fortas had convinced him — but at the cost of voting to affirm Ginzburg's conviction, despite his own comments at conference about its nonobscenity. It was a deal Fortas later regretted, and he rationalized it privately by citing Ginzburg's "slimy" qualities. The short-term effect on the Court was apparent backsliding on the liberal promises of *Roth* — a course further extended the same day in *Mishkin v. New York*, in which Brennan affirmed the conviction of pulp-novel publisher Edward Mishkin, whose books brimmed over with sadomasochism, lesbianism, and other "deviant" sexualities.

Mishkin drew dramatically less public attention than *Ginzburg*, but the collective response to the cases was outrage among liberals. By 1966, even the Hollywood studios had begun depicting women's bared breasts in films, albeit tentatively and in noneretic circumstances (in Sidney Lumet's Holocaust-themed *Pawnbroker* in 1965). Below the mainstream, exploitation and nudist films depicted far more raw images of sexuality; such works as *White Slaves of Chinatown* and *The Defilers* lined the grindhouse theaters of Times Square and various decaying urban downtowns, embodying themes in line with Mishkin's books but more visceral. Ralph Ginzburg, tawdry as his tactics may have been, had a background in respectable journalism and addressed socially relevant themes in *EROS* and the *Housewife's Handbook*. Press coverage, from the *Village Voice* to law reviews, was scathing toward the Court. A group of artists and intellectuals banded together as the Committee to Protest Absurd Censorship took out a full-page *New York Times* ad against the *Ginzburg* decision.

Almost the only praise for *Ginzburg* and *Mishkin* came from Citizens for Decent Literature, which celebrated them in its *National Decency Reporter* as steps in the right direction at last. Brennan, a central player in the Court's support for African American civil rights cases, must have winced to receive supportive letters with congratulations for suppressing *EROS*'s interracial embrace. "Give the negro freedom and you will be a grandmother to half white and half negroe [*sic*] children," one wrote.

By 1966 the sexual revolution was in full swing. That *Roth* had facilitated its emergence and public shape was beyond question. But that it also set the parameters, contained the "revolution" within the boundaries of *normalcy* (as defined through its apparent opposites *prurience* and — after *Mishkin* — *deviance*), and colluded in the continued incarceration of those who stepped beyond its blurry boundaries was just as undeniable. There was a unifying logic that flowed through the Court's opinions, but it was the logic of heteronormativity. At a doctrinal level, *Roth* remained not only an unfulfilled promise, but, it increasingly seemed, a false one.

Even William Brennan himself was beginning a rethinking that would ultimately bring him to this conclusion. The Court had still not articulated a compelling reason for excluding obscenity from the First Amendment, and a decade after *Roth*, it began the process of removing itself from the problem. It seemed to work, for a while. The process hinged on unspoken and unwritten per curiam opinions, though, meaning that when a newly conservative Court took shape only a few years later, the effort had left no powerful precedent to sustain itself. By the 1970s, *Roth* was under attack — first, from conservatives mobilizing against pornography, then from feminists who took a radical analysis no less critical of the straight male justices' limited perspectives. *Roth* staggered through the 1970s under attack from multiple angles and survived only in vestigial form, disowned by its own author.

From Porno Chic to New Critiques

Conservatives, Feminists, and
Backlash to Obscenity

The tenth anniversary of *Roth v. United States* went uncelebrated. One of the appellants from the original conjoined cases, David Alberts, had long since shifted into real estate. Samuel Roth, finally released from prison just as the 1960s dawned, returned to his old ways, but thanks to the case that bore his name he could freely sell the works of the Marquis de Sade and a tawdry volume called *Violations of the Child Marilyn Monroe*. Roth still faced legal obstacles from the post office in the 1960s, though now the fraud orders had nothing to do with obscenity, but rather the medically dubious *Diatitis: Cancer Prevention and Cure*, a book he had — in his own irascibly entrepreneurial manner — contracted to a fellow prisoner he had met while serving his prison term. Neither Roth nor Alberts had great cause to commemorate the anniversary.

Meanwhile, the Supreme Court, still caught in the doctrinal web spun by *Roth*, sought a way out. Following its mid-1960s debacles, the Court forged a new course by effectively overturning nearly every obscenity conviction that reached it, as sex — even its *prurient* form — was finally afforded access to the imagined marketplace of ideas. This libertarian approach found support from social scientists, who collectively argued that smut had no identifiable bearing on juvenile delinquency, crime, or the loosely defined "sexual deviation." By the early 1970s the physical manifestation of these trends was etched across the landscape of urban America, as storefront theaters showing hardcore pornography (depicting graphic, unsimulated sex acts) rapidly proliferated.

As quickly as hardcore porn emerged, so too did a backlash. Conservative political mobilization on the basis of "morality" had already begun by the late 1960s, and even played a role in reshaping the Court. These political currents flowed into legal doctrine. With President Richard Nixon's four Supreme Court appointments, the Court's trajectory veered to the right on a number of issues. When it came to obscenity, the pivotal moment arrived in 1973, as the Court overhauled *Roth* in a newly conservative manner—even as the hardcore film *Deep Throat* captivated the American public.

This "porno chic" moment drew criticism not only from conservatives, but also feminists, already alerted to the gendered inequities of sexual "revolution." As pornography came under scrutiny, a powerful and prominent feminist antipornography movement took shape in the late 1970s, developing a critique of porn that was philosophical and cultural, but legal as well. The attack did not stop with porn itself, but extended further into the obscenity doctrine that regulated it. In the sharp analyses of such scholar-activists as Andrea Dworkin and Catharine MacKinnon, *Roth* was simply another piece of a patriarchal puzzle that, when put together, revealed the insidious tools of men's historical subjugation of women.

In the midst of these debates, *Roth* found few defenders. Derided by social scientists as irrational for criminalizing harmless materials, bemoaned by conservatives for its amoral permissiveness, and condemned by antiporn feminists for upholding a system of gender-based domination, *Roth* could not even muster the support of its own author. In the most striking aspect of the 1973 cases, William Brennan himself renounced *Roth*—not for the conservative reasons shared by the Court majority, but because he finally concluded obscenity could not fairly or effectively be regulated through the criminal justice system. At long last, Justice Douglas (and Hugo Black, who had recently retired) had an ally, though the impact was rather muted when faced with a five-justice majority. That the doctrine *Roth* had established trudged through this ideological carnage altered but fundamentally intact was perhaps less tribute to Brennan's own brilliance in the opinion than to the inability of any of the competing factions to effectively create a new social consensus. Altered and absorbed by *Miller* though it was, *Roth* persisted.

From *Redrup* to Hardcore

After coming under so much fire for its 1966 opinions, the Court was hardly eager to revisit obscenity in the next term, even deciding at a conference to stop taking obscenity cases. But the cases kept arriving, and the justices had little choice but to deal with them. As Abe Fortas wrote in a memo to his colleagues, "I no longer believe that we can appropriately rest on our laurels." The Court had assigned itself this responsibility when it entered the obscenity fray, and it could hardly abandon those who fell under the law's sway now.

Unable to agree on much of anything, the justices consolidated cases from New York, Arkansas, and Kentucky under *Redrup v. New York* in 1967, and issued a short, unsigned per curiam opinion that once again reframed obscenity doctrine. *Redrup* consisted of two brief sections. The first laid out the facts of the cases in about three sentences each. None involved "a specific and limited state concern for juveniles." None contained "an assault upon individual privacy by publication in a manner so obtrusive as to make it impossible for an unwilling individual to avoid exposure to it." And "in none was there evidence of the sort of 'pandering' which the Court found significant in *Ginzburg*."

What this litany meant became clear in the second section, which primarily consisted of a thick paragraph outlining the Court's internal deadlock before concluding, "Whichever of these constitutional views is brought to bear upon the cases before us, it is clear that the judgments cannot stand. Accordingly, the judgment in each case is reversed." The Court had just done two things. It effectively abandoned doctrine entirely, simply suggesting consensus on constitutional logic could not be reached but obscenity cases would be reversed nonetheless, and it had offered a seeming roadmap for both distributors and those policing them: laws could target the sale of smut to minors, public display, and pandering. Other forms of smut regulation, the Court did not say but strongly suggested, would not stand.

Only Harlan and Clark dissented. Most strikingly, *Roth* was mentioned only in a footnote. Had the Court forsaken it? It certainly intended *Redrup* as a statement of position, if not doctrine, and in the two years after it, the Court reversed nearly every obscenity conviction to cross its path. *Roth* fell off the radar entirely. In nearly three dozen per curiam reversals of 1967 and 1968, the Court simply cited *Redrup* without elaboration. Nudist magazines seized by Baltimore customs officers; the sleazy pseudodocumentary film *Mondo Freudo* in Tennessee; *Lust Hungry*, *Sin Hooked*, *Shame Shop*, and several other novels in Kansas; the novel *Sex Life of a Cop* in Michigan; a short stag film simply known as *O-7* in California: all were cleared by the Court, without comment. Legal scholars began using "Redrup" as a verb: the Court Redrupped obscenity cases when it reversed convictions without explanation.

Among adult obscenity cases, only a California case involving the short film *Un Chant d'Amour*, French author Jean Genet's dreamlike and visually striking meditation on male prison sex, was affirmed by the Court during this period, a reminder of the limitations its liberal disposition still carried. Still, by 1969 the Court was ready to take *Redrup*'s implications to the next level. In *Stanley v. Georgia*, recent appointee Thurgood Marshall debuted on the obscenity stage, putting recent obscenity trends into conjunction with the Court's recent recognition of a fundamental right to privacy in the contraceptive case of *Griswold* to conclude, "the First and Fourteenth Amendments prohibit making mere private possession of obscene material a crime." If the First Amendment meant anything, Marshall contended, it meant that "a State has no business telling a man, sitting alone in his own house, what books he may read or what films he may watch." For the first time, in *Stanley*, the Court had protected admittedly obscene material.

Marshall rejected Georgia's claim that obscenity "may lead to deviant sexual behavior or crimes of sexual violence," finding "little empirical basis for that assertion." By the late 1960s, the overwhelming social science consensus agreed. The single strongest such assessment of pornography arrived in 1970, with the publication of the President's Commission on Obscenity and Pornography. Legislated into existence by Congress in 1967, the commission had begun with a mandate to study the perceived smut crisis. To the surprise of many, instead of adopting a tone of moral outrage or emphasizing the social harms of such material, the commission staked its analysis on the empirical work of dozens of psychologists, sociologists, and other scholars, who roundly rejected the idea that pornography caused crime, violence, or "sexual deviation." Its report caused such a stir that Bantam Books published a paperback version — quite a rare phenomenon for a 700-page governmental study.

Beginning from the perspective that "discussions of obscenity and pornography in the past have often been devoid of fact," the report sought to correct this trend. Exposure to sexually explicit materials simply could not be linked to social problems, the teams of researchers concluded, based on numerous studies that used methodologies ranging from prisoner interviews to juvenile-delinquency case files to physiological testing of responses to images. Instead, much of the "problem" regarding pornography — and the commission itself used quotation marks to set off the word as suspect — "stems from the inability or reluctance of people in our society to be open and direct in dealing with sexual matters." Ultimately, the commission proposed decriminalizing obscenity completely for consenting adults and focusing social concern about sexuality on effective, comprehensive sex education that would prevent pornographers from capitalizing on the veil of ignorance surrounding sexuality even in modern America.

Though arousing great moral indignation from many social conservatives (discussed further below), the Commission on Obscenity and Pornography accurately represented the state of social science in 1970. With both the law and social scientific understandings clearly hostile to obscenity law, the time was ripe for testing the boundaries. By 1967, the cutting edge of sexual expression had shifted from the Grove Press's booklist to imported foreign films that ranged from art-house cinema to "sexploitation," often bridging the gap between the levels as artistically minded films were marketed for their cheap thrills. In the wake of *Redrup*, censorial suppression amounted to a rearguard action. Obscenity convictions could still be obtained in local courts, but faced very likely reversal by higher courts. Grove Press lawyer Charles Rembar even titled his 1968 book *The End of Obscenity*, and it sounded plausible at the time. With few legal barriers standing in the way, entrepreneurial gambling could prove quite lucrative, as witnessed that year by one Swedish import film, *I Am Curious (Yellow)*. Though director Vilgot Sjoman had impeccable artistic aspirations, emulating his national film icon Ingmar Bergman in the starkly black-and-white, serious film about late-sixties social change in Sweden, what truly drew American attention was the bold full-frontal male and female nudity and uninhibited sexuality of the film. Grove Press, smartly expanding its operations, imported and distributed the film in the United States. After it was seized by customs as obscene, its court challenge became a test of the new legal openness.

I Am Curious (Yellow) won that test, both legally and culturally. The federal court of appeals reversed customs 2–1 in late 1968, even as it acknowledged the "greater explicitness than has been seen in any other film produced for general viewing." Not even the "scenes of oral-genital activity," concluded the court, prevented *I Am Curious* from holding redeeming social importance. Cleared for American screens, it immediately established itself as a box-office bonanza. In the *New York Times*, critic Vincent Canby called it "a good, serious movie about a society in transition," its sex scenes "honest and so unaffectedly frank as to be nonpornographic." Even former first lady Jacqueline Kennedy Onassis attended the film.

The only line left to cross was graphic, detailed images of unsimulated sexual activity, which *I Am Curious* stopped just short of. As the *New York Times* noted in 1968, Samuel Roth's publications "would now be considered bush-league erotica." By 1970, the legal and scientific contexts merged with technological and urban developments to bring such images to American screens; 16-millimeter film lowered production and distribution costs, and the urban decay wrought by middle-class disinvestment left the urban landscape ripe for the emergence of small storefront theaters willing to experiment with screening such films. Though hardcore pornography dated back to the invention of the camera, only in this new context did it move aboveground. A year after *Stanley*, the same year the President's Commission on Obscenity and Pornography delivered its libertarian report, hardcore surfaced.

The West Coast led the way, with the Los Angeles–shot *Mona*, about a young woman pursuing sexual adventures before her marriage, and the San Francisco–lensed *Tomatoes*, following a door-to-door salesman's hijinks, generally identified as the first American hardcore features. Meanwhile, underground filmmakers straight and gay sought to create what film historian Elena Gorfinkel calls "the utopian sexual public sphere," attempting to translate radical politics and countercultural sexual values into cinematic form, while Scandinavian imports continued to reflect the decriminalization of sexual materials under way there.

Many early hardcore films presented themselves as scientific, informational endeavors, intended to carry the work of Alfred Kinsey or recent sexological superstars William Masters and Virginia Johnson into the cinematic arena. These "white-coaters," as they became known, featured introductions and commentary by doctors and other experts, using them as alibis to confer the requisite social importance on the films. While the sincerity could be questioned, the effectiveness could not. In one of the first important hardcore obscenity cases in 1970, involving the Swedish white-coater *Language of Love*, the Second Circuit Court of Appeals overturned a customs ban. Observing that at least eight other similar films were already playing in New York City, the court decided that not even its "maximal explicitness" stood in the way of allowing "that segment of the public interested in observing sexual activity in the quiet darkness of a movie theatre to do so." *Roth*, *Redrup*, and *Stanley* converged to create a legal safety zone for those willing adults.

These intertwined directions of law and culture culminated in the stunning popular success of the hardcore pornographic film *Deep Throat* in 1973. Shot on the cheap in Miami the year before and featuring star Linda Lovelace as an adventurous but frustrated woman who learns that her inability to climax stems from a misplaced clitoris located in her throat, the film centered on her ambitious acts of fellatio, pleasurable to both her and the string of satisfied men she encounters. Admittedly more clever than the average hardcore comedy and expressly engaged with social questions of sexuality, desire, and pleasure, *Deep Throat* carried a catchy title that helped draw national attention. While earlier porn performers had flown well below the mainstream cultural radar, Lovelace suddenly found herself a guest on Johnny Carson's *Tonight Show*, an instant household name.

Celebrities endorsed *Deep Throat*; college students and middle-class suburban married couples attended in droves. The startling visibility of the film spearheaded a moment quickly labeled "porno chic" by the media, as other films closely followed and attempted to dismantle the wall between porn and art. *The Devil in Miss Jones*, by *Deep Throat* auteur Gerard Damiano, took a remarkably effective existentialist tone not far removed from the plays of French philosopher Jean-Paul Sartre, while Radley Metzger directed *The Opening of Misty Beethoven*, a lavish, opulent narrative based on esteemed playwright George Bernard Shaw's *Pygmalion*.

None of this went uncontested by local obscenity charges, even against *Deep Throat*, that extended from New York City to Little Rock, Arkansas, but once more, they seemed like near afterthoughts.

The war had been won, obscenity law was obsolete, and consenting adults were free to enjoy whatever prurient interests on screen or in text they so wished, as long as no pandering, minors, or unwilling spectators were involved. This coincided with expanded Court definitions of free speech that included antiwar high school students wearing armbands in protest, a young man in a "Fuck the Draft" jacket, and newspapers publishing the classified Pentagon Papers that revealed governmental deception in the war against Vietnam. Both the First Amendment and the sexual revolution seemed triumphant. Gay and lesbian rights and visibility were on the ascent in the wake of the riotous 1969 Stonewall rebellion against homophobic police in New York. In 1972, the Supreme Court extended contraceptive rights to unmarried singles, and Congress finally passed the Equal Rights Amendment, to secure constitutional equality for women, a half century after its introduction. The next year the Court established women's fundamental right to abortion in *Roe v. Wade*. An observer could be forgiven for thinking the battles over sexuality were over, and the liberals had won.

Such an assessment, however, would prove rather facile. A conservative countermobilization had been underway for years, and with four Supreme Court appointments from a presidential administration openly hostile to the sexual revolution, change was already under way — politically, to be sure, but also doctrinally. Even as Americans congratulated themselves for their liberated attitudes in attending porno chic films, a new obscenity doctrine was being written, one that would reverse the *Redrup* trajectory and return to a more restrictive reading of *Roth*.

Miller Time

Conservative resistance had never been absent or invisible as liberalization had seemingly dominated the direction of law and culture from the late 1960s through the mid-1970s. It emanated from diverse sources. Religious moralism, of course, took exception to the normalization of what it perceived as immoral or perverted. Not unrelated, but distinct in articulation, concerned citizens worried about the perceived excesses of the sexual revolution, which threatened to

{ *Chapter 9* }

destabilize the centrality of the traditional family in American life. It was both a symbolic anxiety and also a very real and tangible one for people with emotional stakes in preserving and passing on their ways of life. The concern over children that Anthony Comstock voiced in the 1870s recurred in the words of J. Edgar Hoover, Charles Keating, and every other antismut conservative in the intervening century.

Another undeniable source of moral outrage in the obscenity debates came from politicians in desperate need of new political platforms, especially in the wake of the African American civil rights movement. Enterprising southern politicians had realized early on that the states' rights arguments that had been seemingly demolished by *Brown v. Board of Education* could be repackaged in other venues. Already by 1959 Mississippi senator James Eastland had expressed indignation over the Supreme Court's "mortal blow to the power of a State to maintain within its borders minimum standards of decency and morality" when it forced New York to allow the film of *Lady Chatterley's Lover*. Hinting at his other concerns, Eastland worried that the Court might follow similar logic in regard to "bigamy, or sodomy, or miscegenation, or even rape," the third term being particularly fraught for southerners obsessed with maintaining the color line. With a coterie of segregationist compatriots including South Carolina's Strom Thurmond and Georgia's Herman Talmadge, Eastland proposed a constitutional amendment barring the Supreme Court from hearing cases involving "public policy questions of decency and morality," which would remain state concerns.

The proposed amendment went nowhere, but it showed how a states' rights agenda with clear racial concerns could be articulated as a simple moral agenda. Others would pursue this theme throughout the 1960s, including James Kilpatrick, a Virginia journalist, activist, and supporter of massive resistance against school integration, who championed John Marshall Harlan's obscenity federalism of weak federal and strong state powers—again, a template with clear implications for the politics of race. For most of the decade, obscenity occupied a minor role in conservative attacks on the Court. The Warren Court simply offered too many other targets, from its separation of church and state doctrine under the First Amendment's establishment clause, which could be presented as hostile to religion despite chief architect Hugo Black's unquestionable personal faith and devotion, to the criminal justice procedure opinions such as *Miranda v. Arizona* that empowered those accused of crimes, presented as hostile to law enforcers.

While the tireless activism of Charles Keating and Citizens for Decent Literature kept obscenity alive as a social issue across the years, 1968 brought its grand return to center stage in the politics of law when President Lyndon Johnson attempted to replace outgoing Chief Justice Earl Warren with sitting associate justice Abe Fortas. A wave of conservative indignation over the liberal Fortas failed to gain much broader traction, until CDL called attention to his obscenity votes. With Thurmond screening stag films in the Senate building and conservative journalists like James Kilpatrick relaying the scandalous Fortas votes, public opinion finally shifted.

Though backroom political deals had already ensured the failure of his nomination, the smut cases provided the rhetorical surface and resonated with citizens and voters. This coincided with the enormous political shifts of the 1960s, as the Voting Rights Act of 1965 finally made good, a century late, on the promises of the Fifteenth Amendment to black America. With voting demographics changing rapidly in the South, politicians such as Thurmond or North Carolina's Jesse Helms, and religious leaders such as Virginia's Reverend Jerry Falwell, who had accused Martin Luther King Jr. of being a communist dupe, sped away from their racist pasts as fast as they could. Moral politics provided one safe avenue, where some of the structural content of states' rights arguments could be preserved, but in a nonracial form. The Supreme Court offered a good target, one already resented by many whites. They need not entirely understand the institutional structures of American politics to identify the Court as defender of smut. "Please get legislation against obscenity and pornography," one Memphis woman wrote Hugo Black in 1969; "we want the laws changed — pornography is sick."

Not every antismut politician was fleeing a racist past, of course. The foremost spokesman for this developing movement was Richard Nixon, elected in 1968, and a racial moderate as the Republican Party moved quickly to capture southern disillusionment with the Demo-crats for supporting the civil rights movement. Cynically obsessed with manipulating the press for better coverage, Nixon capitalized on smut as a way to sell himself to the American people as the defender of what he famously termed "the silent majority," those decent Americans distraught by the various social upheavals of the 1960s. Nixon railed against porn constantly, using it as a wedge issue to demonize liberals by equating support for free speech with support for hardcore pornography. At one point, he even considered attending a play in New York simply so he could stand and walk out in disgust over the nudity, to best "dramatize his feelings," as chief of staff H. R. Haldeman recorded.

When the President's Commission on Obscenity and Pornography released its report in 1970, Nixon was ready. He had already appointed Citizens for Decent Literature head Charles Keating to the commission for the specific purpose of undermining it from within and generating media attention, and he lambasted the final report, calling pornography a "threat to our social order as well as to our moral principles." Rejecting the commission's recommendation to decriminalize obscenity, Nixon instead promised to amp up governmental efforts against it, instructing his attorney general and postmaster general to prioritize it. It was such a winning issue that political opponents found it impossible to dispute without fear of appearing to condone smut, so the Senate condemned the report, rejecting its conclusions in a bipartisan 60–5 vote. Porn played well in storefront theaters, but not in the halls of Congress.

Nixon's bluster inspired more headlines than actual results, which is exactly what he wanted. The most lasting change he actually incurred in the obscenity debates came from his four Supreme Court appointments. After the Fortas fiasco, Nixon won the chance to replace Earl Warren as chief justice, choosing conservative Court of Appeals judge Warren Burger. Almost immediately upon ascending to the chief justiceship, Burger began dissenting from the Court's Redrupped reversals, arguing that states should have greater powers to regulate obscenity. He gradually picked up allies, as Nixon appointed three more justices. After two failed nominations of strikingly inept judges, Nixon settled on Minnesotan appellate judge Harry Blackmun, an old friend of Burger, then Virginia corporate lawyer Lewis Powell, known for his moderate racial views during polarized times. Finally, to reinstate more overt ideology into the Court, Nixon added William Rehnquist from his own justice department. Controversy surrounded a memorandum Rehnquist had written while a clerk to Robert Jackson in the 1950s arguing against overturning *Plessy v. Ferguson*'s "separate but equal" standard, but Nixon valued Rehnquist's loyalty (even if he couldn't always remember his name in private conversations).

As evident as the Court's disposition had been from 1967 to the early 1970s, nowhere had there been a particularly substantive doctrinal exposition. The *Redrup* era was more *pattern* than *doctrine*, and it left no binding precedent to oblige the Nixon justices' adherence. With Warren, Fortas, Harlan, and Black gone, no one among Court watchers expected the pattern to persist.

Redrup's fade could be charted subtly across the Burger Court's early years. As the Court continued to Redrup obscenity convictions in 1970, Burger began appending brief dissents, arguing for more flexible state-level standards. By 1972, *Redrup* was gone; when the Court reversed a Wisconsin conviction of an underground newspaper in a per curiam opinion, the governing citation had reverted back to *Roth v. U.S.*, which appeared to satisfy the new Nixon appointees — at least for the moment.

That it was time for a new obscenity regime seemed clear, though what the new doctrine might be remained far less so. The justices heard the case of Marvin Miller, a southern California smut dealer whose graphic books like *Sex Orgies Illustrated* and *Intercourse* had earned him an obscenity conviction in January 1972. Perplexed as to how best to resolve the issue, they set the case for reargument in November and spent the year circulating a flurry of memoranda to stake out their positions.

Chief Justice Burger took charge, advocating a denationalization of obscenity doctrine that allowed states and localities to define obscenity by their own terms. "I do not see it as a threat to genuine First Amendment values to have commercial porno-peddlers feel some unease," he wrote to William Brennan in June; "a little 'chill' will do some of the 'pornos' no great harm and it might be good for the country." An outraged Brennan saw the chief as interjecting moralism into the First Amendment. In a strongly worded memo to the brethren, he contended that Burger's suggestions would "worsen an already intolerable mess." Concluding that obscenity doctrine had failed to work, Brennan wrote, "only a drastic change in applicable constitutional principles promises a way out."

When that change came, it was not what Brennan had in mind. The Nixon appointees sided with Burger, and as *Deep Throat* packed theaters across the nation in June 1973, the Supreme Court undid fifteen years of interpreting *Roth*. Delivering the majority opinion in *Miller v. California*, the chief justice brushed aside those years. "The Court now undertakes to formulate standards more concrete than those in the past," he began. Burger correctly noted that, since *Roth*, no five-justice majority had ever again agreed on a standard for obscenity. For a new majority consisting of himself, his three fellow Nixon appointees, and Byron White, Burger could thus speak authoritatively, without fear of violating the traditional Court decorum that held it improper to reverse too recent a precedent. Simply put, there was no solid doctrine to reverse.

So, when Burger declared community standards to be no longer national in scope, he needed waste little time on *Jacobellis v. Ohio*, the 1964 case in which Brennan had asserted that they were. *Jacobellis* had been highly fractured, and *Miller* was not. "It is neither realistic nor constitutionally sound," Burger explained, "to read the First Amendment as requiring that the people of Maine or Mississippi accept public depiction of conduct found tolerable in Las Vegas, or New York City."

States did not have infinite leeway under *Miller*. The new constitutional standards limited obscenity to "works which, taken as a whole, appeal to the prurient interest in sex, which portray sexual conduct in a patently offensive way, and which, taken as a whole, do not have serious literary, artistic, political, or scientific value." Burger even offered possible statutes as examples, setting "hard core" as the crucial boundary. No longer would a single smidgeon of socially redeeming value rescue a work that otherwise lacked a claim to serious value.

Burger declined to further flesh out the notions of "hard core" or "serious value," content to leave them to legislators. He explicitly presented *Miller v. California* as a reaffirmation of *Roth*, though the new opinion dramatically shifted the burden of proof onto the accused, to establish their literary, artistic, political, or scientific value. If Brennan had shown only a thin interest in history in *Roth*, Burger showed even less in *Miller*. "There is no evidence, empirical or historical, that the stern 19th century American censorship of public distribution and display of material relating to sex . . . in any way limited or affected expression of serious literary, artistic, political, or scientific ideas," he wrote, rather blithely brushing aside the experiences of Ida Craddock, Ezra Heywood, and the numerous other sex radicals imprisoned under the Comstock Act.

What *Miller* meant in practice was clarified through its companion cases, handed down the same day. *Kaplan v. California* involved a Los Angeles obscenity conviction for the proprietor of the Peek-A-Boo Bookstore, solely on the basis of *Suite 69*, a pulpy porn novel with no images whatsoever but simply a procession of verbal sex scenes. Burger agreed with the California court that the novel was obscene. "A state could reasonably regard the 'hard core' conduct described by *Suite 69* as capable of encouraging or causing antisocial behavior, especially in its impact on young people," Burger wrote. The overwhelming social-science consensus that had been laid out in the 1970 President's Commission on Obscenity and Pornography report rejected that claim, but Burger paid it little heed. In yet another case, *Paris Adult Theatre I v. Slaton*, he elaborated, citing the dissenting commission report written by Catholic priest Morton Hill to suggest "there is at least an arguable correlation between obscene material and crime." Thus the state of Georgia, from which the case came, might "quite reasonably determine that such a connection does or might exist."

"We categorically disapprove the theory," Burger opined, "that obscene, pornographic films acquire constitutional immunity from state regulation simply because they are exhibited for consenting adults only." Two more cases restricted transportation of obscene materials, clarifying that *Stanley* ended at the doorway of the home. All five of the cases that introduced the new *Miller* standards came from the same five-justice majority of the Nixon quartet plus White. Burger wrote for the majority in all cases, with the others signing on fully without qualifying concurrences. As much as he insisted the Court had reaffirmed *Roth*, it had also gutted the entirety of the obscenity framework built on *Roth*. Unsurprisingly, the dissenting justices fumed. William O. Douglas's absolutist dissents, if even more scathing than ever, were to be expected. The true surprise was the new doctrine of William Brennan.

In addition to presiding as key architect of Supreme Court obscenity doctrine for fifteen years, Brennan was also the justice who had first explained the exclusion of obscenity from First Amendment protection. As the new *Miller* standards were handed down, Brennan rejected his own creation. He had drafted a *Miller* dissent but instead made *Paris Theatre* the place of his major statement, since the case involved such clear conditions of nonintrusive pornography screened only for adults who sought it out. In a long, candid, and searching dissent, Brennan reviewed the history of modern obscenity doctrine, assessed the various possible options, and finally decided, "Our experience with the *Roth* approach has certainly taught us that the outright suppression of obscenity cannot be reconciled with the fundamental principles of the First and Fourteenth Amendments." Accusing Burger of vagueness and of creating "an invitation to widespread suppression of sexually oriented speech" in the new standards, Brennan felt "forced to conclude" that obscenity was a failed doctrine. While not quite reaching Douglas's absolutism, Brennan called for a limitation of state action to obscene materials displayed to minors or unconsenting adults. All else should receive First Amendment protection, no matter how pornographic or devoid of value.

That the key author of modern obscenity doctrine should so decisively renounce it was bitterly ironic, given that it came at the very moment when Brennan had so clearly lost his liberal majority. The window in which *Redrup* might have been formalized into an actual, binding doctrine was surely closed, if it had indeed ever been open. Like Dr. Frankenstein watching his own monstrous creation wander off to a path of destruction, Brennan could but sit on the bench powerless to intervene in the new *Miller* era.

The destruction, when it came, proved fleeting. *Miller* did indeed, as its critics and dissenters feared, invite immediate repression. Provincial prosecutors threatened newsdealers over items as innocuous as *Playboy*; Hollywood producers abandoned a planned film of Hubert Selby Jr.'s notorious novel *Last Exit to Brooklyn*; many adult theaters replaced hardcore films with softcore; and the gay and lesbian press expressed fear of yet another crackdown. Even the critical and commercial hit film *The Exorcist* drew obscenity charges in Jackson, Mississippi.

Warren Burger had accomplished his "little chill." But it was a bit *too* chilly for the Court, as local courts overreached. Burger's conservatism was not extremism, and he had attempted to make clear in

Miller that even the newly flexible local standards rested on a "hard-core" bed. The *Miller* standards were not meant to apply to something like Mike Nichols's *Carnal Knowledge*, a mainstream film with Jack Nicholson and Art Garfunkel. Though the film loosely paralleled *Deep Throat* structurally, with scenes of two male friends discussing their romantic and sexual troubles with women interspersed with their various encounters, the sex was strictly simulated and the nudity more discreet than hardcore's maximum visibility.

When a theater manager was convicted on obscenity charges for screening *Carnal Knowledge* in Albany, Georgia, shortly after *Miller*, the Court needed to clarify matters. Reversing the Georgia courts that had upheld the conviction, William Rehnquist explained that "nudity alone is not enough to make material legally obscene under the *Miller* standards." As Brennan noted in a resigned concurrence, that left the Court back where it had started, stuck as a review board for lower courts as they hashed out the vaguely defined notion of obscenity.

Obscenity doctrine in 1974, then, was more conservative than it had been several years earlier, but not necessarily more clear. At this impasse, what John Marshall Harlan had years ago called "the intractable problem" of obscenity, culture superseded law. With the universal awareness of *Deep Throat* even lending itself to the alias for the man whose secret information helped topple the criminal Nixon administration after the bungled Watergate break-ins, pornography had become less stigmatized. *Miller* seemingly made prosecutions easier, but in fact this cultural drift made convictions harder to obtain. Juries were tougher to shock, more reluctant to send people to prison for obscenity. A more liberal culture reined in the more conservative doctrine.

What this meant, in practice, was that pornography had won over obscenity law, at least for the most part. National politics affirmed this. Many cities shifted from obscenity busts to using zoning laws to contain porn. While Nixon had embraced porn-busting as a means of displaying his conservative bona fides, Democrat Jimmy Carter, elected in 1976, showed little interest in continuing that trend. Other than signing a bill against child pornography, Carter kept quiet on the topic. Though his Justice Department initiated a major investigation, known as MIPORN, it was much more interested in the Mafia structures that increasingly ran the business than in moralistic obscenity busts.

As if to mark the passing of an era, Samuel Roth had died in July 1974, the year after *Miller v. California*. His final years had been quiet ones, with Roth surely deriving satisfaction from his family's upward mobility back into respectability. Grandson James Kugel even published a book, *The Techniques of Strangeness: A Study of Symbolist Poetry*, with prestigious Yale University Press in 1971, dedicating it to Sam. Upon his death, the *New York Times* ran a respectful obituary that called him a "poet, translator, and publisher." Time, distance, and sexual revolution had helped obscure some of Roth's more troubling aspects, allowing him placement in a simpler narrative of the fight for free expression.

Snuffing Obscenity Law?

With obscenity law fading in relevance by the late 1970s, a powerful and innovative critique of the doctrine emanated out of the emerging feminist antipornography movement. While primarily committed to combating porn itself, the movement's intellectual leaders also developed a new analysis of obscenity in order both to distinguish themselves from moralists like Comstock and also to theorize fresh methods of employing the law against the subjugation of women. Generally remembered as a grassroots political movement, feminist antiporn activism also deserves inclusion in the legal history of obscenity as a necessary intervention into a discussion that had been largely dominated by men with little interest in interrogating sexual politics.

In the wake of the 1976 exploitation film *Snuff* and its advertising, which promised spectacular, sexualized violence against women, feminist energies began coalescing around porn. A robust dialogue across feminist periodicals earlier in the decade had expressed nuance and ambivalence, but new groups like Women Against Violence in Pornography and Media signaled a shift, positioning *Snuff* in the context of ongoing feminist efforts against media violence; its East Coast splinter group Women Against Pornography (WAP) superseded the group but reduced its critique in scope, as its name suggested. As WAP conceptualized it, *all* pornography was violence against women — if not in literal, physical terms, then in ideological ones. As movement leader Andrea Dworkin put it in her 1981 landmark *Pornography: Men*

Possessing Women, "Male power is the raison d'etre of pornography; the degradation of the female is the means of achieving this power." This analysis won extensive media attention, as WAP drew upwards of 5,000 supporters to its marches and rallies.

The feminist antiporn movement drew internal criticisms from other feminists, some of whom found it overly broad in painting women as victims, problematic in the ways it conflated pornography and violence, and insensitive to the concerns of lesbians and women of color, among other key critiques. Much of the memory of the movement was shaped by the internal "sex wars" of the 1980s it launched among feminists, which expanded beyond pornography to address BDSM sexuality (a composite abbreviation for bondage and discipline, dominance and submission, and sadomaschism), lesbian butch/femme identities, and more. This set of conflicts, too large and complicated to be fully recounted here, is definitively examined in historian Carolyn Bronstein's *Battling Pornography*. Less remembered is the specifically *legal* analysis pioneered by antiporn feminists.

From the start, antiporn feminists were intent on distinguishing their project from that of obscenity law. Questions of free speech were troubling, and editor Laura Lederer devoted several essays in the important 1980 anthology *Take Back the Night: Women on Pornography* to the issue. Approaches differed. Susan Brownmiller, who had applauded *Miller* in a 1973 op-ed, suggested that "contemporary community standards" were precisely "what we're trying to redefine," by fighting pornography whose intent was to "humiliate, degrade, and dehumanize the female body for the purpose of erotic stimulation and pleasure." Another author defined pornography as "any use of the media which equates sex and violence," and agreed that the First Amendment should not protect it. Attorney Wendy Kaminer produced the most compelling essay, reminding that only the government could violate the First Amendment, and feminists could "protest pornography with impunity under the First Amendment as long as they do not invoke or advocate the exercise of government authority." Surveying possible approaches like the clear and present danger test, Kaminer concluded that the solution needed to remain a nonstate one, carried out through activism and education rather than legal suppression.

More than any other figure, law professor Catharine MacKinnon pulled these threads together into a cohesive feminist legal theory of pornography. Having established herself as a masterful feminist legal thinker in pioneering work that led to the legal recognition of sexual harassment, she now turned to porn. Rejecting obscenity law as a tool of male power, she also refused to stay beholden to the First Amendment. Writing on the sexual politics of that cherished constitutional centerpiece, she claimed the "social preconditions, the presumptions, that underlie" it "do not apply to women." The amendment, after all, "essentially presumes some level of social equality among people and hence essentially equal social access to the means of expression." As MacKinnon pointedly put it in another essay, the First Amendment was "conceived by white men from the point of view of their social position. Some of them owned slaves; most of them owned women."

Since patriarchal society had never allotted women a full voice as a social class, they owed little fealty to the liberal fetish of free speech. Her answer, though, was not a recourse to obscenity doctrine. The law of obscenity, as MacKinnon saw it, "reproduces the pornographic point of view on women." Acting as a site of male power, obscenity "helps keep pornography sexy by putting state power—force, hierarchy—behind its purported prohibition on what man can have sexual access to." In a 1984 *Yale Law and Policy Review* article, MacKinnon deconstructed the logic of obscenity from a feminist perspective. "Feminism doubts," for instance, "whether the average person, gender neutral, exists"; prurient interest she understood as meaning "to give a man an erection." As she memorably put it elsewhere, "obscenity is more concerned with whether men blush, pornography with whether women bleed—both producing a sexual rush."

Ultimately obscenity was nothing more than a "moral idea," while pornography "is a political practice." The one thing obscenity law got right was that "pornography is more act-like than thought-like." Rejecting obscenity law entirely, MacKinnon nonetheless argued that pornography lacked free-speech claims. Like "white only" signs that did the dirty work of segregation, pornography was not *about* the subjugation of women; it did not *depict* the subjugation of women; it *was*, in literal fact, the actual subjugation of women in practice. As evidence, she cited Linda Lovelace, who had recently published an autobiography, *Ordeal*, which claimed she had been forced into *Deep Throat* and porn by an abusive husband.

MacKinnon went beyond theorizing. Teaching at the University of Minnesota, she and Andrea Dworkin attempted to put their ideas into practice. They cowrote a Minneapolis city ordinance in 1983, classifying pornography not as a free-speech issue, but as one of civil rights. Their definition and finding of facts offered a sweeping reconceptualization:

> Pornography is a systematic practice of exploitation and subordination on sex that differentially harms women. The harm of pornography includes dehumanization, sexual exploitation, forced sex, forced prostitution, physical injury, and social and sexual terrorism and inferiority presented as entertainment. The bigotry and contempt pornography promotes, with the acts of aggression it fosters, diminish opportunities for equality of rights in employment, education, property, public accommodations, and public services . . . [and ultimately] restricting women in particular from full exercise of citizenship and participation in public life.

On those grounds, pornography in which "sexually explicit subordination of women, graphically depicted, whether in pictures or in words," included women "presented dehumanized as sexual objects," as "sexual objects who enjoy pain or humiliation," or as "sexual objects who experience sexual pleasure in being raped," or "presented in postures of sexual submission" fell under the ordinance's purview. Some of the language was quite broad; other clauses included "women are presented as whores by nature" and "women are presented being penetrated by objects or animals," leaving unclear the line between depictions of physical violence and mere sexual explicitness.

Some of the activities barred by the ordinance were already actionable under existing laws, such as "coercion into pornographic performances." The Dworkin-MacKinnon ordinance also invited civil action against "discrimination by trafficking in pornography," which not only included unwilling spectators' forced exposure to porn but also declared, "The formation of private clubs or associations for purposes of trafficking in pornography is illegal and shall be considered a conspiracy to violate the civil rights of women." The ordinance invited civil actions in the form of injunctions against such "conspir-

acies" and financial damages to parties who could show injury resulting from pornography.

Free-speech activists were horrified by the Minneapolis ordinance,
with some of the fiercest criticism coming from other feminists.
Defining themselves as "sex-positive" feminists, such critics as Nan
Hunter, Carole Vance, and Lisa Duggan saw in the legislation a threatening reinscription of gender roles that froze women as passive victims and stripped them of sexual agency. As if to disprove Dworkin
and MacKinnon by counterexample, new lesbian magazines *Bad Attitude* and *On Our Backs* (parodying long-running, and antiporn, *off our
backs*) embraced prurience and explicitness as self-affirming assertions
of lesbian identity. Feminist scholars, meanwhile, devised an interpretation of women's historical experience of sexuality based on *Plea -
sure and Danger*, as one prominent 1984 anthology was titled. This
framework acknowledged that women had been oppressed by patri-
archy, but emphasized that they nonetheless retained the capacity to
experience power and pleasure *within* the constraints of gender
inequality—including, at times, erotic tastes that antiporn feminists
seemingly reduced to mere effects of sexist indoctrination.

As the sex wars raged, the Minneapolis city council passed the ordinance, but it was twice vetoed by Mayor Donald Fraser on free-speech
grounds. The ordinance found better reception in Indianapolis, where
a more openly conservative local government passed a slightly modified version in 1984. Its feminist reinterpretation of pornography
never had the chance to be implemented. A consortium led by the
ACLU, librarians, and publishers filed for an immediate injunction.
Challenging the law in court, they won before federal district judge
Sarah Evans Barker, who found the ordinance unconstitutionally
vague and overbroad. Showing some sympathy for the goals of the
ordinance, Barker nonetheless ruled that pornography remained a
form of speech rather than an action. The Supreme Court ultimately
affirmed without comment. MacKinnon and Dworkin would be free
to argue against pornography in words and actions, but not through
law in this way. Several other local emulations occurred, but most
failed, and none withstood court challenge. Feminists grew increasingly wary of the approach as it became clear that the radical gender
ideals of Dworkin and MacKinnon were all too easily co-opted by

social conservatives who actually opposed feminism but were willing to use its rhetoric to support old-fashioned smut-busting.

Ultimately unimplemented as it was, the Dworkin-MacKinnon ordinance represented the last great intervention into obscenity doctrine. The Supreme Court had exempted child pornography from the First Amendment as a new legal category independent of obscenity in 1982, but otherwise the real battlegrounds of the never-ending porn debates were located in the political arena. Judge Barker's opinion against the feminist antiporn ordinance served as a telling reminder of *Roth*'s place in the legal discourse of the 1980s: it wasn't cited at all or by the circuit court on appeal. Though *Roth* remained the major landmark in obscenity doctrine, it had been absorbed into the new *Miller* standards so completely that little reason existed to invoke *Roth* directly.

Receding into invisibility, renounced by its own author, rejected by feminists, and reconfigured by *Miller*, *Roth v. United States* nonetheless remained the governing framework for obscenity. Cultural change meant that the content of the battles had shifted from important novels to exclusively hardcore pornography, but the fundamental structure remained intact: obscenity was not protected by the First Amendment.

Epilogue
After Obscenity?

Eight decades after Random House challenged obscenity law by publishing James Joyce's *Ulysses*, its Vintage imprint brought another author across the Atlantic to America. E. L. James carried less critical weight than Joyce, coming not out of the literary avant-garde but rather the Internet world, where her *Fifty Shades of Grey* trilogy (as of 2012) had begun life as smutty fan fiction based on the popular *Twilight* series. As feminists debated the sexual politics of the series' bondage-themed relationship between a young woman and an older, wealthier man, conservatives expressed moral indignation about the popularity of the books, with their graphic and somewhat unconventional sexuality. Libraries across the nation split over whether to stock them.

In some ways, not much had changed since the days of Samuel Roth. James's notoriously clunky prose, combined with her clear interest in pushing the boundaries of socially accepted sexuality, carried a Roth-like quality. One legacy of *Roth v. United States* was evident in the controversies over *Fifty Shades of Grey*. Commentators like television self-help guru Dr. Drew Pinsky might dismissively call the series "pathological," but no one within mainstream circles would call the books obscene. That battle appeared to have been fought, and won, by the forces of sexual expression.

Yet another legacy of *Roth* more silently inhered in the debate: in the early twenty-first century, obscene materials remain unprotected by the First Amendment. No less than the head of the National Coalition Against Censorship weighed in against libraries refusing to carry *Fifty Shades* in May 2012, telling the *New York Times* that libraries should not police adult reading, "other than the restrictions on obscenity and child pornography." Apparently the exclusion of obscene materials (made by and for consenting adults, as opposed to child porn) from the First Amendment had also been accepted as something other than censorship.

This condition is highly unlikely to change in any imaginable future. For a brief moment after the Supreme Court finally declared sodomy laws for consenting adults in private spaces unconstitutional in *Lawrence v. Texas* (2003), there appeared to be some doubt about governmental jurisdiction over private morality. Conservative justice Antonin Scalia's impassioned dissent in *Lawrence* relied on slippery-slope reasoning to worry that the decision might abolish obscenity laws, along with other moral regulations including laws against prostitution and even, to the surprise and amusement of many Court watchers, masturbation. Yet when a Pennsylvania federal court applied *Lawrence* to obscenity in overturning the conviction of the operators of California porn firm Extreme Associates in 2005, the opinion was quickly overturned. Whatever advances *Lawrence* made for LGBT rights, those changes would not affect obscenity.

Thus in the years since the early 1980s, obscenity as a legal doctrine has largely remained in the shadows of pornography as a political and cultural issue. On those fronts, it has never been far from the public consciousness. The Reagan administration of the 1980s used pornography tactically to curry favor with conservative evangelical Christians, who had coalesced around the Republican Party after experiencing disappointment with the liberal social policies of Jimmy Carter in the late 1970s. Though Carter was America's first born-again Christian president and Reagan a divorced, relatively unreligious man, he was elected with major support from what political scientists labeled the "Christian Right." After disappointing many members with his preference for free-market economic policies over antigay or antiabortion efforts, Reagan took action against smut in 1985 with the creation of the Attorney General's Commission on Pornography.

Generally known as the Meese Commission, after Attorney General Ed Meese, the body was given an explicit mandate to overturn the conclusions of the libertarian 1970 President's Commission on Obscenity and Pornography report. Instead of social science research, it held emotionally intense hearings, in which various "victims" of pornography, from female models to male consumers, testified about the harmful impact porn had on their lives. The Meese Commission also adopted the language of antiporn feminism, invoking the subjugation of women, although no fair observer would mistake its socially conservative agenda for sharing much common ground with feminism. When it issued its report in 1986, linking adult pornography to child pornography, violence against women, and other social ills, social scientists like the University of California, Santa Barbara's Edward Donnerstein published strong rebukes, noting that the Meese Commission had deliberately distorted their research, which did not support its conclusions. "The single most important problem in the media today, as clearly indicated by social science research," Donnerstein and colleague Edward Linz insisted, "is not pornography but violence."

While the media mostly mocked the Meese Commission report, it did provide support for the Reagan Justice Department to place more emphasis on obscenity prosecutions. While the legal doctrine had not shifted, the laws of enforcement did. The Reagan era marked the onset of increasingly punitive laws, especially relating to such perceived social threats as drugs, leading to the mass incarceration of hundreds of thousands, disproportionately young men of color. Obscenity enforcement, too, received a boost from the application of RICO, the Racketeer Influenced and Corrupt Organizations Act, which allowed the government to confiscate the property of those convicted as a "syndicated racket" — including even family-owned video stores that had adult-only back rooms for porn movies. Meanwhile, the Justice Department under Reagan also relied on deliberate attrition tactics, charging mail distributors in numerous, always conservative venues, on the logic that even without convictions they might be driven out of business by the sheer costs of defending themselves in, say, Utah, Alabama, and North Carolina simultaneously.

Eventually, a federal court denounced the Reaganite attrition prosecutions as unconstitutional, and Reagan's vice president and successor George H. W. Bush showed little enthusiasm for such moral grandstanding (a fact that cost him dearly in his failed bid for reelection — a lesson not lost on his son). Bill Clinton, elected in 1992 on a socially liberal platform, had even less. His Justice Department followed an expressed policy of pursuing child pornography cases, but deescalating consenting-adult obscenity cases.

In this deregulated atmosphere, pornography moved further into the mainstream than it had since its brief flirtation with public acceptance in the porno-chic moment of the early 1970s. Certainly the relaxed law-enforcement protocol of the 1990s set a safe foundation for this development, but other forces were also at work. The corporatization of porn, for instance, perfected new public-relations techniques. The Meese Commission had worked hard to link porn with the criminal Mafia underworld in 1986, and while it wasn't exactly wrong, it was looking to the past rather than the future. Already by the 1980s firms such as VCX and Vivid had emerged from the shady back alleys of capitalism and into the main currents. They practiced the same habits as other media-savvy enterprises: branding, diversified product lines, multimedia advertising, and the like. Thus by the turn of the century, consumers could watch porn star Ron Jeremy on reality television, read Jenna Jameson's autobiography, or purchase sex toys intimately molded by Lexington Steele or Belladonna.

Perhaps the major factor underlying the mainstreaming of pornography by the twenty-first century, though, was technology, particularly the ascent of the Internet to a place of daily centrality in American lives. Home video in the 1980s had already removed porn from the urban landscape, as VHS tapes and later DVDs replaced the more public adult theaters, but the Internet perfected the privatization of porn, reducing the need to even leave the house for it. Porn had played a major role in online culture from its very inception and would stay ubiquitous; by 2012 even a Google image search for as innocuous a term as "housewife" would result in a deluge of pornographic images, provided its family-friendly SafeSearch was turned off. As the Internet began its ascent in the mid-1990s, it had triggered an outpouring of anxiety about protecting children from its dangerously sexualized clutches. The rhetoric frequently echoed the very concerns popularized by Anthony Comstock a century earlier and led to a series of efforts to regulate cyberspace, beginning with the Communications Decency Act in 1996 and continuing well into the early twenty-first century. Such efforts tended to fare poorly in court or as regulatory tools, but did serve as reminders of the role child-protection sentiment continues to play in American understandings of obscenity.

Meanwhile, the Internet decentralized everything about porn — not just the consumption, but also the production. Competing with the corporate porn world was an entire galaxy of self-produced smut, some of it done in the name of commerce (such as successful web sites like Suicide Girls, with its heavily tattooed models in librarian glasses), much simply for noncommodified exhibitionistic pleasure, shot on webcams and cell phones and posted to sites such as XTube. Much online smut replicated sexist and misogynist attitudes of earlier incarnations, but other venues provided access for previously marginalized voices to assert themselves. "There is power in creating images, and . . . for a woman of color and a queer to take that power," explained Shine Louise Houston, head of San Francisco–based Pink and White Productions, whose *Crash Pad* series and other Internet-based work focused on "the complexities of queer sexual desire" — combining both feminist theory *and* prurience. Meanwhile, Morty Diamond's films like *Trannyfags* and *Trans Entities* offered empowered, eroticized representations of transgender bodies and identities still demeaned in mainstream culture. Both Houston and Diamond won frequent online praise from feminist blogs, showing that sex-positive feminism had superseded antiporn feminism in the younger generation.

Cultural narratives of obscenity reflected this trajectory. In films that dealt with the subject, prosecutors were, without fail, presented negatively. Narrative films like *The People vs. Larry Flynt* (1996) and *Howl* (2010), as well as documentaries like *Inside Deep Throat* (2003) and *Obscene* (2007, about Grove Press publisher Barney Rosset), portrayed those who challenged obscenity laws as rebellious heroes who paved the way for the future. Of course, no films lionized Samuel Roth. When *Howl*, which dramatized the 1957 San Francisco obscenity trial of Allen Ginsberg's groundbreaking poem, flashed an onscreen quotation of the *Roth* standards, it simply credited them to "U.S. Supreme Court" without citing the case by name.

Porn, it seemed, had lost much of its threatening edge. Larry Flynt and porn actress Mary Carey both placed in the top ten among the numerous candidates for the surreal California gubernatorial recall election of 2003 — and few even found it noteworthy that winner Arnold Schwarzenegger in the 1970s had posed nude for physique photographs that would have challenged obscenity law just a decade before that. By the time independent filmmaker Steven Soderbergh cast porn actress Sasha Grey in his moody art-house film *The Girlfriend Experience* (2009), it was perceived as neither shocking nor even an act of stunt-casting. "Porn is beyond everywhere now," Soderbergh explained in an interview. "Everybody on television looks like they're in porn, you know?"

Not everyone joined in this acceptance of the new cultural norm. Antiporn feminists like Gail Dines maintained active speaking engagements, while the Christian Right continued in its socially conservative push. The legal policies of the George W. Bush administration reflected the limitations of this resistance. Wholly pledged to the Christian Right, Bush delivered when it came to restricting abortion access and fighting against LGBT rights. But on porn, even the biblically inclined president found himself stuck. Declaring "Protection from Pornography Week" in 2003, he accused smut of "debilitating effects on communities, marriages, families, and children." Bush committed his Justice Department to a revival of adult obscenity prosecutions.

Yet the best he was able to achieve, even with a new Obscenity Prosecution Task Force that brought back some of the very Reagan-era bureaucrats who had been chided for their unconstitutional attrition tactics, was a string of victories against marginal purveyors of "extreme porn," featuring simulated rape, real vomit and other bodily functions, or bestiality. Though the Bush Justice Department seemed to return to another era in prosecuting Pennsylvanian Karen Fletcher for her web site Red Rose Stories, which featured descriptive but unillustrated stories about intergenerational sex, the mainstream porn industry remained safe and legally secure — as a disappointed Christian Right observed.

The election of Barack Obama in 2008 brought the Bush prosecutions to an end. Obama replayed the Clinton years in many ways, including bringing the former president's deputy attorney general, Eric Holder, back with a promotion to the top Justice Department post. Neither Obama nor Holder showed any interest in pursuing adult obscenity cases, and with the last major Bush effort, against Evil Angel Productions head John Stagliano, thrown out of court by an irate federal judge in 2010, obscenity law receded again to the background.

Yet it never disappeared. Campaigning on a hard-line social-conservative platform for the Republican presidential nomination in 2012, former Pennsylvania senator Rick Santorum called for a return to vigorous obscenity enforcement. He lost his bid, but not before compelling frontrunner Mitt Romney to make a similar pledge. Nothing in the historical record suggests anything but that a return of a conservative administration will mean more obscenity cases—if not successful legally, then more so politically, as a display of moral values.

Roth v. United States, too, remains dormant but ever present. If *Miller v. California* has superseded it in defining the doctrine of obscenity, *Roth* still pertains as the moment where the Court declared obscenity outside the range of the First Amendment's protections. When Antonin Scalia upheld the criminalization of even *virtual* child pornography (involving no real minors) in the 2008 case *U.S. v. Williams*, *Roth* appeared as his first citation. The citation served as a reminder: if *Roth* was a failure, as even its own author ultimately concluded, nothing better has yet come along in obscenity doctrine.

What that says about obscenity law probably depends on the perspective of the reader. For this book, Samuel Roth gets the last thought. Challenging his latest postal ban in 1948, he asked, "Is this blood the Postmaster General is complaining of, or is it ketchup? The mute, substantial testimony of these thousands of men and women from every village, town, city, and religious denomination in the United States is lost sight of by the Post Office Department in its mad war against all public discussion of sex." Sex has won, but the war continues. As Roth would surely point out, those citizens continue to vote for prurience with their eyes and money, and for politicians who allow its criminalization with their ballots. Obscenity law does the dirty work of cleaning up the mess.

Abrams v. U.S., 250 U.S. 616 (1919)
Adams Newark Theater Co. v. Newark, 120 A.2d 496 (1956); reversed, 126 A.2d 340 (1956); affirmed, 354 U.S. 931 (1957)
Adams Theatre Co. v. Keenan, 96 A.2d 519 (1953)
American Booksellers Association v. Hudnut, 598 F. Supp. 1316 (1984)
Bantam Books v. Sullivan, 372 U.S. 58 (1963)
Beauharnais v. Illinois, 343 U.S. 250 (1952)
Bridges v. California, 314 U.S. 252 (1941)
Burstyn v. Wilson, 343 U.S. 495 (1952)
Butler v. Michigan, 352 U.S. 380 (1952)
Chaplinsky v. New Hampshire, 315 U.S. 568 (1942)
Commonwealth v. Isenstadt, 62 N.E.2d 840 (1945)
Commonwealth v. Sharpless, 2 Serg. & Rawle 91 (1815)
Debs v. U.S., 249 U.S. 211 (1919)
Dennis v. U.S., 341 U.S. 494 (1951)
Ex Parte Jackson, 96 U.S. 727 (1877)
Excelsior Pictures Corp. v. Regents, 144 N.E.2d 31 (1957)
Gent v. State, 393 S.W.2d 219 (1965)
Ginsberg v. New York, 390 U.S. 629 (1968)
Ginzburg v. U.S., 383 U.S. 463 (1966)
Gitlow v. New York, 268 U.S. 652 (1925)
Grimm v. U.S., 156 U.S. 604 (1895)
Hadley v. State, 172 S.2d 237 (1943)
Halsey v. N.Y.S.S.V. 136 N.E. 219 (1922)
Hannegan v. Esquire, 327 U.S. 146 (1946)
Holmby Productions v. Vaughn, 350 U.S. 870 (1955)
Jacobellis v. Ohio, 378 U.S. 184 (1964)
Jenkins v. Georgia, 418 U.S. 153 (1974)
Kingsley Books, Inc. v. Brown, 354 U.S. 436 (1957)
Kingsley International Pictures v. Regents, 151 N.E.2d 197 (1958)
Manual Enterprises v. Day, 370 U.S. 478 (1962)
Memoirs v. Massachusetts, 383 U.S. 413 (1966)
Miller v. California, 413 U.S. 15 (1973)
Minersville School District v. Gobitis, 310 U.S. 586 (1940)
Mishkin v. New York, 383 U.S. 502 (1966)
Near v. Minnesota, 283 U.S. 697 (1931)
Paris Adult Theatre I v. Slaton, 413 U.S. 49 (1973)
Parmalee v. U.S., 113 F.2d 729 (1940)
Patterson v. Colorado, 205 U.S. 454 (1907)

People v. Brainard, 183 N.Y.S. 452 (1920)

People v. Pesky, 243 N.Y.S. 193 (1930)

People v. Ruggles, 8 Johns. 290 (1811)

People v. Winters, 63 N.E.2d 98 (1945)

Redrup v. New York, 386 U.S. 767 (1967)

Reynolds v. U.S., 98 U.S. 145 (1878)

Rosen v. U.S., 161 U.S. 29 (1896)

Roth v. Goldman, 172 F.2d 788 (1949)

Roth v. U.S., 237 F.2d 796 (1956), affirmed, 354 U.S. 476 (1957)

Schenck v. U.S., 249 U.S. 47 (1919)

Schindler v. U.S., 208 F.2d 289 (1953)

Smith v. California, 361 U.S. 147 (1959)

Stanley v. Georgia, 394 U.S. 557 (1969)

State v. Becker, 272 S.W.2d 283, 1954

Sunshine Book Company v. McCaffrey, 112 N.Y.S. 2d 476 (1952)

Sunshine Book Company v. Summerfield, 128 F. Supp. 564 (1955), reversed, 355
    U.S. 372 (1958)

Swearingen v. U.S., 161 U.S. 446 (1896)

Thornhill v. Alabama, 310 U.S. 88 (1940)

Times Film Corporation v. Chicago, 355 U.S. 35 (1957)

Times Film Corp. v. Chicago, 365 U.S. 43 (1961)

U.S. v. 35mm. Film Entitled "Language of Love," 432 F.2d 705 (1970)

U.S. v. Bennett, 24 F.Cas. 1093 (1879)

U.S. v. Kennerley, 209 F. 119 (1913)

U.S. v. Levine, 83 F.2d 156 (1936)

U.S. v. One Book Called "Ulysses," 5 F. Supp. 182 (1933), affirmed, 72 F. 2d 705
    (1934)

U.S. v. One Obscene Book Entitled "Married Love," 48 F. 2d 821 (1931)

U.S. v. One Package, 86 F.2d 737 (1936)

U.S. v. Williams, 553 U.S. 285 (2008)

Walker v. Popenoe, 149 F.2d 511 (1945)

West Virginia State Board of Education v. Barnette, 319 U.S. 624 (1943)

Whitney v. California, 274 U.S. 357 (1927)

Winters v. New York, 333 U.S. 507 (1948)

CHRONOLOGY

1727	Obscenity enters English common law (as obscene libel) in *Regina v. Curll*
1791	First Amendment added to the U.S. Constitution, adopted as part of the Bill of Rights
1798	Sedition Act passed; expires in 1801 without its constitutionality being tested
1820s	States begin codifying obscenity, moving it from the common law to statutory law
Early 1840s	Prosecutions of flash-press publications in New York City signal both official resistance to "obscene" materials and relative unimportance of First Amendment
1865–1870	Reconstruction Amendments (Thirteenth, Fourteenth, and Fifteenth) show increasing role of the federal government
1868	British case *Regina v. Hicklin* introduces "deprave and corrupt" test for obscenity; materials to be evaluated on the basis of their parts and effects on the most vulnerable
1873	Comstock Act makes the mailing of obscene material a federal crime; New York antivice crusader Anthony Comstock appointed special agent of the Post Office to help enforce it
1875	National Liberal League begins to coalesce free-speech activism
1893	Samuel Roth born
1896	Supreme Court explicitly adopts *Hicklin* standards in *Rosen*; also restricts obscenity to matters of "sexual impurity" in *Swearingen*, then retreats from obscenity for next six decades
1902	Ida Craddock commits suicide in response to persecution by Anthony Comstock
1902	Free Speech League formed, takes radical libertarian approach to freedom of speech
1913	A jury refuses to convict Mitchell Kennerley of obscenity for publishing popular novel *Hagar Revelly*, reflecting increasing sexual liberalism among the public

1915	Anthony Comstock dies; leadership of New York Society for the Suppression of Vice passes to John Saxton Sumner
1917–1918	Espionage Act and Sedition Act lead to wartime government crackdown on dissent
March 1919	*Schenck v. U.S.* upholds Espionage Act against First Amendment challenge; Justice Oliver Wendell Holmes articulates "clear and present danger" for first time, though does not yet assign great importance to the phrase
November 1919	In *Abrams v. U.S.*, Holmes gives new weight to "clear and present danger" in his dissent, though Court majority affirms convictions of revolutionaries under Sedition Act
1920	American Civil Liberties Union takes shape, growing out of World War I pacifist activism
1925	*Gitlow v. New York* incorporates the First Amendment for the first time, making it relevant at the state level
1927	Samuel Roth's unauthorized version of James Joyce's *Ulysses* leads to his exile from reputable literary circles and a career in smut
1928	Arrested for selling works including *Lady Chatterley's Lover*, Roth receives his first prison sentence, of three months
1933	Judge John Woolsey allows importation of *Ulysses* despite customs officials' efforts to ban it as obscene; his opinion weakens *Hicklin* standards
1936	Roth returns to prison for longest term yet, three years
1942	*Chaplinsky v. New Hampshire* upholds ban on "fighting words," and Justice Frank Murphy lumps obscenity with them in a passing comment
1946	*Hannegan v. Esquire* restricts postal authority to bar nonobscene magazines from second-class mailing privileges
1948	*Sexual Behavior in the Human Male* (the first Kinsey Report) sparks national discussion of sexual practices, along with much controversy over its findings
1949	Supreme Court refuses to hear Roth's challenge of postal authorities in *Roth v. Goldman*
Early 1950s	Intertwining of Cold War and domestic sexual conservatism results in more repressive sexual politics; both homosexuality and obscenity increasingly targeted, both linked to communism by opponents

1951	Supreme Court signals retraction of First Amendment in *Dennis v. U.S.*, upholding Smith Act prosecutions of Communist Party leaders and weakening "clear and present danger" standard
1953	Second Kinsey Report, *Sexual Behavior in the Human Female*, generates even greater outcry than the first, reflecting tenor of the times
May 1955	Samuel Roth called before Kefauver Committee, is vilified in press
February 1956	Roth convicted by federal jury on four obscenity counts based on *Good Times* and *American Aphrodite*; Judge John Cashin sentences him to five years' imprisonment and $5,000 fine
September 1956	Second Circuit Court of Appeals rejects Roth's appeal, with concurrence from Judge Jerome Frank urging the Supreme Court to take the case
January 1957	Supreme Court grants certiorari in *Roth v. U.S.*
February 1957	In *Butler v. Michigan*, Supreme Court overturns state statute based on *Hicklin* standards, but avoids larger questions of obscenity per se
June 1957	Supreme Court issues *Roth v. U.S.*, bound with *Alberts v. California*, establishing William Brennan's obscenity doctrine
January 1958	Effects of *Roth* seen in *ONE v. Oleson*, where Court delivers first ever gay-rights Supreme Court victory in homophile magazine's case against postal authorities; lack of written opinion hampers impact, however
1958–1959	Several Court opinions show liberalizing attitude, with *Roth* as primary basis
1962	*Manual Enterprises v. Day* sides with male physique magazines over postal authorities
1964	*Jacobellis v. Ohio* makes clear that *Roth* "community standards" are national, not local
1966	Trio of cases (*Memoirs v. Massachusetts*, *Ginzburg v. U.S.*, *Mishkin v. New York*) reflects inability of Court to articulate clear, consistent standards for obscenity
1967	*Redrup v. New York* begins new Court tactic of reversing obscenity convictions without signed opinions
1968	Citizens for Decent Literature plays central role in

derailing Lyndon Johnson's nomination of Abe Fortas to chief justiceship of the Supreme Court, reflecting growing conservative mobilization against smut

1970   Hardcore pornography appears in storefront theaters across the nation

1972   *Deep Throat* begins the "porno chic" moment of mainstream pornography

1973   *Miller v. California* announces new conservative spin on obscenity doctrine, led by Richard Nixon's appointees; Justice Brennan renounces his own earlier efforts at obscenity doctrine, moves toward free speech absolutism. *Miller* supplants *Roth* as the new definitive precedent, but does not reverse it, only clarifies it

1976   Exploitation film *Snuff* helps inspire formation of Women Against Violence in Pornography and Media; spinoff group Women Against Pornography takes lead in feminist antipornography movement a few years later

1984   Law professor Catharine MacKinnon leads efforts to pass feminist antipornography ordinances in Minneapolis, then Indianapolis

1984   *On Our Backs* debuts as pro-sex lesbian erotic magazine in opposition to feminist antiporn movement

1986   Meese Commission report shows continued use of pornography as a rallying point for conservative politicians

2003   *Lawrence v. Texas* opinion against sodomy laws briefly suggests a broader challenge to obscenity, but federal courts reject its application on that front

2003   President George W. Bush declares Protection from Pornography Week, commits Justice Department to reviving adult obscenity prosecutions

BIBLIOGRAPHICAL ESSAY

Note from the Series Editors: The following bibliographical essay contains the major primary and secondary sources the author consulted for this volume. We have asked all authors in the series to omit formal citations in order to make our volumes more readable, inexpensive, and appealing for students and general readers. In adopting this format, Landmark Law Cases and American Society follows the precedent of a number of highly regarded and widely consulted series.

As an avowed footnote fetishist, part of me mourns their absence here. But a bibliographical essay is something to relish, and it provides juicy compensation to write. I have organized this essay thematically, highlighting the archival sources, published primary sources, and secondary scholarship that constitute the research base of this book. Some important sources cut across categories, though, so I begin with the general.

Works that deal broadly with the histories of obscenity and pornography are many, but I would single out a few. Edward de Grazia, *Girls Lean Back Everywhere: The Law of Obscenity and the Assault on Genius* (New York: Random House, 1992), is such an enormous book that few nonspecialists will read it, but its encyclopedic scope is matched by its sharp eye, befitting one who was not just a scholar but an active participant (as defense attorney) in these battles. Richard Kuh comes from the other side of the courtroom, but provides more insider perspective in *Foolish Figleaves? Pornography In and Out of Court* (New York: Macmillan, 1967). Felice Flannery Lewis's *Literature, Obscenity, and the Law* (Carbondale: Southern Illinois University Press, 1976), remains exemplary in its balancing of legal analysis against literary, and Richard Hixson delivers a more focused but useful narrative in *Pornography and the Justices: The Supreme Court and the Intractable Obscenity Problem* (Carbondale: Southern Illinois University Press, 1996). Almost everything one could imagine and much that one could not is covered in Joseph Slade's three-volume *Pornography and Sexual Representation: A Reference Guide* (Westport, Conn.: Greenwood, 2001). Finally, a marvelous and thus far rather overlooked study, Christopher Novlin, *Judging Obscenity: A Critical History of Evidence* (Montreal: McGill-Queen's University Press, 2003), examines both the United States and Canada.

While numerous works on the history of sexuality are cited below, it remains amazing that a broad synthetic text *predated* much of the field, yet John D'Emilio and Estelle Freedman's *Intimate Matters: A History of Sexuality in America* (New York: Harper and Row, 1988), did just that. It is from D'Emilio and Freedman that I take the idea of sexual liberalism, so important in this book.

The Samuel Roth Papers at Columbia University are perhaps the central source for this book. The collection, only recently opened, is an absolute boon to scholars, full of personal correspondence, legal documents, examples of Roth's advertising circulars that landed him in so much trouble, and more, including his FBI file. It was truly a thrill to comb through. A thick vertical file on Roth at the Kinsey Institute for Research in Sex, Gender, and Reproduction at Indiana University usefully complemented the Roth Papers.

Before the work of Jay Gertzman, little had been written on Roth. Leo Hamalian, *The Secret Careers of Samuel Roth* (Saratoga Springs, N.Y.: Harian Press, 1969), and the overlapping "Nobody Knows My Name: Samuel Roth and the Underside of Modern Letters," *Journal of Modern Literature* 3 (1974), are useful if not entirely accurate, and a good mini-biography appears in Gay Talese, *Thy Neighbor's Wife* (New York: Dell, 1980), but it was the arrival of Gertzman's *Bookleggers and Smuthounds: The Trade in Erotica, 1920–1940* (Philadelphia: University of Pennsylvania Press, 1999), that truly brought the elusive Roth into focus, in a stunning 80-page chapter. The rest of the book is also a remarkable contribution to the history of obscenity. Gertzman has continued to explore Roth, in such pieces as "The Promising Jewish Poetry of a Pariah: Samuel Roth," *Studies in American Jewish Literature* 28 (2009), and "Not Quite Honest: Samuel Roth's 'Unauthorized' *Ulysses* and the 1927 International Protest," *Joyce Studies Annual* (2009). His "A Scarlet Pansy Goes to War: Subversion, Schlock, and an Early Gay Classic," *Journal of American Culture* 33 (2010), recovers a significant book that Roth published, and Gertzman's forthcoming biography, *Samuel Roth, Infamous Modernist*, will be a major work.

A few other scholars have begun to pursue Roth. Mark Gaippa and Robert Scholes, "She 'Never Had a Room of Her Own': Hemingway and the New Edition of Kiki's *Memoirs*," *Hemingway Review* 19 (1999), examines one of Roth's many dubious republications, and Joshua Lambert's stellar dissertation, "Unclean Lips: Obscenity and Jews in American Literature" (PhD diss., University of Michigan, 2009), positions Roth among the many other Jews on both sides of the bench in the history of obscenity. For background on Roth's identity as a Jewish immigrant, see Eric Goldstein, *The Price of Whiteness: Jews, Race, and American Identity* (Princeton, N.J.: Princeton University Press, 2006).

Because this book casts a wide net into law and culture, many of its published primary sources come from both the mainstream press and the world of the law review. While major sources are cited by name below, the broad research base included *Harper's*, *New Republic*, *Redbook*, *Science News Letter*, *Playboy*, *Saturday Review*, *America*, *Los Angeles Times*, *New York Times*, *Time*, *Washington Post*, *Commentary*, *Variety*, and *New Yorker*, as well as *Journal of Criminal Law, Criminology, and Police Science*, *Duke Law Journal*, *Vanderbilt Law Review*, *Harvard Law Review*, *Temple Law Quarterly*, *Ohio State Law Journal*, *Brooklyn Law Review*, *Minnesota Law Review*, *Columbia Law Review*, and *Virginia Law Review*.

Early Obscenity

For a primer on the prehistory of American obscenity law, see the essays in Lynn Hunt, ed., *The Invention of Pornography: Obscenity and the Origins of Modernity, 1500–1800* (New York: Zone Books, 1996); Joan DeJean, *The Reinvention of Obscenity: Sex, Lies, and Tabloids in Early Modern France* (Chicago: University of Chicago Press, 2002); Lisa Sigel, *Governing Pleasures: Pornography and Social Change in England, 1815–1914* (New Brunswick, N.J.: Rutgers University Press, 2002). Less specialized but very smart is Walter Kendrick, *The Secret Museum: Pornography in Modern Culture* (Berkeley: University of California Press, 1987). To watch obscenity emerge out of British law, consult Colin Manchester, "Lord Campbell's Act: England's First Obscenity Statute," *Journal of Legal History* 9 (1988), and the quite useful James Alexander, "*Roth* at Fifty: Reconsidering the Common Law Antecedents of American Obscenity Law," *John Marshall Law Review* 41 (2008).

Scholars have not lavished great attention on early American obscenity, but see Peter Wagner, *Eros Revived: Erotica of the Enlightenment in England and America* (London: Secker and Warburg, 1988), and Marcus McCorison, "Printers and the Law: The Trials of Publishing Obscene Libel in Early America," *Papers of the Bibliographical Society of America* 104 (2010). Leonard Levy's *Blasphemy: Verbal Offense against the Sacred from Moses to Salman Rushdie* (New York: Knopf, 1993), too, sets important context. Clare Lyons's excellent *Sex among the Rabble: An Intimate History of Gender and Power in the Age of Revolution, Philadelphia, 1730–1830* (Chapel Hill: University of North Carolina Press, 2006), inventively reconstructs the circulation of erotic texts outside a strictly legal framework. On the limitations of the First Amendment in the early republic, see Peter Charles Hoffer, *The Free Speech Crisis of 1800: Thomas Cooper's Trial for Seditious Libel* (Lawrence: University Press of Kansas, 2011).

The nineteenth century, on the other hand, has seen an explosion of studies related to obscenity. Paving the way, and still fresh, are Paul Boyer's two landmarks, *Purity in Print: The Vice-Society Movement and Book Censorship in America* (New York: Scribner, 1968), and *Urban Masses and Moral Order in America, 1820–1920* (Cambridge, Mass.: Harvard University Press, 1978). So influential were Boyer's books that scholars have only recently begun to look earlier in the century. The fruits of this exploration include Donna Dennis, *Licentious Gotham: Erotic Publishing and Its Prosecution in Nineteenth-Century New York* (Cambridge, Mass.: Harvard University Press, 2009), and Patricia Cline Cohen, Timothy Gilfoyle, and Helen Lefkowitz Horowitz, *The Flash Press: Sporting Male Weeklies in 1840s New York* (Chicago: University of Chicago Press, 2008). All three of those authors have also published highly relevant books of top-notch quality. Especially relevant here are Timothy Gilfoyle, *City of Eros: New York City, Prostitution, and the Commercialization of*

Sex, 1790–1920 (New York: Norton, 1992), and Helen Lefkowitz Horowitz, *Rereading Sex: Battles over Sexual Knowledge and Suppression in Nineteenth-Century America* (New York: Knopf, 2002). See also Joseph Ridgeley, "George Lippard's *The Quaker City*: The World of the American Porno-Gothic," *Studies in the Literary Imagination* 7 (1974), and Christopher Looby, "George Thompson's 'Romance of the Real': Transgression and Taboo in American Sensation Fiction," *American Literature* 65 (1993).

In the Comstock-era canon, I would place Nicola Beisel, *Imperiled Innocents: Anthony Comstock and Family Reproduction in Victorian America* (Princeton, N.J.: Princeton University Press, 1997); Alison Parker, *Purifying America: Women, Cultural Reform, and Pro-Censorship Activism, 1873–1933* (Urbana: University of Illinois Press, 1997); and Leigh Ann Wheeler, *Against Obscenity: Reform and the Politics of Womanhood in America, 1873–1935* (Baltimore: Johns Hopkins University Press, 2004), fantastic books all. Gaines Foster, *Moral Reconstruction: Christian Lobbyists and the Federal Legislation of Morality, 1865–1920* (Chapel Hill: University of North Carolina Press, 2002), crucially links moralism to the rise of modern federalism. On the development of sexual liberalism, see Sharon Ullman's excellent study, *Sex Seen: The Emergence of Modern Sexuality in America* (Berkeley: University of California Press, 1997).

Other useful and important works consulted for this book include Sarah Barringer Gordon, "Blasphemy and the Law of Religious Liberty," *American Quarterly* 52 (2000); Jesse Battan, " 'You Cannot Fix the Scarlet Letter on My Breast!': Women Reading, Writing, and Reshaping the Sexual Culture of Victorian America," *Journal of Social History* 37 (2004); April Haynes, "The Trials of Frederick Hollick: Obscenity, Sex Education, and Medical Democracy in the Antebellum United States," *Journal of the History of Sexuality* 12 (2003); Shirley Burton, "Obscene, Lewd, and Lascivious: Ida Craddock and the Criminally Obscene Women of Chicago, 1873–1913," *Michigan Historical Review* 19 (1993); Andrea Tone, "Black Market Birth Control: Contraceptive Entrepreneurship and Criminality in the Gilded Age," *Journal of American History* 87 (2000); Roderick Bradford, "D. M. Bennett," *American History* (December 2005); Janice Wood, *The Struggle for Free Speech in the United States, 1872–1915: Edward Bliss Foote, Edward Bond Foote, and Anti-Comstock Operations* (New York: Routledge, 2008); and Leigh Eric Schmidt, *Heaven's Bride: The Unprintable Life of Ida C. Craddock, American Mystic, Scholar, Sexologist, Martyr, and Madwoman* (New York: Basic, 2010).

Primary sources for the Comstock era include, of course, Anthony Comstock, whose *Traps for the Young* (New York: Funk & Wagnalls, 1883), remains enthralling reading nearly a century and a half later. George Thompson's *City Crimes* (1849) and *Venus in Boston* (1849) were republished by the University of Massachusetts Press in 2002. All accessible online and also still remarkable are Ezra Heywood, *Cupid's Yokes* (1877), D. M. Bennett, "An Open Letter to

Jesus" (1875), D. M. Bennett, *An Open Letter to Samuel Colgate* (1879), and Robert Ingersoll, "The Circulation of Obscene Literature" (1879). Ida Craddock's writings, including "The Wedding Night" and even her suicide notes, are available at the useful www.idacraddock.com.

Free Speech and Sexual Liberalism

Perhaps the single most important work on the emergence of free speech in the United States is David Rabban, *Free Speech in Its Forgotten Years* (New York: Cambridge University Press, 1997), a truly daunting feat of research and analysis. My other main secondary sources are Paul Murphy, *World War I and the Origins of Civil Liberties in the United States* (New York: Norton, 1979); Samuel Walker, *In Defense of American Liberties: A History of the ACLU* (New York: Oxford University Press, 1990); Mark Graeber, *Transforming Free Speech: The Ambiguous Legacy of Civil Libertarianism* (Berkeley: University of California Press, 1991); Roger Cottrell, *Roger Nash Baldwin and the American Civil Liberties Union* (New York: Columbia University Press, 2000); and Judy Kutulas, *The American Civil Liberties Union and the Making of Modern Liberalism, 1930–1960* (Chapel Hill: University of North Carolina Press, 2006). See too the exciting recent work of Leigh Ann Wheeler, "Where Else but Greenwich Village? Love, Lust, and the Emergence of the American Civil Liberties Union's Sexual Rights Agenda, 1920–1931," *Journal of the History of Sexuality* 21 (2012).

Primary sources on the early free-speech movement include such works by its major figures as Theodore Schroeder, *"Obscene Literature" and Constitutional Law* (privately printed, 1911); Zechariah Chafee Jr., *Freedom of Speech* (New York: Harcourt, Brace, 1920); Chafee, *Government and Mass Communications* (Chicago: University of Chicago Press, 1947); Alexander Meiklejohn, *Free Speech and Its Relation to Self-Government* (New York: Harper, 1948); Morris Ernst and William Seagle, *To the Pure . . . A Study of Obscenity and the Censor* (New York: Viking, 1929); and Ernst and Alexander Lindey, *The Censor Marches On: Recent Milestones in the Administration of the Obscenity Law in the United States* (New York: Doubleday, Doran, 1940). As well, the papers of the American Civil Liberties Union at Princeton University are a gold mine of documents and information regarding tactics, decision-making, specific cases, and organizational policy. I have used them extensively here.

The free-speech movement developed in tandem with sexual liberalism, and the single best scholarly work linking that to obscenity is Andrea Friedman's *Prurient Interests: Gender, Democracy, and Obscenity in New York City, 1909–1945* (New York: Columbia University Press, 2000), a book I never tire of praising. Also useful here is Leslie Taylor, " 'I Made Up My Mind to Get It': The American Trial of *The Well of Loneliness*, New York City, 1928–1929," *Journal of the History of Sexuality* 10 (2001), and Stephen Gillers, "A Tendency to Deprave and Corrupt: The Transformation of American Obscenity Law from *Hicklin* to *Ulysses II*," *Washington University Law Review* 85 (2007), which focuses primarily on New York but thus sets a nice backdrop for Roth. Constance Chen matches nice storytelling with astute analysis in *"The Sex Side of Life": Mary Ware Dennett's Pioneering Battle for Birth Control and Sex Education* (New York: Free Press, 1996), and Brian Hoffman has written one of the best recent extensions of this narrative in " 'A Certain Amount of Prudishness': Nudist Magazines and the Liberalisation of American Obscenity Law, 1947–58," *Gender & History* 22 (2010).

The emergence of motion pictures links to both free speech and sexual liberalism. From the vast literature on the topic, see especially Lee Grieveson, *Policing Cinema: Movies and Censorship in Early-Twentieth-Century America* (Berkeley: University of California Press, 2004), and Laura Wittern-Keller, *Freedom of the Screen: Legal Challenges to State Film Censorship, 1915–1981* (Lexington: University Press of Kentucky, 2008).

Primary sources for this early-twentieth-century period I've used include Daniel Carsons Goodman, *Hagar Revelly* (New York: Mitchell Kennerley, 1913), not a great novel by any means but a historically interesting one; Margaret Sanger's fiery *My Fight for Birth Control* (New York: Farrar & Rinehart, 1931); Mary Ware Dennett, *Who's Obscene?* (New York: Vanguard Press, 1930); and of course the works of Samuel Roth. For this book I specifically used *First Offering: A Book of Sonnets and Lyrics* (New York: Lyric, 1917); *Europe: A Book for America* (New York: Boni & Liveright, 1919); *Now and Forever: A Conversation with Mr. Israel Zangwill on the Jew and the Future* (New York: McBride, 1925); (as Hugh Wakem) *Diary of a Smut-Hound* (Philadelphia: William Hodgson, 1930); *Lady Chatterley's Lover: A Dramatization of His Version of D. H. Lawrence's Novel* (New York: William Faro, 1931); *The Private Life of Frank Harris* (New York: Faro, 1931); *Jews Must Live: An Account of the Persecution of the World by Israel on All the Frontiers of Civilization* (New York: Golden Hind, 1934); *Peep-Hole of the Present: An Inquiry into the Substance of Appearance* (New York: Philosophical Book Club, 1945); *Bumarap* (New York: Arrowhead, 1947); (as Norman Lockridge) *Waggish Tales of the Czechs* (New York: Candide Press, 1947); and (as Lockridge) *The Sexual Conduct of Men and Women* (New York: Hogarth House, 1948). The most easily available version of *Jews Must Live* is a 1964 reprint missing several chapters. Fortunately for historical purposes, if unfortunately as a comment on society, the original full text can be found with minimal searching on a white-supremacist web site.

Works published by Roth though not necessarily written by him include the periodicals *Beau*, *Two Worlds Monthly*, *Casanova Jr.'s Tales*, *American Aphrodite*, and *Good Times*. Also Giovanni Boccaccio, *Pasquerella and Madonna Babetta* (New York: Biblion, 1927); Octave Mirabeau, *Celestine: Being the Diary of a Chambermaid* (New York: William Faro, 1930), *The Intimate Journal of*

Rudolph Valentino (New York: Faro, 1931); *Lady Chatterley's Friends* (New York: Faro, 1932); Rhys Davies, *A Bed of Feathers & Tale* (New York: Black Hawk Press, 1935); Marie Lorenz, *Tina and Jimmy Learn How They Were Born* (New York: Boar's Head, 1949); and A Flesh Peddler, *Beautiful Sinners of New York* (New York: Boar's Head, 1949).

As far as I can tell, the Kinsey Institute appears to be the only public repository for some of the more obscure and pornographic works sold by Sam and Pauline Roth in the 1930s and beyond. Its holdings include Dr. Desernet, *Nirvana* (n.p.: Valhallian Sectarian Press, 1934); the anonymous *Wide Open* (privately printed, 1935); Jimmy Harrington, *Memories of an Hotel Man* (n.p.: Art-Guild Press, 1935); and much, much more.

Archival sources beyond the Roth Papers that I found useful included the James J. Walker and Fiorella LaGuardia Mayoral Papers at the New York Municipal Archives, helpful in establishing the local backdrop of city politics in Roth's hometown. As well, the John Saxton Sumner Papers at the Wisconsin Historical Society, housed at the University of Wisconsin in Madison, contain useful information on the policing of smut by Roth's longtime nemesis.

Roth *in Court*

The centerpiece of my reconstruction of *Roth v. U.S.* is undoubtedly the Library of Congress in Washington, D.C., which holds the personal papers of several key Supreme Court justices. Of particular use were the papers of William Brennan, William O. Douglas, and Earl Warren, full of opinion drafts, memoranda, conference notes, and other backstage materials that provide valuable understanding of the Court's internal dynamics. Somewhat less rich than those collections, but still used in this study, were the papers of Hugo Black, Harold Burton, Felix Frankfurter, Robert Jackson, Thurgood Marshall, and Wiley Rutledge, all of which still shed useful light on key cases. The John Marshall Harlan Papers at Princeton University were also quite illuminating.

Case files including briefs and sometimes transcripts can be found in *The Making of Modern Law: U.S. Supreme Court Records and Briefs, 1832–1978*, a scholarly online database, or at the law library at the Library of Congress. Oral arguments in *Roth* and *Alberts* are published in *Obscenity: The Complete Oral Arguments before the Supreme Court in the Major Obscenity Cases*, ed. Leon Friedman (New York: Chelsea House, 1970), and can also be heard in audio format online at the Oyez Project.

There is a massive Supreme Court historiography, but of particular use for this book were such general studies as Melvin Urofsky, *Division and Discord: The Supreme Court under Stone and Vinson, 1941–1953* (Columbia: University of South Carolina Press, 1997); William Wiecek, *The Birth of the Mod-*

ern Constitution: The United States Supreme Court, 1941–1953 (New York: Cambridge University Press, 2006); Mark Tushnet, ed., *The Warren Court in Historical and Political Perspective* (Charlottesville: University Press of Virginia, 1993); Lucas Powe Jr., *The Warren Court and American Politics* (Cambridge, Mass.: Harvard University Press, 2000); and Michal Belknap, *The Supreme Court under Earl Warren, 1953–1969* (Columbia: University of South Carolina Press, 2005). Though the book remains controversial for its secretive sourcing and contested content, *The Brethren: Inside the Supreme Court* (New York: Simon and Schuster, 1979), by journalists Bob Woodward and Scott Armstrong, provides both insight and frequent amusement into otherwise invisible Court debates over obscenity in the 1970s. Joyce Murdoch and Deb Price add an important element in *Courting Justice: Gay Men and Lesbians v. the Supreme Court* (New York: Basic, 2001), and the single most important recent contribution is Marc Stein's brilliant *Sexual Injustice: Supreme Court Decisions from* Griswold *to* Roe (Chapel Hill: University of North Carolina Press, 2010).

Biography is a common approach to the Court, and of the many words spilled on William Brennan, the standard for the foreseeable future is likely to remain Seth Stern and Stephen Wermiel, *Justice Brennan: Liberal Champion* (Boston: Houghton Mifflin Harcourt, 2010). Also worthy of note are James Simon, *The Antagonists: Hugo Black, Felix Frankfurter, and Civil Liberties in Modern America* (New York: Simon & Schuster, 1989); Howard Ball and Philip Cooper, *Of Power and Right: Hugo Black, William O. Douglas, and America's Constitutional Revolution* (New York: Oxford University Press, 1992); Ed Cray, *Chief Justice: A Biography of Earl Warren* (New York: Simon & Schuster, 1997); and Laura Kalman, *Abe Fortas: A Biography* (New Haven, Conn.: Yale University Press, 1990).

For establishing the biographies of some of the judges and attorneys involved in Roth's cases, online sources such as the *Biographical Directory of Federal Judges* as well as the archives of the Jewish Telegraphic Agency provided much help. One rare scholarly study, not involving Roth's case but setting an interesting backdrop, is Phillip Deery, "'A Divided Soul'? The Cold War Odyssey of O. John Rogge," *Cold War History* 6 (2006).

Tracking Roth's legal history backward, down the judicial ladder, I found the case files from the Southern District of New York federal court and the Second Circuit Court of Appeals tremendously valuable, including arrest records, indictments, trial transcripts, and other legal documents. Though some remain elusive or incomplete, the case files for most of Sam and Pauline Roth's criminal and civil cases from the 1920s through the late 1950s can be found at the National Archives and Records Administration New York City branch. Specifically, see files C53-79 (Sam and Pauline, 1929); C81-159 (Pauline, 1931); C97-413 (Pauline, 1935); Civ.46-185 (*Roth v. Goldman*); C134-338 (*Beautiful Sinners* case, 1951); and C148-9 (the case that became *Roth v. U.S.*).

The iconoclastic Jerome Frank figures prominently in Roth's legal history, and the Jerome Frank Papers at Yale University contain striking private correspondence between the appellate judge and his colleagues regarding Roth's cases. On Frank, see Morton Horwitz, *The Transformation of American Law, 1870–1960: The Crisis of Legal Orthodoxy* (New York: Oxford University Press, 1992).

David Alberts, whose case was subsumed by *Roth v. U.S.*, is far less remembered than Samuel Roth and trickier to track. I sought him out in the online archive of the *Los Angeles Times* through ProQuest's Historical Newspapers and the clippings morgue of the *Los Angeles Examiner* housed at the University of Southern California, but the only direct trace of the man I could locate was a single letter to his lawyer, written after the fact of his case in 1964, in the Stanley Fleishman Papers at UCLA, which fortunately contained his credit report. Much work remains to be done on midcentury smut pioneers such as Alberts, Edward Mishkin, or Irving Klaw. For the best existing portrait, of Cleveland's Reuben Sturman, see Eric Schlosser, *Reefer Madness: Sex, Drugs, and Cheap Labor in the American Black Market* (Boston: Houghton Mifflin, 2003).

Some of the key legal discussions that informed and responded to *Roth* were William Lockhart and Robert McClure, "Literature, the Law of Obscenity, and the Constitution," *Minnesota Law Review* 38 (1954); Lockhart and McClure, "Obscenity in the Courts," *Law and Contemporary Problems* 20 (1955); Harry Kalven, "Obscenity and the Law," *Library Quarterly* (July 1957); O. John Rogge, "Congress Shall Make No Law . . . ," *Michigan Law Review* 56 (1958); and Harry Kalven, "The Metaphysics of the Law of Obscenity," *Supreme Court Review* (1960).

Cold War

Elaine Tyler May ushered in studies of Cold War sexual politics with *Homeward Bound: American Families in the Cold War Era* (New York: Basic, 1988), still a great read. See also Robert Dean, *Imperial Brotherhood: Gender and the Making of Cold War* (Amherst: University of Massachusetts Press, 2001); David K. Johnson, *The Lavender Scare: The Cold War Persecution of Gays and Lesbians in the Federal Government* (Chicago: University of Chicago Press, 2004); and Margot Canaday, *The Straight State: Sexuality and Citizenship in Twentieth-Century America* (Princeton, N.J.: Princeton University Press, 2009); as well as Andrea Friedman's wonderful essays "Sadists and Sissies: Anti-Pornography Campaigns in Cold War America," *Gender & History* 15 (2003), and "The Smearing of Joe McCarthy: The Lavender Scare, Gossip, and Cold War Politics," *American Quarterly* 57 (2005). For a general cultural backdrop, see Stephen Whitfield, *The Culture of the Cold War* (Baltimore: Johns Hopkins University Press, 1991).

Some of the conservatism of the 1950s began earlier. On censorial efforts emanating out of the Depression but still carrying currency in the 1950s, see Gregory Black, *Hollywood Censored: Morality Codes, Catholics, and the Movies* (New York: Cambridge University Press, 1994); Black, *The Catholic Crusade against the Movies, 1940–1975* (New York: Cambridge University Press, 1997); and Frank Walsh, *Sin and Censorship: The Catholic Church and the Motion Picture Industry* (New Haven, Conn.: Yale University Press, 1996). A great counterpoint to the Catholic pressure tactics comes from this very series, in Laura Wittern-Keller and Raymond Haberski Jr., *The Miracle Case: Film Censorship and the Supreme Court* (Lawrence: University Press of Kansas, 2008). See also Amy Kiste Nyberg, *Seal of Approval: The History of the Comics Code* (Jackson: University Press of Mississippi, 1998); Thomas Waugh, *Hard to Imagine: Gay Male Eroticism in Photography and Film from Their Beginnings to Stonewall* (New York: Columbia University Press, 1996); and Gregory Lisby, " 'Trying to Define What May Be Indefinable': The Georgia Literature Commission, 1953–1973," *Georgia Historical Quarterly* 84 (2000). On an influential Roth enemy with serious cultural power, see Neal Gabler, *Winchell: Gossip, Power, and the Culture of Celebrity* (New York: Knopf, 1994).

The government made no secret of its sexual politics during the Cold War. See the following congressional documents, all published by the Government Printing Office in Washington, D.C.: *Report of the Select Committee on Current Pornographic Materials* (1952); *Juvenile Delinquency (Obscene and Pornographic Materials)*, hearings (1955); *Subcommittee to Investigate Juvenile Delinquency, Interim Report, Obscene and Pornographic Literature and Juvenile Delinquency* (1956); Committee on the Judiciary, *Scope of Soviet Activity in the United States, Part 23* (1956); Subcommittee on Postal Operations, House, *Obscene Matter Sent through the Mail* (1959); also *Circulation of Obscene and Pornographic Material* (1960); as well as, once more, *Obscene Matter Sent through the Mail* (1962). The most naked expression of the decade's moral panic in nongovernmental form remains Fredric Wertham, *Seduction of the Innocent* (New York: Rinehart, 1954).

Sexual Revolution and New Right Response
On the sexual revolution see Beth Bailey, *Sex in the Heartland* (Cambridge, Mass.: Harvard University Press, 1999), and David Allyn, *Make Love, Not War: The Sexual Revolution, an Unfettered History* (Boston: Little, Brown, 2000). Specific to pornography and obscenity, see Eric Schaefer, "Gauging a Revolution: 16mm Film and the Rise of the Pornographic Feature," *Cinema Journal* 41 (2002); Elena Gorfinkel, "Wet Dreams: Erotic Film Festivals of the Early 1970s and the Utopian Sexual Public Sphere," *Framework* 47 (2006); Jeffrey Escoffier, *Bigger Than Life: The History of Gay Porn Cinema from Beefcake to Hardcore* (Philadelphia: Running Dog Press, 2009); and Timothy Nutt,

" 'Somebody Somewhere Needs to Draw the Line:': *Deep Throat* and the Regulation of Obscenity in Little Rock," *Arkansas Historical Quarterly* 69 (2010).

From the time itself, the best sources are Charles Rembar, *The End of Obscenity* (New York: Harper & Row, 1968); *The Report of the Commission on Obscenity and Pornography* (New York: Bantam, 1970); and Kenneth Turan and Stephen Zito, *Sinema: American Pornographic Films and the People Who Make Them* (New York: Praeger, 1974). The most significant social science work funded by the commission is Louis Zurcher and R. George Kirkpatrick, *Citizens for Decency: Antipornography Crusades as Status Defense* (Austin: University of Texas Press, 1976).

On porn and the New Right, see Whitney Strub, *Perversion for Profit: The Politics of Pornography and the Rise of the New Right* (New York: Columbia University Press, 2011). On the racial dimensions of conservative antismut activism, see Strub, "Black and White and Banned All Over: Race, Censorship and Obscenity in Postwar Memphis," *Journal of Social History* 40 (2007), and also Anders Walker's insightful "A Horrible Fascination: Sex, Segregation, and the Lost Politics of Obscenity," *Washington University Law Review* 89 (2012).

More broadly on the sexual politics of the New Right, see Didi Herman, *The Antigay Agenda: Orthodox Vision and the Christian Right* (Chicago: University of Chicago Press, 1997); Janice Irvine, *Talk about Sex: The Battles over Sex Education in the United States* (Berkeley: University of California Press, 2002); and Gillian Frank, "Save Our Children: The Sexual Politics of Child Protection in the United States, 1965–1990" (PhD diss., Brown University, 2009). The best single source on the Nixon era is Rick Perlstein's sweeping, majestic *Nixonland: The Rise of a President and the Fracturing of America* (New York: Scribner, 2008).

Feminism and the Sex Wars

The key primary sources of the feminist antipornography movement are Laura Lederer, ed., *Take Back the Night: Women on Pornography* (New York: Bantam, 1979); Andrew Dworkin, *Pornography: Men Possessing Women* (New York: Perigee, 1981), and *Intercourse* (New York: Free Press, 1987); Catharine MacKinnon, *Feminism Unmodified* (Cambridge, Mass.: Harvard University Press, 1987), *Toward a Feminist Theory of the State* (Cambridge, Mass.: Harvard University Press, 1989), and *Only Words* (Cambridge, Mass.: Harvard University Press, 1993); and Susan Griffin, *Pornography and Silence: Culture's Revenge Against Nature* (New York: Harper & Row, 1981). The Minneapolis and Indianapolis ordinances are contained in Dworkin and MacKinnon, *Pornography and Civil Rights: A New Day for Women's Equality* (Minneapolis: Organizing Against Pornography, 1988),

On sex-positive feminism, see Lisa Duggan and Nan D. Hunter, *Sex Wars:*

Sexual Dissent and Political Culture (New York: Routledge, 1995). For the conservative appropriation of feminist rhetoric, see Attorney General's Commission on Pornography, *Final Report* (Washington, D.C.: Department of Justice, 1986). Scholarly work on the feminist antiporn movement began with Donald Alexander Downs, *The New Politics of Pornography* (Chicago: University of Chicago Press, 1989), but the defining work thus far is Carolyn Bronstein, *Battling Pornography: The Feminist Anti-Pornography Movement, 1976–1986* (New York: Cambridge University Press, 2011).

Finally, on obscenity and pornography up to and in the Internet era, see Frederick Lane III, *Obscene Profits: The Entrepreneurs of Pornography in the Cyber Age* (New York: Routledge, 2000); Marjorie Heins, *Not in Front of the Children: "Indecency," Censorship, and the Innocence of Youth* (New York: Hill & Wang, 2001); Stephen Patrick Johnson, "Staying Power: The Mainstreaming of the Hard-Core Pornographic Film Industry, 1969–1990" (Ph.D. diss., University of Maryland, 2009); as well as Strub, *Perversion for Profit*, ch. 8.

INDEX

obscenity laws and, 195; on *Roth*, 195

Heinecke, Alfred, 193

Helms, Jesse, 210

Hemingway, Ernest, 44, 54, 56

Henkin, Louis, 194

Heteronormativity, 184, 200

Heterosexuality, 107, 108, 115, 184

Heywood, Angela, 21

Heywood, Ezra, 21, 23, 28, 29, 214

Hicklin standards, 23, 24, 46, 54, 59, 100, 101, 128, 130, 151, 153, 168, 179, 233, 234, 235; breakdown of, 77–78; obscenity and, 43; Supreme Court and, 43, 47

Hill, Morton, 214

Hitler, Adolf, 78, 79, 110

Hogarth House, 85

Holder, Eric, 228

Holmby Productions v. Vaughn (1955), 231

Holmes, Oliver Wendell, 126; *Abrams* and, 36, 37; clear and present danger and, 234; First Amendment and, 36; free speech and, 35; opinion of, 33–34; repressive speech cases and, 35; *Schenck* and, 34–35, 36

Homophobia, 107, 208

Homosexual Life, 154

Homosexuality, 2, 63, 111, 147, 185, 192, 193, 234; communism and, 107; pornography and, 118; threat of, 108

Hoover, Herbert, 117

Hoover, J. Edgar, 67, 117, 195, 209

House Committee on the Revision of Laws, 28

House Un-American Activities Committee (HUAC), 110, 177

Housewife's Handbook on Selective Promiscuity, The, 197, 199

Houston, Shine Louise, 227

Howl, 227

Hughes, Charles Evans, 38, 39

Hungarian Catholic League of America, 122

Hunter, Louis, 109

Hunter, Nan, 221

I Am Curious (Yellow), 205–206

I Was Hitler's Doctor (Roth), 74

Immigrants, 14, 33

Immigration Department, 120

Immorality, 14, 17, 55, 151

Imperiled Innocents (Beisel), 19

Individual rights, 2, 34, 36, 38

Industrial Workers of the World (IWW), 34, 38

Ingersoll, Robert, 28, 29

Inside Deep Throat, 227

Inside Hitler, 73–74

Intercourse, 212

International Mark Twain Society, 85

Intimate Journal of Rudolph Valentino, The, 62

IWW. *See* Industrial Workers of the World

Jackson, Andrew, 143

Jackson, Robert, 97, 98–99, 101, 212

Jacobellis v. Ohio (1964), 186, 187, 188, 194, 213, 231, 235

James, E. L., 223

Jameson, Jenna, 1, 226

Jazz Age, 43, 49, 63, 115

Jefferson, Thomas, 8, 140

Jehovah's Witnesses, 75, 95, 97

Jenkins v. Georgia (1974), 231

Jeremy, Ron, 226

Jesus Christ, 22, 116

Jewett, Helen, 11

Jewish Welfare Board, Roth and, 50–51

Jews, 50, 66

Jews Must Live (Roth), 66, 67, 181

Jim Crow laws, 94, 156

Johnson, Lyndon, 210, 236

Johnson, Virginia, 206

Jones, James, 113

Journal of Criminal Law, Criminology, and Police Science, 178

Joyce, James, 44, 46, 58, 113, 171, 223, 234; artistry of, 47; Roth and, 57

career of, 48; challenge by, 181; citizenship status of, 121; convicting, 68, 234; death of, 217; economic trials for, 67; imprisonment of, 4, 59, 61, 70, 71, 79, 137, 160, 183, 186, 190, 201; legal obstacles for, 4, 56, 59–60, 102, 113, 132–137, 201; legalistic writing and, 181; library of, 58; literary interests of, 50, 52; marriage of, 51; personal obsessions of, 49; petition by, 103, 104; respectability of, 74; sentence for, 58, 70, 71, 169, 180–181; story of, 3–4, 53; trial of, 132–137; war years and, 72–75; youth of, 50, 233

Roth test, 194, 197, 198, 201

Roth v. Goldman (1949), 89, 104, 139–140, 168, 232, 234

Roth v. United States (1957), 5, 24, 138, 153, 157, 163, 164, 165, 212, 229, 232, 235; attention for, 1, 156; condemning, 2, 202; conservative side of, 184, 189–200; framing, 143–147; hearings for, 158; legacy of, 2, 161, 176, 181, 201, 207, 222, 223–224; liberal side of, 184–189, 199; overhauling, 202; readings of, 181, 187, 208; reception for, 175–182

Rubenstein, Joseph: on morality, 180

Rubin, Abraham, 119

Ruggles, John, 8–9

"Rules for Bringing about Revolution," 122

Rutledge, Wiley, 96, 99, 102, 124; *Doubleday* and, 125; *Roth* and, 104

Sabbatarian movement, 8

Sacco and Vanzetti, 95

Sadomasochism, 192, 199, 218

Sandburg, Carl, 56

Sanford, Edward, 37

Sanger, Margaret, 41, 42, 69

Sanger, William, 42

Santorum, Rick, 228

Sartre, Jean-Paul, 207

Saturday Press, 38

Saturday Review, 114

Scalia, Antonin, 224, 229

Scarlet Pansy, A (Scully), 62

Schenck, Charles, 34

Schenck v. U.S. (1919), 34–35, 36, 232, 234

Schindler v. U.S. (1953), 232

Schroeder, Theodore, 29–30, 38, 40, 63, 131–132; civil libertarians and, 44; radical libertarianism of, 46

Schwarzenegger, Arnold, 227

Science News Letter, 111, 121

Scienter, 171

Scopes, John, 45

Scopes Monkey Trial, 44

Scorpion, The (Weirauch), 112

Scully, Robert, 62

Search and seizure, protection against, 103, 152

Sears, Roebuck, 19

Second Circuit Court of Appeals, 69, 88, 141, 207; Roth and, 138–139, 235

Secret Life of Walter Winchell, The (Stuart), 117

Secret Museum of Anthropology, 69

Secret Places of the Human Body, The, 67

Securities and Exchange Commission, 96, 104

Sedition Act (1798), 8, 233

Sedition Act (1917), 30, 35, 234

Seduction of the Innocent (Wertham), 141

Segregation, 94, 149, 185, 219

Selby, Hubert, Jr., 215

Self-Defense for Women, 85

Separate but equal, 94, 212

Sex, 64, 65, 115; court confusion over, 127–132; court-sanctioned, 70; direct representations of, 145, 182, 183; forced, 220; intergenerational, 228; male prison, 204; obscenity and, 162, 167, 178; pre-/extramarital, 39, 41, 186; procreation and, 19, 108; singular doctrine and, 184–189; social dialogue and, 195

Sex, 65

Sex crimes, 92, 118, 121

Sex education, pornography and, 205

Sex Life, 65

Sex Life of a Cop, 204

Sex Orgies Illustrated, 212

Sex radicals, 28, 29, 214

Sex Side of Life, The, 42, 45

Sex wars, feminists and, 218

Sexology, 65

Sexual activity, 70, 88, 91, 108, 183, 207

Sexual Behavior in the Human Female (Kinsey Report), 109, 235

Sexual Behavior in the Human Male (Kinsey Report), 88, 108, 234

Sexual Conduct of Men and Women (Lockridge), 92

Sexual conservatism, 10, 234

Sexual expression, 56, 141, 169, 183, 184, 223; freedom of speech and, 166–167

Sexual harassment, 219

Sexual liberalism, 2, 28, 40–41, 42, 43, 46, 53, 69, 70, 75, 79, 98, 108, 112, 118, 131, 166, 168; influence of, 47, 162; modern, 118, 183; obscenity and, 78, 151; Roth and, 61; Victorian norms and, 60

Sexual normalcy, 107, 108

Sexual pleasure, 11, 116–117

Sexual politics, 19, 95, 170, 182, 195, 217, 219, 223; Cold War and, 114, 119–120, 129, 169; foreign policy and, 107; obscenity and, 4; Roth and, 122

Sexual revolution, 4, 186, 217; cultural memory and, 183; First Amendment and, 208; pornography and, 202; rolling back, 184; *Roth* and, 182, 183, 189, 200

Sexual-rights doctrine, 184

Sexual thoughts, 140, 173, 174

Sexuality, 2, 19, 28, 39–48, 63, 92, 105, 205, 207, 208; African American, 62; assassination and, 39; BDSM, 218; commodified, 75; deviant, 27, 70, 115, 169, 223; marriage and, 25; masculine, 87; national dialogue over, 88; public expressions of, 10; scientific study of, 69; social liberalization toward, 101; socially accepted, 223

Sexually Adequate Male, The, 123

Shame Shop, 203

Sharpless, Jesse, 10

Shaw, George Bernard, 207

Sherman, Roger, 143

Sinclair, Upton, 73–74

Sjoman, Vilgot, 205

Slavery, 13, 14

Slaves of the Lash, 154

Smith, Joseph, 29

Smith, Lillian, 77

Smith Act (1940), 124, 125, 126, 177

Smith v. California (1959), 232

Smith v. Georgia (1969), 232

Smoot, Reed, 64

Smut, 1, 2, 4, 11, 12, 30, 141, 158, 163, 190, 196, 210–211, 212, 228; behavior and, 140; Cold War and, 110; concern about, 25, 118–119, 122; juvenile delinquency and, 121, 139; peddling, 60, 132, 150, 203; producing, 114, 226; suppressing, 16–17, 18, 72, 160, 197, 222

"Smut Held to Cause Delinquency" (*New York Times*), 121

Smutmongers, 15, 72–75, 106

Snuff, 217, 236

Social change, 9, 52, 164, 165, 205

Social conservatism, 43, 225, 228

Social control, 17, 18, 19

Social importance, 165, 169, 179, 195, 206

Voltaire, 66
Voting Rights Act (1965), 210

Waggish Tales of the Czechs
    (Lockridge), 85–86, 87, 88, 93,
    102, 103, 104, 131; criticism of, 91;
    obscenity of, 89, 90
Wagner Act (1935), 80
Wakem, Hugh, 60
Walker, Jimmy, 64–65
Walker v. Popenoe (1945), 84, 232
Wallet Nudes, 133, 137
WAP. *See* Women Against Porn
Warren, Earl, 151, 168, 173, 179, 193,
    210, 212; *Alberts* and, 171;
    appointment of, 149, 160, 170;
    Brown and, 170; community
    standards and, 187; Douglas and,
    174; First Amendment and, 159,
    170; liberalism and, 188;
    moralism of, 170; *Roth* and, 162,
    198
Warren Court, 170, 188, 192, 209
Washington, D.C., Court of Appeals,
    76
Washington Post, 177
Watch and Ward Society, 44, 55
Watts, Rowland, 147
WCTU. *See* Women's Christian
    Temperance Union
Wedding Night, The, 25
Weinfeld, Edward, 113
Weirauch, Anna, 112
Well of Loneliness, The (Hall), 45, 60,
    81
Wertham, Frederic, 110, 141
*West Virginia State Board of Education
    v. Barnette* (1943), 232
Whichello, Fred, 159
Whip, 11
White, Byron, 213, 214
White, Stanford, 39, 40
White Circle League of America, 126
"White slave" films, 40
White Slaves of Chinatown, 199
Whitman, Walt, 21, 50

Whitney, Anita, 37, 38
Whitney v. California (1927), 37, 38, 232
Whittaker, Charles Evans, 149, 160,
    168, 176, 191
Who's Obscene? (Dennett), 45
Wide Open, 68
William Faro, Inc., 61, 62–63, 65–66
Wilmot, John, 116
Wilson, Edmund, 10, 100, 101
Wilson, Woodrow, 31, 35
Winchell, Walter, 117, 133
Winters, Murray, 72, 77, 98–99, 100,
    102
Winters v. New York (1948), 99, 102,
    128, 165, 232
Wise, John B., 29
Woman Rebel, The, 41
Women: civil rights of, 220;
    constitutional equality for, 208;
    subjugation of, 202, 217, 219, 220
Women Against Porn (WAP), 217,
    218, 236
Women Against Violence in
    Pornography and Media, 217,
    236
Women's Christian Temperance
    Union (WCTU), 25, 66
Wood, Clement, 66
Woodhull, Victoria, 15, 24, 28
Woodhull & Claflin's Weekly, 15
Woollcott, Alexander, 86
Woolsey, John, 46, 47, 76, 234
"Word You Can't Say, The" (Lees), 79
Words in Pearl for the Married, 20
Wylie, Philip, 79

Yale Law and Policy Review, 219
Yale University Press, 217
Yeats, William Butler, 116
Young Men's Christian Association
    (YMCA), 15, 16
Youth Protection Committee, 122

Zangwill, Israel, 52, 57
Zenger, John Peter, 7
Zionism, 52